ACHIEVING DIVERSITY

A How-To-Do-It Manual
for Librarians

Edited by
Barbara I. Dewey
Loretta Parham

**HOW-TO-DO-IT MANUALS
FOR LIBRARIANS**

NUMBER 140

NEAL-SCHUMAN PUBLISHERS, INC.
New York, London

Published by Neal-Schuman Publishers, Inc.
100 William St., Suite 2004
New York, NY 10038

Copyright © 2006 Neal-Schuman Publishers, Inc.
Individual Chapters © 2006 by the contributors.

All rights reserved. Reproduction of this book, in whole or in part, without written permission of the publisher, is prohibited.

Printed and bound in the United States of America.

The paper used in this publication meets the minimum requirements of American National Standard for Information Sciences—Permanence of Paper for Printed Library Materials, ANSI Z39.48-1992.∞

Library of Congress Cataloging-in-Publication Data

Achieving diversity : a how-to-do-it manual for librarians / edited by Barbara I. Dewey, Loretta Parham.
    p. cm. —(How-to-do-it manuals for librarians; no. 140)
    Includes bibliographical references and index.
    ISBN 1-55570-554-5 (alk. paper)
  1. Libraries and minorities. 2. Minority librarians—Recruiting. 3. Libraries—Special collections—Minorities. 4. Academic libraries—Services to minorities. 5. Multiculturalism. 6. Diversity in the workplace. 7. Libraries and minorities—United States—Case studies. I. Dewey, Barbara I. II. Parham, Loretta, III. How-to-do-it manuals for libraries ; no. 140.
    Z711.8.A25 2006
    027.6'3—dc22   2006003072

CONTENTS

List of Figures v

Foreword vii

Preface.. ix

I. How to Create a Successful Diversity Plan 1

1. **Assessing Your Library's Diversity and Organizational Climate** 3
   by Jane Williams

2. **Making Diversity a Goal through Strategic Planning** 16
   by Rhea Ballard-Thrower and Grace M. Mills

3. **Best Practices for Placing Diversity at the Center of Your Library** ... 33
   by Tracie D. Hall

4. **Practical Strategies for Building a Library Diversity Program** 46
   by Molly Royse

5. **Diversity in Libraries—A Canadian Perspective** 51
   by Ganga B. Dakshinamurti

II. How to Recruit and Retain a Diverse Workforce 59

6. **Creating a Diverse Library Staff** 61
   by Hannelore B. Rader

7. **Fostering Diversity in Recruitment, Staffing, and Retention** 69
   by Emma Bradford Perry

8. **Diversity and Recruiting Practices: How LIS Schools and Practitioners Work Together** 76
   by Jametoria Burton and W. Michael Havener

9. **Diversity and Research Libraries: The CIRLA Fellows Program** 93
   by Irene M. Hoffman

10. **Reaching High School Students: Sowing the Seeds of Librarianship** ... 102
    by Jessica Kayongo, LeRoy LaFleur, and Ira Revels

III. How to Improve Diversity through Services, Collections, and Collaborations 115

11. **Diversity and the Digital Divide at an HBCU: The University of Maryland Eastern Shore** 117
    by Sharon D. Brooks, Marvella Rounds, Theodosia F. Shields, and Teri B. Weil

12. **Developing Approaches for Working with Diverse User Populations** 126
    by Deloice G. Holliday

13. **Tips and Practices for Quality Library User Services in a Diverse Environment** 137
    by Justina O. Osa

14. **Making Peer Research Advisors a Reality at NCSU Libraries** 152
    by Laura Blessing, Karen M. Brown Letarte, and Amy VanScoy

15. **Special Collections as an Integral Part of a Library's Diversity Initiative** 163
    by Tomaro I. Taylor and Lorel K. Reinstrom

16. **The Past Is Never Dead. It's Not Even Past: The Role of the Department of Archives and Special Collections during the "Open Doors" Commemoration of the Fortieth Anniversary of Integration at the University of Mississippi** 169
    by Jennifer Aronson and Jennifer Ford

17. **The HBCU Library Alliance and SOLINET: Partners in Inclusion** 182
    by Loretta Parham, Janice R. Franklin, and Kate Nevins

18. **The Diversity Librarians' Network** 187
    by Kawanna Bright, Jayati Chaudhuri, and Maud Mundava

19. **Final Thoughts on Diversity in Libraries** 203
    by Loretta Parham

20. **Celebrating Diversity in Libraries: A Selected Bibliography** 205
    by Molly Royse

IV. Samples of Successful Diversity Documents 213

Index 225

About the Editors 239

About the Contributors 241

LIST OF FIGURES

Figure 2-1	Howard University Law Library Strategic Plan (2002–2005)	28
Figure 3-1	A Scenario Planning Exercise	44
Figure 5-1	Quotable Quotations on Diversity	55
Figure 9-1	CIRLA Fellows Program Brochure	98
Figure 10-1	Sample Schedule—Cornell University Library's Junior Fellows Summer Program 2002	104
Figure 10-2	Demographic Characteristics of 2002 Cornell University Library Junior Fellows	105
Figure 10-3	Notre Dame High School Summer Program Interview Questionnaire	108
Figure 10-4	Notre Dame Summer Program Sample Work Schedule	109
Figure 10-5	Notre Dame Summer Program Exit Interview Responses	109
Figure 16-1	U.S. Military Troops Surround Lafayette County Court House, 1962	170
Figure 16-2	James H. Meredith and University of Mississippi Students, 2002	172
Figure 16-3	"Ghost of Robert E. Lee" Telegram, 1962	173
Figure 16-4	University of Mississippi Staff and Donated Items, 2002	174
Figure 16-5	Road Blockade, 1962	175
Figure 16-6	Jackson's Chapel School, Grenada County, Mississippi, April 1955	178
Figure 16-7	Del Mont Seminary, Oxford, Mississippi 1927	179
Figure 18-1	Diversity Librarians' Network Web Page	188
Figure 18-2	Diversity Librarians' Network Brochure	191
Figure 18-3	Diversity Librarians' Network Poster	196

FOREWORD

If we strive to create an environment within libraries that reflects and serves the rich diversity of humankind, why does this goal often remain unmet? To help answer this question and move the effort forward, *Achieving Diversity: A How-To-Do-It Manual for Librarians* identifies practical solutions that will pull down the barriers that remain. This is a book that no librarian with a commitment to social justice and a belief in the inherent value of equality can afford to ignore.

This book was inspired, in part, by ideas and experiences presented at the recent biennial National Diversity in Libraries Conference in Atlanta, Georgia, co-hosted by the Association of Research Libraries (ARL), the Association of Southeastern Research Libraries (ASERL), the Historically Black Colleges and Universities (HBCU) Library Alliance, and the Southeastern Library Network (SOLINET). At this conference, for the first time, leaders from public libraries, small and medium-sized academic libraries, and special/corporate libraries converged with staff from research libraries. *Achieving Diversity: A How-To-Do-It Manual for Librarians* seeks to capture the wisdom and energies of the participants and expand on their ideas with practical approaches. In the process, it admirably explores some of the many ways that libraries embrace and foster diversity with innovative services, recruitment strategies, collection approaches, and other specialized initiatives, and it does a remarkable job of capturing the many facets of diversity efforts in information science today.

The editors, Barbara Dewey, dean of Libraries, University of Tennessee, and Loretta Parham, director of the Woodruff Library, Atlanta University Center, are recognized leaders in librarianship and diversity. The strength of their well-justified reputations and their acknowledged commitment attracted excellent thinkers from around the country to participate in this important endeavor. *Achieving Diversity* both captures the rich content of the outstanding conference which inspired it and surpasses it. Compiling the book you now hold in your hands has clearly been a labor of love for Barbara and Loretta, one arising from their sincere desire to recognize and serve our diverse constituencies. The chapters provide a practical roadmap for librarians who want to make real progress in advancing their libraries' diversity efforts. Some of the brightest voices in the field offer achievable, measurable means to engender an orientation toward inclusion and to integrate diversity into day-to-day activities throughout the library.

John Burger,
Executive Director
Association of Southeastern Research Libraries
Atlanta, Georgia

PREFACE

Diversity is not realized simply by bringing more "people of color" into traditionally homogeneous settings. It is a far broader concept encompassing dimensions both interpersonal and intellectual. We firmly believe that this concept must be embedded in all aspects of planning, programs, and collections. It must play a central role in our virtual and physical environment if we want to remain relevant in our increasingly multicultural world. We edited *Achieving Diversity: A How-To-Do-It Manual for Librarians* as a compilation of great ideas and action-oriented programs designed to advance both the practices and theories of diversity consciousness in the library.

The contributors of the individual chapters come from many higher education institutions and backgrounds. Collectively they bring together a wealth of expertise that should be a tremendous boon to all librarians interested in advancing their own organizations' diversity programs. Unlike many other attempts to cover this topic, their efforts remain focused on *practical* strategies and approaches, striving at all times to provide real-world solutions to even the most complex problems.

Achieving Diversity: A How-To-Do-It Manual for Librarians concentrates on three broad areas. Part I, "How to Create a Successful Diversity Plan," contains five chapters: Chapter 1, "Assessing Your Library's Diversity and Organizational Climate"; Chapter 2, "Making Diversity a Goal through Strategic Planning"; Chapter 3, "Best Practices for Placing Diversity at the Center of Your Library"; Chapter 4, "Practical Strategies for Building a Library Diversity Program"; and Chapter 5, "Diversity in Libraries—A Canadian Perspective." They target strategies to develop institutional consciousness of, and appreciation for, difference as such. Insofar as no one solution can ever be universal, what works in one setting may have little effect in another. Accordingly, Part I addresses ways to carefully examine and assess a library's existing attitudes and orientations to better determine what must be changed. An international perspective is also included through an examination of the Canadian context in Chapter 5—offering a fresh perspective of the issues at hand.

Part II, "How to Recruit and Retain a Diverse Workforce," includes a variety of initiatives designed to decrease uniformity of libraries' staffs. Recognizing the importance of strategies tailored to fit particular needs, the chapters cover a wide range of approaches. In Chapter 6, "Creating a Diverse Library Staff," the author makes suggestions about how to actively pursue and hire individuals and groups of all types. Chapter 7, "Fostering Diversity in Recruitment, Staffing, and Retention," and Chapter 8, "Diversity and Recruiting Practices: How LIS Schools and Practitioners Work Together," examine recruitment and retention strategies in institutions of numerous sizes and scopes. Chapter 9, "Diversity and Research Libraries: The CIRLA Fellows Program," and Chapter 10, "Reaching High School Students: Sowing the Seeds of Librarianship," explore the varied perspectives of library educators, library science students, and librarians in minority residency and fellowship programs, providing the reader with a wide array of tools to meet the changing needs of the workplace.

Part III, "How to Improve Diversity through Services, Collections, and Collaborations," expands the scope of the book beyond questions of equal employment. Here, we discuss exciting programs and initiatives that help to infuse library services and collections with heterogeneous vitality. They highlight innovative collaborations and partnerships that take advantage of both new technologies and "traditional" collections. These nine chapters, including Chapter 11, "Diversity and the Digital Divide at an HBCU: The University of Maryland Eastern Shore"; Chapter 12, "Developing Approaches for Working with Diverse User Populations"; Chapter 13, "Tips and Practices for Quality Library User Services in a Diverse Environment"; and Chapter 14, "Making Peer Research Advisors a Reality at NCSU Libraries," focus on the particular needs of users. They examine and describe services and programs ideally suited to serve today's complex modern communities. Chapters 15 and 16 show how special collections departments celebrate diversity through collections and exhibits. Chapters 17 and 18 talk about national diversity-related collaborations through library alliances and between librarians holding residency or diversity-related positions.

Chapter 19, "Final Thoughts on Diversity in Libraries," provides summary thoughts that emphasize the imperative to make a positive, practical difference by changing the way we conceptualize diversity.

The final chapter of *Achieving Diversity* features a bibliography celebrating significant writings that further discuss the themes.

Part IV, "Samples of Successful Diversity Documents," offers nine examples of materials already in use in diversity programs. It includes diversity plans, Web sites, promotional ideas, mission statements, surveys, and more.

There is a perpetual need to reaffirm our dedication to diversity. We hope the ideas and suggestions presented here will inspire you to turn the ambition that underlies that commitment into a reality.

Barbara I. Dewey,
Loretta Parham
Editors

HOW TO CREATE A SUCCESSFUL DIVERSITY PLAN

ASSESSING YOUR LIBRARY'S DIVERSITY AND ORGANIZATIONAL CLIMATE

by Jane Williams

INTRODUCTION

This chapter's objectives are to show that diversity initiatives can be assessed—i.e., that an organization can determine how real its diversity and organizational climate are—and that those assessments can be used as tools to manage and identify areas of growth and development for organizational change (Love 2001). Assessment can be used as a way to realize the benefits of real, productive diversity. *Real* signifies integration into the organization of the principles and values of inclusion, respect, personal responsibility and empowerment, high performance, and commitment to the organization. Real diversity says, "We are all on the same team, *with* our differences, not *despite* them" (Thomas and Ely 1996, 86). The primary example will be the University of Maryland Libraries' experience with two major assessments.

DEFINING DIVERSITY

Diversity can be an elusive term. As DeEtta Jones wrote in the Association of Research Libraries' publication *Leading Ideas*:

> Early affirmative action legislation focused on a narrow set of groups; over time, the discussion has become more inclusive. To endorse a broad definition of diversity, some libraries have created diversity statements. The University of Michigan is among the pioneers in this work and adopted this language: "Diversity is all the characteristics that can be used to describe humans. We are all diverse in many ways. Unique intersections of these characteristics define each individual's diversity. Examples—in alphabetical order—are:
>
> | | |
> |---|---|
> | age | marital/partnered status |
> | ancestry | nationality |
> | cognitive style | disability (mental, learning, physical) |
> | cultural background | physical appearance |

economic background	political affiliation
ethnicity	race
gender	religious beliefs
geographic background	sexual orientation"
language(s) spoken	(Jones 2000, 8–9)

For any meaningful assessment, an organization must first have defined its diversity initiative, what goals it wants to gain and how those goals are to be reached—i.e., the concept of managing diversity. R. Roosevelt Thomas, Jr. posits that managing diversity is different from affirmative action or the approach of valuing differences. He sees managing diversity as a "way of thinking toward the objective of creating an environment that will enable all employees to reach their full potential in pursuit of organizational objectives" (Thomas 1996, 41). Another take on it is, "This diversity framework highlights the reality of the diversity forest that is greater than an individual's pet diversity tree" (Thomas 1995, 261).

In his book *Building a House for Diversity: How a Fable about a Giraffe and an Elephant Offers New Strategies for Today's Workforce*, Thomas writes that context is everything. A compelling motive must be developed in three key areas: workforce, workplace, and marketplace. Without this motive, efforts are seen as extraneous, and commitment is minimal (Thomas 1999). Thomas' approach moves diversity away from being a program or a movement or a trend. It becomes a way of life. It becomes real diversity. The challenge for all is determining whether real diversity exists.

RATIONALE FOR DIVERSITY ASSESSMENT

Developing diverse workforces in supportive and productive work environments is reported to be a major concern of many libraries, as attested to by the numerous conferences, conference presentations, and initiatives sponsored by the American Library Association and the Association of Research Libraries. However, diversity assessment has only recently become a tool in libraries for measuring and planning change, and as a result, assessment of diversity initiatives is still scattered. Librarianship is certainly not the only profession in which this is true. For example, a member of the Association for Assessment in Counseling noted in *Issues in Advancing Diversity through Assessment*: "This title suggests an important focus which is recent in our profession; using assessment as a proactive tool to initiate change rather than in a more passive, defensive way to insure that we aren't harming someone" (Sedlacek 1993, 1).

The thesis of this chapter is that, for large libraries, anecdotal or observational evidence of how the organization is faring with diversity efforts is inadequate and that systematic, reliable assessments must be undertaken. Large libraries include, but are not limited to, those belonging to the Urban Libraries Council or the Association of Research Libraries. Library systems with multiple sites are also good candidates for systematic assessment.

A library may need to undertake a systematic diversity assessment in order to meet the requirements or suggestions of its parent organization or to show leadership to the parent organization by undertaking an assessment before it is suggested or required that a library undertake such research.

Thomas argues for auditing an organization's culture by noting:

> If the goal is not to assimilate diversity into the dominant culture but rather to build a culture that can digest unassimilated diversity, then you better

start by figuring out what your present culture looks like. Since what we're talking about here is the body of unspoken and unexamined assumptions, values, and mythologies that make your world go round, this kind of cultural audit is impossible to conduct without outside help. It's a research activity. (Thomas 1990, 114)

CURRENT RESEARCH AND EFFORTS IN DIVERSITY ASSESSMENT IN LIBRARIES

In a chapter of the 2001 monograph *Diversity Now*, Johnnie Love reported on reviewing the literature and finding that, "other than reporting the number of new employees hired, few libraries have found ways to assess and document diversity progress" (Love 2001, 75).

Because of the lack of models for assessing diversity in the academic library, Love drew on corporate resources to develop a survey instrument with nine variables: awareness of diversity issues, shifting of power, diversity of opinion, lack of empathy, tokenism, learning, participation, overcoming inertia, and racism. These variables were developed to assess all services and operations of the library. The objective was to assess observable and unobservable behaviors and attitudes (Love 2001, 90). The survey was used with three pilot groups.

The data from her study showed diversity assessment as a viable tool for diagnosing how prepared academic libraries are to integrate their diversity initiatives into all services and operations. She reported, "The academic libraries in the study were not meeting the needs of all staff members, thereby not making the workplace a welcoming environment" (Love 2001, 97).

Another notable assessment of diversity climate took place in the Fairfax County Public Library (FCPL) system. Fairfax staffers wrote, "Evaluating diversity initiatives is still a new phenomenon, with only a few academic and public libraries attempting such studies" (Coats, Goodwin, and Bangs 2000, 149). The authors said Fairfax County may have been the first public library to do an assessment. The Columbus Metropolitan Library system in Ohio used the Fairfax model to perform a similar study as well.

The motivators for the Fairfax study were Diversity Committee members who wanted feedback on how they were doing. They wanted to evaluate their success and think about new directions. The idea for a survey originated with the Diversity Committee. A survey was designed in-house and was divided into four sections:

1. FCPL Practices and Policies
2. Diversity in the Workplace
3. Staff/Patron Interaction
4. FCPL's Diversity Program

The Fairfax authors concluded with these statements: "What Fairfax County Public Library discovered from its Diversity Climate Survey was not only what needed to be improved, but what it was doing right and also where new diversity activities should be headed.... Future plans include a possible follow-up survey in three to five years.... Other libraries should find such evaluation tools extremely useful in the new demographics of the twenty-first century" (Coats, Goodwin, and Bangs 2000, 152).

The Fairfax approach may be unusual in that the assessment was done in-house. It appears more common to contract out for such studies. Indeed, the Association of Research

Libraries (ARL) has sponsored at least one workshop, "The Role of Assessment in Advancing Diversity for Libraries," the stated goal being "to provide participants with vocabulary that will facilitate their interaction with researchers and consultants who systematically collect information and do survey research" (ARL 2002). ARL has also offered this workshop online several times in recent years, as part of its Online Lyceum. Of course, if individuals are comfortable doing surveys in-house, they might consider shorter, less formal surveys, done periodically, to take the "temperature" of the organization and see how it compares over time.

UNIVERSITY OF MARYLAND LIBRARIES' EXPERIENCE WITH TWO MAJOR ASSESSMENTS

REASONS FOR THE INITIAL ASSESSMENT

In November 1995, the University of Maryland (UMD) Dean of Libraries appointed a Coordinator of Services to Diverse Populations and a Diversity Committee. The staff person's title was later renamed to "Diversity Coordinator." The three main goals of the UMD Libraries' Diversity Initiative, as then stated, were:

1. To hire and retain a diverse workforce
2. To foster a work environment where all employees are valued for their uniqueness and personal contributions
3. To provide services and collections that meet users' individual and diverse needs

In 1998 and 1999, the Diversity Committee began planning for a diversity training component in staff development programs that would address diversity issues. The diversity assessment was initiated with the goal of determining whether there was a need within the libraries to conduct diversity training and, if so, what content areas should be included. In September 1999, the libraries' manager of Staff Training and Development approached the chair of the campus Industrial/Organizational (I/O) Psychology Department about conducting a diversity needs assessment for the libraries.

The parallel and underlying purpose of the diversity assessment was to provide a snapshot of where the UMD Libraries were then in achieving the principles of diversity, particularly focusing on individual attitudes and beliefs, organizational culture, and management practices and policies. A formal assessment would provide baseline data against which the organization's future progress could be measured. Because diversity issues are only one aspect of the whole organizational system, the libraries soon determined that it would be necessary to collect information about the general organizational culture in addition to information about diversity issues.

APPROACH AND TOOLS USED

The I/O Psychology Department research team, which consisted of three doctoral students assigned to the project, began with focus groups, the goal being to sample at least 15 percent of the employee population. Eight focus groups were held with forty total employees, who responded to five questions regarding general climate perceptions and diversity at the libraries:

1. Please tell us about your experiences while working in the Libraries and the kind of climate in which you work (i.e., the kinds of events and/or practices that are rewarded and are expected of employees).
2. Can you tell me about the interpersonal relations between employees in this organization?
3. Please tell me about any problems that you have seen in this organization that are related to diversity issues.
4. How do you think employees feel about the Diversity Initiative and how do you think they feel about diversity issues in general?
5. What recommendations do you have for the Libraries' Diversity Initiative? (Nishii, Raver, and Domingue 2000)

A survey for all library employees was then constructed. The researchers did a literature review to determine what important predictor and outcome variables to include. They also developed questions and included published scales that reflected the themes that emerged from the focus groups. One purpose of the survey was to examine whether or not the issues that surfaced in the focus groups were representative of the library employee population at large and to link employee perceptions of organizational culture and diversity to organizational outcome variables. The survey's questions and scales dealt with topics such as organizational commitment, job satisfaction, distributive fairness (the perception that rewards and resources are distributed in accordance with the recipients' contributions), ethnic and gender harassment, and perceptions of fair interpersonal treatment.

Since the goal was to assess the attitudes and experiences of all library employees through the survey, the UMD Libraries aimed to administer it to as many employees as possible. The survey was not sent out to employees. Instead, the researchers administered the survey in a large conference room, set up with tables and chairs and with snacks provided. The survey was administered on four different days and took an average of 45 minutes to 1 hour to complete. Library employees received a letter from the dean in advance, requesting their participation. In addition, employees who could not participate during any of the four days could fill out the survey and mail it to the researchers. Two hundred and sixty staff members (82 percent of library employees) participated and every division in the libraries was well represented.

The survey consisted of two types of scales. The first reflected the themes encountered in the focus groups, as well as items that reflect common themes found in the diversity literature. This type of scale was designed to reflect whether the libraries have a climate for diversity. The second major type of scale included those drawn from previous organizational research. These scales included the following: Ethnic Harassment, Gender Harassment, Armed Forces Ethnic Experiences Inventory, Job Satisfaction, Organizational Commitment, Organizational Withdrawal, Perceptions of Fair Interpersonal Treatment, Distributive Justice, Continuous Learning Culture, Managerial Practices, and Work Group Conflict. Each of these scales was used to evaluate an aspect of the libraries' organizational culture or individuals' experiences (Nishii, Raver, and Domingue 2000).

RESULTS OF THE INITIAL ASSESSMENT

In sum, the primary recommendation of the researchers was for the libraries to be cognizant of the critical role that organizational culture plays in the effective management of all human resources in the libraries and to be willing to challenge the existing culture. The researchers made the following recommendations for planning and change:

- The assessment data provided in this report should be utilized to enact a detailed, well-defined, long-term diversity plan that clearly defines all objectives and the steps necessary to attain the objectives of a multicultural organization.
- This diversity plan should also include an explicit definition of diversity as it will be applied within the University of Maryland Libraries.
- Management should work together with the Diversity Committee to establish the strategies necessary to implement the diversity plan. The libraries' Diversity Committee should play a role that is more critically linked to organizational processes. The definition of the Diversity Committee should be expanded to include a broader range of functions and duties.
- The change process began when the libraries solicited the opinions of all employees; thus the administration must follow through on the results of this survey. (Nishii, Raver, and Domingue 2000)

The researchers additionally had these specific recommendations for action:

- Assessment results suggest that the UMD Libraries would benefit from managerial training. Over 90 percent of survey respondents agreed that managers should be required to attend interpersonal skills training. Such training would be important for addressing many issues that arose in the assessment, including the standardization of procedures across groups, fairness in the distribution of rewards, intercultural sensitivity and communication, how to encourage employee participation and voice, how to build effective teams, and how to play an active role in subordinates' development and mentoring. Diversity and awareness would play a part in such training but would not be the primary focus.
- Both focus group and survey results indicated that many employees perceived that the library administration should pay further attention to ensuring that the libraries' policies, practices, and procedures are standardized across groups. Two critical areas of concern are the performance review and development process and the procedures for awarding merit increases.
- The literature review indicated that the primary way to increase the proportion of ethnic minorities in upper management is to hire more minorities who have the background necessary to advance. More aggressive recruiting efforts need to be implemented in order to broaden the applicant pool. In addition, training should be provided for interviewers at all levels of the organization in order to minimize rater biases in the selection process.
- Library employees expressed an interest in having more voice and being more empowered in the decision-making process. One of the most important guidelines for building trust is to follow through on one's commitments. If employees are to feel more empowered, then decision making must be collective, and employees must be able to see that their suggestions are translated into actions.

- There is clear evidence in the literature that mentoring serves a very important function in an individual's career success. Formal mechanisms for monitoring the progress of mentoring relationships should be established.
- A suggestion from the focus groups was that employees should be given more opportunities to socialize in a nonwork environment (i.e., opportunities other than the holiday party in December). Over 65 percent of survey respondents agreed that the libraries should sponsor social activities for employees.
- Management should also be particularly aware of the high levels of reported satisfaction with co-workers across all groups and use this finding to its full advantage. More specifically, the cultural survey and the focus groups both revealed that employees generally have positive relationships with co-workers in their immediate work groups. Furthermore, library employees tend to react positively to group- or team-based initiatives. The libraries are a prime example of an organization that could benefit from team-based structures and initiatives.
- Feedback regarding the Advisory Group in Public Services has been extremely positive, and focus group and survey results suggest that other divisions would also benefit from such an opportunity.
- The results of this assessment indicate that the problems related to diversity in the libraries are intricately linked to other organizational processes; hence the researchers suggested that the processes be examined as a system. They thought that the implementation of training that isolates diversity from other organizational processes would not be the best avenue for the libraries at that time.
- Many library employees reported dissatisfaction with the requirement at that time of placing an African American on every search committee. While understanding the administrative constraints placed by the university, the researchers recommended the libraries continue their role as a leader in diversity on campus by expanding the definition of diversity. (Nishii 2000)

INTERVENTIONS, CHANGES, AND ACCOMPLISHMENTS AS A RESULT OF THE 2000 ASSESSMENT

Once the survey analysis was complete and the final report issued, the Diversity Committee and the Library Executive Council (the dean and division heads) met jointly to review the results of the study. In October 2000, two forums were held to afford all library staff an opportunity to discuss the results of the cultural assessment and its implications for diversity in the libraries. (Those forums for general communication and sharing information continue to date as monthly all-staff meetings.) In the fall of 2000 the libraries began work to follow up on the study's findings and recommendations. This work is evidenced by interventions that have taken place along a variety of fronts.

The UMD Libraries not only addressed the need for managerial training. In May 2001 they inaugurated the Learning Curriculum, a comprehensive learning and education plan of over 150 content hours that focuses on individual and organizational development. The Learning Curriculum is comprised of ten components which in turn include a number of modules. The components are the following:

1. Introduction: Development of the Organization
2. Defining Customer Service
3. Measurement, Evaluation and Continuous Improvement for Planning and Decision-Making
4. Development of Self, Teams, and Workgroups
5. Exploring Leadership and Followership
6. Individual Improvement
7. Computer Skills
8. Library Basic Skills
9. Leadership Development
10. Train-the-Trainer

Workshops have been offered in all these areas, with the emphasis to date being on leadership development, customer service, supervisory skills, and computer skills. Notably, in 2003 a "Summer for Supervisors" series was offered which included a "Dealing with Differences" component. This program focused on methods to more effectively manage cultural differences in the workplace. In that same extended series, workshops on conflict management were offered in the spring of 2004.

In 2002, the UMD Libraries formalized support for participation in professional development and learning activities via an administrative memo informing staff members that they can use approximately 8 hours per month of work time to participate in workshops and other learning activities of their choice. That decision grew out of an earlier effort where several of the libraries' units and committees co-sponsored video showings of PBS's *Race and Diversity* and *Diversity and the Arts* series. Staff could use up to 3 hours of work time to view and discuss those videos.

The UMD Libraries have continued other efforts at open communication. One example from August 2001 was when a total of ninety-six library staff participated in two town hall meetings entitled: "Bridging the Gap: Overcoming Us vs. Them." The program was designed as a means to surface issues and concerns and to create an open climate in which to begin discussing perceived barriers to moving the library forward as an organization.

The UMD Libraries have strengthened support for staff and answered some of the findings of the 2000 assessment by describing and filling a new position in 2001—that of Coordinator of Personnel Programs. The coordinator works with others to ensure that library employees have a productive, challenging work environment and that work planning and performance review and other personnel programs are similarly handled throughout the libraries. This individual has begun several important programs, among them a Support Group for Advanced Studies, a pilot group of library staff who are interested in furthering their studies. It began with a core group of fourteen staff members and currently has approximately nineteen members. She also coordinates mentoring programs, both for library staff and for faculty librarians.

Since the 2000 survey, social occasions for library employees that are held on work time have increased. For example, the Diversity and Goodwill Committees have co-sponsored new staff/welcome-back luncheons annually since October 2002. The Diversity Committee also sponsors various activities like monthly video "brown-bag" lunch programs, on a variety of diversity-related topics from disability awareness to *Brown v. Board of Education* to left-handedness. In 2003, the group published a cookbook of recipes contributed by various members of the multicultural staff.

The libraries' planning has improved as well. There are library-wide diversity plans, as required by the university. Beyond this, the libraries' Diversity Committee has developed its own work plans that are more detailed for its purposes.

In short, acting on the findings and recommendations of the 2000 assessment, the UMD Libraries have tried to address learning time, social time, information sharing and communication, and standardization of policies and procedures.

THE SECOND ORGANIZATIONAL CULTURE AND DIVERSITY ASSESSMENT IN 2004

The UMD Libraries invested much effort in acting on the findings and recommendations of the 2000 study. From the outset the libraries intended to have a second assessment to know what has succeeded and why or why not and what needs to be done in the future.

The libraries returned to the Industrial/Organizational Psychology Department on campus, which was again interested in undertaking the study with and for the libraries. The same pattern was followed as with the 2000 assessment—i.e., focus groups and then a written survey conducted in May 2004. The libraries wanted to test several important areas:

- How the views and experiences of staff who were here in 2000 and participated in that survey have changed
- How the views and experiences of staff who were not here in 2000 differ from those who were here in 2000 and who participated in that survey
- How the spread of a team-based environment has changed individuals' perspectives and accomplishments

The libraries recognized the risk of having the assessment colored by the external environment of the past several years, during which time budgets have been reduced, there have been no merit or cost-of-living salary increases, and positions have had to be held open. On the other hand, it was important to measure what the internal efforts had produced, employees' individual attitudes and beliefs, the libraries' organizational culture, and current management practices as they relate to diversity. Participants were assured that they could take the survey on work time and that their responses would be confidential.

The survey was again administered over several days and staff came to a large room to fill out the survey rather than having it mailed to them. While approximately 19.4 percent of library staff participated in focus groups, 71.1 percent participated in the survey. The Assistant Dean for Organizational Development, the Manager of Staff Learning and Development, the Coordinator of Personnel Programs, and the Director for Planning and Administrative Services coordinated logistics for the assessment. They also worked with the Library Executive Council to gain staff awareness of, support for, and participation in the assessment.

RESULTS OF THE 2004 ASSESSMENT

In November 2004, the lead researcher, who is the chair of the I/O Psychology Department, briefed staff on preliminary study findings at two all-staff meetings. In December 2004 he met with the Library Executive Council to review additional findings and to plan for further discussion and follow-up on the findings and recommendations of the assessment. The final report will be presented to the UMD Libraries in January 2005.

The executive summary of the final draft report notes that, based on overall respondent averages, the assessment results indicate that the UMD Libraries:

- Have a positive work environment for diversity
- Lack racial barriers
- Successfully disseminate information
- Support and value diversity
- Have nondiscriminatory practices and apply these practices and procedures uniformly
- Value and support effective teamwork (Hanges, Leslie, and Keller 2004)

Further, based on overall responses, respondents appear to be committed to the organization, be somewhat satisfied, perceive fairness in their interpersonal treatment by supervisors, perceive fairness in the amount of information that is shared, and go out of their way to help fellow library employees (Hanges, Leslie, and Keller 2004).

However, despite the overall positive trends identified in the survey, there were differences among subgroups in terms of the degree to which they support the average assessment. "In particular, there were consistent ethnic group differences and division differences in how the Climate and Culture of the UM Libraries were described" (Hanges, Leslie, and Keller 2004, 5).

COMPARISON OF RESULTS OF THE 2000 AND 2004 ASSESSMENTS

The 2004 report also compared the scale scores of fifteen scales held in common between the 2000 and 2004 surveys. Those common scales included measures of organizational commitment, managerial practices, and perceptions of fair interpersonal treatment. The comparisons revealed a number of positive changes over the past four years. Respondents who completed both the 2000 and 2004 surveys showed statistically significant improvements in the beliefs that:

- The UMD Libraries support diversity.
- Employees are kept well-informed.
- The UMD Libraries have nondiscriminatory practices.
- Employees are fairly treated. (Hanges 2004)

The significant change that occurred between 2000 and 2004 was in organizational commitment. The frequency with which respondents think about leaving the UMD Libraries statistically increased in 2004.

The executive summary ends with this statement: "Overall, this analysis reveals that the UM Libraries climate and culture has undergone some significant improvements over the past 4 years" (Hanges, Leslie, and Keller 2004, 6).

PLANS TO FOLLOW UP ON THE 2004 ASSESSMENT

The 2004 researchers have said their final report will not contain the type of detailed recommendations found in the 2000 assessment. Rather, the researchers will point to the results that they think need further examination and will recommend that the libraries do that follow-up. The findings of most concern are the divisional (departmental) and ethnic differences from the overall positive trends and the decline in organizational commitment.

The Library Executive Council, the Diversity Committee, and the Staff Education Coordinating Team will play key roles in the follow-up. The first order of business will be to plan how to present findings to all staff work groups. Next will be to plan how to organize focus groups or other avenues to get at root causes of the findings of concern, noted previously. The large effort beyond that will be to change the organizational climate and culture to address the concerns.

The I/O researchers have repeatedly reminded the libraries that changing an organization's climate and culture creates negative results in the short term. In the short term there is increased uncertainty, and perceptions lag behind the reality of changes. The libraries will keep working in the direction of the last several years, mindful that organizational change is a long-term effort and determined to understand and work to resolve the negative findings in 2004.

ADAPTABILITY OF RESEARCH AND OTHER LIBRARIES' STUDIES

There are several factors for other organizations to keep in mind when considering whether to adapt the published research on diversity assessment and the University of Maryland's approach:

- *What outcomes you seek*: Do you have a venerable diversity initiative that needs new life and direction? Do you want to start an initiative but need to know first what problems or opportunities it needs to address?

- *Which variables are most important to you*: For example, you may be interested in questions of justice. In your organization, is interpersonal, procedural, distributive, or information justice more important to you? Where do you need to target your questions? In other words, measure the right things. Measure what is important in your organization (Cox 2001).

- *What interventions may be needed to make diversity as a way of life real in your libraries*: Are managerial and supervisory training and development needed? Is there a need for more open and consistent systems of communication? Do you need to pay more attention to how work planning and performance review take place across the organization and, if so, what will that intervention look like?

Contracting with outside experts for a diversity and organizational culture assessment is recommended. A library in a college or university will likely have some built-in resources on campus, found in such places as the business or human resources programs and psychology or human development schools. A library in a city or town in which there is a university or college may have access to those same resources. For public libraries, city or county governments' departments of human resources are sources of expertise as well. The Urban Libraries Council, the Association of Research Libraries, or the various divisions or offices of the American Library Association may also serve as starting points for locating resources in the field of assessment.

There are several other suggestions that may seem obvious but cannot be taken for granted if an assessment is to yield broad participation and reliable information. A successful assessment program requires:

- Support from senior managers and the head of the library
- Assurance of anonymity of survey participants
- Clear definition of diversity, diversity initiative, organizational culture, or other terms used in the survey
- Definition of the environment one is to consider in answering the survey—e.g., one's immediate work unit, one's department, the whole library system
- Availability of budgetary and personnel resources to carry out recommendations made in the assessment

Libraries also need to be sure that their efforts are consistent with those of their parent organization.

CONCLUSION

The Association of Research Libraries identifies its assumptions about organizational assessment in its online course, "The Role of Assessment in Advancing Diversity for Libraries":

- Assessment is a subprocess of a larger system.
- The goal of assessment is to provide data about the reality in which individuals and organizations exist.
- Assessment without action can negatively impact organizational climate.
- Assessment methods should be honestly and thoroughly described before, during, and after the process.
- Planning for diversity should be based on an underlying knowledge of the organization. (ARL 1999)

ARL adds, "Effective assessment gives feedback to the organization that informs decisions related to resource allocation and areas for growth and enhancement. Most importantly, understanding organizational strengths and areas for improvement allows administrators to make adjustments that impact the organization's performance" (ARL 1999).

Johnnie Love sums up the effort this way: "Constructing and implementing diversity initiatives involves continuous experimentation, assessment, modification, and innovation. Assessment of diversity is an ongoing lifetime process of improvement" (Love 2001, 101). It is the commitment of the institution to this long-term process that makes diversity real.

BIBLIOGRAPHY

Association of Research Libraries (ARL). 1999. "The Role of Assessment in Advancing Diversity for Libraries." Online Lyceum. Available: http://mccoy.lib.siu.edu/arl/diversity/cintro.html.

Association of Research Libraries (ARL). August 2002. "The Role of Assessment in Advancing Diversity for Libraries." Available: http://www.arl.org/stats/diversity.html.

Chemers, Martin M., Stuart Oskamp, and Mark A. Costanzo, eds. 1995. *Diversity in Organizations: New Perspectives for a Changing Workplace*. Thousand Oaks, CA: SAGE.

Coats, Reed, Jane Goodwin, and Patricia Bangs. 2000. "Seeking the Best Path: Assessing a Library's Diversity Climate." *Library Administration and Management* 14, no. 3 (summer): 148–154.

Cox, Taylor, Jr. 2001. *Creating the Multicultural Organization: A Strategy for Capturing the Power of Diversity*. San Francisco: Jossey-Bass.

Hanges, Paul J., Lisa M. Leslie, and Kirsten Keller. 2004. *The University of Maryland Libraries' Organizational Climate and Culture Survey: Final Draft Report*. College Park: University of Maryland.

Jones, DeEtta. 2000. "Diversity: Where We Are and Where We Came From." *Leading Ideas* 15 (July): 3–10.

Love, Johnnieque B. 2001. "The Assessment of Diversity Initiatives in Academic Libraries." In *Diversity Now: People, Collections, and Services in Academic Libraries*, edited by Teresa Y. Neely and Kuang-Hwei (Janet) Lee-Smeltzer. New York: Haworth.

Nishii, Lisa N., Jana L. Raver, and Alexandria L. Domingue. 2000. *Results of the University of Maryland Libraries' Organizational Culture and Diversity Assessment: Final Report*. College Park: University of Maryland. Available: http://www.lib.umd.edu/PUB/ diversity.html.

Riggs, Donald E., and Patricia A. Tarin, eds. 1994. *Cultural Diversity in Libraries*. New York: Neal-Schuman.

Sedlacek, William E. 1993. *Issues in Advancing Diversity Through Assessment*. College Park: University of Maryland.

Thomas, David A., and Robin J. Ely. 1996. "Making Differences Matter: A New Paradigm for Managing Diversity." *Harvard Business Review* (September–October): 79–90.

Thomas, R. Roosevelt, Jr. 1990. "From Affirmative Action to Affirming Diversity." *Harvard Business Review* (March–April): 114.

Thomas, R. Roosevelt, Jr. 1995. "A Diversity Framework." In *Diversity in Organizations: New Perspectives for a Changing Workplace*, edited by Martin M. Chemers, Stuart Iskamo, and Mark A. Costanzo. Thousand Oaks, CA: SAGE.

Thomas, R. Roosevelt, Jr. 1996. "Managing a Diverse Workforce." *Public Manager: The New Bureaucrat* 25 (winter): 41–43.

Thomas, R. Roosevelt, Jr. 1999. *Building a House for Diversity: How a Fable about a Giraffe and an Elephant Offers New Strategies for Today's Workforce*. New York: American Management Association.

Winston, Mark, ed. 1999. *Managing Multiculturalism and Diversity in the Library: Principles and Issues for Administrators*. New York: Haworth.

2 MAKING DIVERSITY A GOAL THROUGH STRATEGIC PLANNING

by Rhea Ballard-Thrower and Grace M. Mills

INTRODUCTION

Strategic planning has a long and varied history. It has been used in a variety of cultures and organizations. Strategic planning has been defined as the process by which leaders of an organization prepare a framework for the future by developing a plan to achieve set goals. (Goodstein et al. 1993). The purpose of the strategic plan is to answer three questions:

- What is the environment? (internal and external assessment)
- Where are we going? (mission, vision, goals, objectives)
- How do we get there? (resources allocation) (Goodstein et al. 1993)

This chapter explores the importance of strategic planning for diversity in the library environment.

WHAT IS DIVERSITY TODAY?

As America's population changed from an immigrant culture to one where the majority of Americans were native born, people began to question if the melting pot blended into a new distinctive American culture or just an American version of European culture. Voices of protest rose to promote diversity—a concept that demanded not only acknowledgment of differences, but also appreciation for them (Carnevale and Stone 1995). Census statistics confirm that being known as an American is more diverse than it has ever been (U.S. Census Bureau 2000). The 2000 Census characterizes the United States as 75.1 percent white, 12.3 percent black, 12.5 percent Hispanic or Latino, 3.6 percent Asian, 0.9 percent American Indian and Alaska Native, and 0.1 percent Native Hawaiian and Other Pacific Islander (U.S. Census Bureau 2000).

It is not only by race or color that one considers diversity. Increasingly there need to be considerations of religion: Amish, Atheist, Buddhist, Christian (that includes Born-Again, Fundamentalist, Mainline, New Age, Protestant, Roman Catholic, or Traditional), Mennonite, Muslim, Quaker, and Taoist to name only a few (U.S. Census Bureau 2003, 67). There are considerations to be made concerning ability: fully abled, partially abled, handicapped, hearing impaired, or visually impaired. Depending upon the organization there are increasing considerations about status: ageism, medical status, and veteran's status.

Diversity is not limited to the labeling of one group over another. *Webster's New Collegiate Dictionary* gives a fundamental definition of diversity as "an instance or a point of difference" (1975, 334). Increasingly as directors of organizations, and as members of our organizations, one faces (if one is not confronted by) a multiplying variety of people in a variety of circumstances in one organization. With so many "point[s] of difference" found in an organization, one's only hope for continued success of the organization is for one to adapt.

DIVERSITY IN THE WORKPLACE

> A State or its instrumentality may, of course, regulate the use of its libraries or other public facilities. But it must do so in a reasonable and nondiscriminatory manner, equally applicable to all and administered with equality to all.

Brown v. State of Louisiana, (383 U.S. 131, 143 [1966]).

Those words, stated by Supreme Court Justice Abe Fortas in *Brown v. State of Louisiana*, expanded the scope of the Supreme Court's ruling in *Brown v. Board of Education* (347 U.S. 483 [1954]) to prohibit racial segregation in public libraries. Although the *Brown v. Board of Education* case concerned racial segregation in public schools, using that same reasoning, later decisions by the Supreme Court heralded the end of de jure racial segregation in public accommodations (*Johnson v. Virginia* 1963) (courtrooms); *City of St. Petersburg v. Alsup*, 238 F.2d 830 (5th Cir. 1956) (municipal beaches and swimming pools); *Hanes v. Shuttlesworth*, 310 F.2d (5th Cir. 1962) (public parks and recreational facilities).

As a consequence of the civil rights decisions of the Supreme Court, there was an increasing likelihood that the workplace would become more diverse. However, it was the passage of the Civil Rights Act of 1964 that provided the impetus for people of various races, colors, religions, and national origins to interact in the workplace (42 U.S.C. §2000a-1 [2000 and Supp. I 2004]). The Civil Rights Act prohibited discrimination in employment, voting, public places, and federally supported programs. It was that melding of different races, cultures, religions, etc. in the workplace that exposed the difficulties of respecting differences. Prior to the 1960s, the prevailing view of society was that of the melting pot (Zangwill 1975). The idea was that the various cultures in America combined to create an American culture unique unto itself and no longer distinguished by its various parts. Often, it was the European culture that was considered the most acceptable (Jacoby 2004).

In response to the changes in society, businesses have recognized the need for diverse representation in the workplace (Carnevale and Stone 1995). In his book *Beyond Race and Gender: Unleashing the Power of Your Total Workforce by Managing Diversity*, Dr. R. Roosevelt Thomas, Jr. is credited with promoting two distinguishing aspects of workplace diversity—valuing and managing (Thomas 1991). To value diversity is to have a positive response to the various differences (Thomas 1991, 23). To manage diversity is to implement plans whereby the environment is comfortable for all workers (Thomas 1991, 23). Because managing diversity involves empowerment, Dr. Thomas theorizes that managing diversity is a much more difficult task to accomplish. Both valuing and managing diversity require that the majority culture not only change its customs but also welcome the distinctions of others (Carnevale and Stone 1995). Subsequently, diversity training, a proactive examination of the various differences in the workplace and how response to those differences impacts the work environment, became the means whereby employees were introduced to the concept of appreciating workplace diversity (Lasch-Quinn 2001).

During the 1990s, in an effort to better understand and compete with Japanese business productivity, diversity training exploded in the United States (Lasch-Quinn 2001, 164). Today, diversity training is so widely accepted that it has become an industry unto itself (Lasch-Quinn 2001, 163). There are videos, manuals, books, courses, consultants, and even institutes. As the focus on diversity training grew, there were a number of schools of thought developed on the best way to facilitate diversity training. The Sensitivity Training Model proved the most popular (Lasch-Quinn 2001, 65). Using this model, people were placed in groups and asked to express their feelings on various topics involving diversity. Feedback given by a consultant, moderator, or other participants in the group was considered an important element of this model (Lasch-Quinn 2001, 66). Eventually two workshop methods grew out of the sensitivity model.

Today, awareness-based and skill-based training are considered the two most popular workshops for diversity (Mossison 1992). Awareness-based training is when participants are encouraged to increase their sensitivity to diverse issues (Mossison 1992). Skill-based training is when participants are taught the skills needed to work in a diverse environment (Mossison 1992). Having participants attend sessions employing either method is believed to make the workplace a better environment for all. However, as the economy has proven to be less stable, detractors have questioned whether diversity training and workshops have benefited the bottom line (Kochan et al. 2002).

In her book *Race Experts: How Racial Etiquette, Sensitivity Training, and New Age Therapy Hijacked the Civil Rights Revolution*, Lasch-Quinn questions whether sensitivity sessions really solve societal issues or if they make the environment a more difficult place to work (Lasch-Quinn 2001, 193). Although there may not be agreement on the best way to value and manage diversity in the workplace, with the increasing changes in America's ethnic population, and subsequently its workforce, some form of diversity training will still be a necessity. Whether one considers diversity issues as positively or negatively influencing the workplace, these issues have been an important aspect of the environment for several decades. The same can be said concerning the development of a workplace's strategic plan.

HISTORY OF STRATEGIC PLANNING AND DIVERSITY

A strategic plan is very important in defining where the organization is going. Strategic planning and diversity issues are so intertwined that *diversity* is often listed as one of the goals of a strategic plan. Diversity of personnel is a key goal in the strategic plan and the organization's diversity ensures the success of the organization's strategic plan.

Generally, strategic planning is not a new concept. Historical documents reveal an amazing range of plans and planners from Plato's *Republic*, Sun Tzu's *The Art of War*, and Thomas Jefferson's University of Virginia to Alexander the Great's dominance (Rea and Kerzner 1997). Actually, it can be argued that strategic planning is as old as time itself. For those who believe, even God developed and implemented a plan over seven days. In modern times, strategic planning gained popularity in the 1960s (Mintzberg 1994). Often Frederick W. Taylor, the efficiency engineer, is credited with formulating the basis for what was to become strategic planning (Mintzberg 1994). Strategic planning was viewed as a way to contend in an increasingly competitive world (Mintzberg 1994). Taylor surmised that in order to benefit a company's bottom line, a business must devise a plan of goals and then follow it to accomplish the desired objective (Copley 1923). Strategic planning is considered beneficial because it provides a clear plan for the future, identifies problems, sets priorities, and promotes teamwork (Rea and Kerzner 1997).

Throughout time, strategic planning has morphed from one model or type to another. Strategic planning has included, but is not limited to, such models as SWOT (Strengths, Weaknesses, Opportunities, and Threats), core competencies, strategic agility, Porter's Five Forces, etc. (Rea and Kerzner 1997). Of course, no one strategic planning method has worked for every environment. Yet, all strategic plans have a few similar characteristics—creation of long-term goals, allocation of resources to achieve the goals, implementation, review, and revision (Rea and Kerzner 1997). As the benefits of strategic planning have been touted, it too has developed some well-known detractors (Kochan 2002; Mintzberg 1994).

In the book *High Impact Tools and Activities for Strategic Planning: Creative Techniques for Facilitating Your Organization's Planning Process*, the authors suggest that there are many difficulties with strategic planning. First, life is uncertain, so strategic planning does not occur in a vacuum. Second, employees see strategic planning as a special, one-time event. Third, the strategic plan is drafted to maintain control and support the hierarchical structure. Fourth, the people who draft the plan are not responsible for its implementation (Napier et al. 1997).

Management theorist Professor Henry Mintzberg believes that strategic planning generally fails because it is calculating rather than committing. Calculating is when the goals are the priority and anything is done to achieve them. Committing is when the progression of the process is the focus (Mintzberg 1994). Mintzberg laments that over time the practice of strategic planning has been highjacked by professional planners and molded into an analytical, solution-oriented format (Mintzberg 1994, 112). Mintzberg argues that the world is constantly changing and uncertain. Thus, the workplace cannot solely rely on facts and figures for strategic planning. Strategic planners must acquire all types of information if they are to successfully prepare for the future (Mintzberg 1994).

THE UNCERTAINTY OF STRATEGIC PLANNING

Creating a strategic plan is not easy by any means. There are levels of uncertainty, the "unknown," that constantly affect the decision-making process and have to be balanced with the objective of promoting diversity. Often reiterated is the idea that uncertainty is the most difficult element of strategic planning. In *Strategy Under Uncertainty*, the authors suggest that there are four levels of uncertainty that affect strategic planning (Courtney et al. 1997).

THE FOUR LEVELS OF UNCERTAINTY IN STRATEGIC PLANNING

Level 1—"Clear Enough"

This level is considered when extensive fact gathering is used to reduce uncertainty to reveal specific outcomes (Courtney et al. 1997). Scenario: the library administration is concerned that it cannot fund a special project. Research provided by the development office confirms that a donor plans to give the library a financial gift in the next three years which will provide a source of funding for the special project.

Level 2—"Alternative Futures"

This is considered when a goal is set based on the actions taken by an outside force (Courtney et al. 1997). Scenario: a recent court decision requires changes to the library's hiring procedures. A recent county ordinance states that all homeless people living in the county cannot be denied access into a library unless they have received a "trespass" notice three times previously within the last year.

Level 3—"Range of Futures"

This is related to the second level of uncertainty of "Alternative Futures," in that another party has taken action. However, the goals set for this level of uncertainty are of a larger range (Courtney et al. 1997, 10). Scenario: library administration has received word that the budget will be reduced, but the amount is unknown. If the amount is one figure, certain steps can be taken. However, if the amount is another figure, then other steps will be taken.

Level 4—"True Ambiguity"

This is the final and most critical level of uncertainty: "True Ambiguity." This is when nothing is certain (Courtney et al. 1997). Fortunately, this level of instability is *never* permanent. Eventually, "True Ambiguity" changes into one of the other three levels of uncertainty and then a strategic plan can be developed (Courtney et al. 1997). For example, library administration has decided to participate in an exchange program with another country. Unfortunately, a civil war erupts in the host country, postponing the planned exchange.

In regard to traditional strategic planning, the authors state that there is the tendency to consider all levels of uncertainty, as "Clear Enough" (Courtney et al. 1997, 11). Strategic planners believe that with only more research the level of uncertainty can be eliminated (Courtney et al. 1997). However, the authors believe that this approach often leads to unsuccessful strategic planning. The level of uncertainty in strategic planning will more likely be either levels two or three—"Alternative Futures" or "Range of Futures," not "Clear Enough" (Courtney et al. 1997).

ANALYZING YOUR LIBRARY POSTURE

While determining and creating its strategic plan, a library must also analyze its posture. *Strategy Under Uncertainty* describes three types of posture: "Shapers," "Adaptors," and "Reserving the Right to Play" (Courtney et al. 1997, 16).

IS YOUR LIBRARY A SHAPER?

A "Shaper" library is one that manipulates the environment into a new paradigm (Courtney et al. 1997). For example, the Library of Congress creates a new classification system. While many library systems may not be as grand or have such a large organization as this example, any size library can be a "shaper." A county public library system could develop a new method of book delivery to its constituents; a library could develop a new Web system with delivery of reference answers and/or library communication to its users that changes how the library is structured and how the county library users interact with the library.

IS YOUR LIBRARY AN ADAPTOR?

An "Adaptor," the second type of posture, is when the library easily identifies changes in the environment and reacts quickly (Courtney et al. 1997). For example, a library becomes aware that the federal funds for the work-study program will be reduced. The library responds by actively recruiting more library volunteers. In this manner the library takes a reflective look at its internal structure and its personnel and reacts quickly before the change has injurious effects upon the library activities, its personnel, and most importantly, its internal morale.

DOES YOUR LIBRARY RESERVE THE RIGHT TO PLAY?

The last posture type is "Reserving the Right to Play." This is when a library takes incremental steps today, and then waits until the environment becomes more stable before it implements its plan (Courtney et al. 1997). For example, a library builds a new facility with load-bearing floors to accommodate compact shelving in the future.

Because the environment is uncertain, strategic planning for a library is that much more critical. By developing a strategic plan, a library can have a clear understanding of its purpose, awareness of its competition, a strategy that is proactive, and knowledge of its strengths and weaknesses.

> *Questions to Ask Yourself*
>
> - What type of library are you in, Shaper, Adaptor, or Reserve the Right to Play?
> - Does your library organization want to shape the environment in which it is in?
> - Does it have the opportunity to do so?
> - If so, does it want to do so?
> - Are you (or your library organization) aware of any funding issues that can change your environment?
> - Can you work to change your library posture so you do not have to react violently to the changes?
> - Are you able to implement small changes in your present and/or future environment so that you have the ability to change/grow in the future?

WHAT LIBRARIES LOOK LIKE

Libraries are unique in that they are often a microcosm of society. All types of people work at libraries: various races, cultures, religions, political parties, sexual orientations, ages, marital status (with or without children)—the combinations are varied and limitless (U.S. Census Bureau 2003). In most cases these varied types of people manage to work together to provide excellent customer service. Of course, some libraries are more successful in building a diverse staff than others. Larger towns and cities frequently have types of people from a variety of races and cultures. Smaller towns and cities may have clusters of people that are more homogeneous.

This is not a slur or defensive statement for or against either the larger or smaller environments. It is stating something that is relatively obvious and most of us can relate to if in our experiences. Yet that obviousness need not forestall the continued effort to maintain achieved diversity or to increase standards of diversity of staff. For those libraries that have successfully built more diverse staff, diversity and diversity training are often goals in their strategic plans. Yet, as the world becomes more diverse it is no longer acceptable to just have diversity as a goal of a strategic plan. Rather, diversity must be part of every stage of the strategic planning process. Once a library has determined what type of library it is (and determining its type can take months of discussion), the library can use its diversity to create its strategic plan. Using the team-based (Fogg 1994) approach in conjunction with the various levels of uncertainty, diversity can be an integral part of a library's strategic planning process.

DIVERSITY AND TEAM-BASED STRATEGIC PLANNING

Team-based strategic planning begins with the formation of the team. Team members should include all employees who will be responsible for executing the strategic plan. If the library is so large that it is not feasible for every employee to be on the planning team, then the team should include a representative from each library department. It is imperative that the team be a diverse representation of the library. Team members of different races, cultures, religions, etc. will provide various perspectives and input during the planning process. In his book *Team-Based Strategic Planning: A Complete Guide to Structuring, Facilitating, and Implementing the Process*, C. Davis Fogg characterizes an effective team as one that communicates openly, discusses, debates, conflicts, agrees, and is respectful and flexible (Fogg 1994). Team members should be employees who not only have had diversity training but also respect and value diversity. If the library is to have various departments represented on the strategic planning team, a team leader should be selected for each department. For example, a reference librarian is selected as team leader for the reference department. The team leader is responsible for representing the interests of his or her department and keeping his or her colleagues informed (Fogg 1994, 260).

Once the team is created and the leaders identified, the next step is to select a facilitator (Fogg 1994, 44). Like the team leaders, the facilitator should be someone who has had diversity training and values workplace diversity. The purpose of the facilitator is to make sure the team completes all steps of the strategic planning process in a timely manner (Fogg 1994). To ensure impartiality, it is recommended that the facilitator be a professional from outside the organization who has previous experience with strategic planning (Fogg 1994, 57). However, professional strategic planners can be very expensive, so many libraries may not be able to afford someone from outside the organization. Thus, an internal candidate should be selected. *However, it is important to be aware that not every team member is a potential facilitator.* An internal candidate should be selected based on his or her previous experience as a facilitator or his or her perceived abilities to be the best person for the task. It is possible for the library director to be this person. However, to be an effective facilitator, he or she must remember to be neutral, speak last, and not be authoritarian (Fogg 1994, 46). Fogg believes that because the facilitator has such a pivotal role, the facilitator should already possess three important skills before he or she is selected. The skills are process, content, and intervention (Fogg 1994, 44). Process is when the facilitator outlines how the course of action will develop (Fogg 1994, 44). This can include selecting the meeting location and times, providing an agenda, documentation, etc. The next skill the facilitator should possess is content (Fogg 1994, 49–50). The facilitator should have enough knowledge about other libraries so that he or she can provide valuable input about how things are accomplished at comparable institutions. However, if the facilitator does not know such information, he or she should know how to find it. The final and most important is intervention. That is when the facilitator recognizes the team members are at an impasse and the facilitator is able to resolve the issue and get the team working again (Fogg 1994, 50). Once the team has selected a facilitator with these characteristics, the group is one step closer to beginning to strategize.

The strategic planning process is not a "one size fits all" process. To successfully complete a strategic plan it is a very good idea to tailor the process and the plan to fit the organization (Fogg 1994, 59). It is in your organization's best interest to take the time to complete this tailoring process before you do the strategizing work. Why? The preparatory planning could be costly in time, personnel, and money (Fogg 1994, 61).

THE TEAM-BASED STRATEGIC PLANNING PROCESS IN NINE STEPS

With planning and attention to these nine steps and details, a library organization can conceive its own strategic plan. The team-based model involves the following nine steps:

- Situation analysis
- Priority issues
- Mission/vision
- Objectives
- Strategies
- Program development
- Delegation
- Accountability
- Review

STEP ONE: SITUATION ANALYSIS

This is when the organization determines its strengths and weaknesses (internal assessment), as well as what outside factors impact the organization's ability to achieve success (external assessment) (Fogg 1994, 3–10). For the internal assessment, the team should look at its culture, systems, and practices (Fogg 1994, 8–10). What does the library do really well? What does the library not do well? The team can identify four or five things for each of the above aspects. For example, the team could agree that having the staff attend an awareness-based diversity training workshop was productive. Is one of its strengths its commitment to public service? Is it the delivery of public service? Is the catalog fantastic and very user friendly?

For its external assessment, the team should analyze, among other things, its patrons and their sociodemographics, competition, technology, the economy, and politics (Fogg 1994, 5–8). In its external assessment the team should identify four or five things the library does well and the same number of things that the library doesn't do well. For example, the team could surmise that its location in an area where the percentage of minorities is small may be a factor when trying to hire a more diverse staff. The team may consider the population of the area it serves. Are there a substantial number of homeless persons? Are there many children? It is at this stage in the process when the strategic planning team should be mindful of the four levels of uncertainty—Clear Enough, Alternative Futures, Range of Futures, and True Ambiguity (remembering Courtney 1997).

STEP TWO: PRIORITY ISSUES

Out of the list of strengths and weaknesses, the library should determine what main issue is key if it is to be productive (Fogg 1994). Does the library want to improve its delivery of public service to its clientele?

STEP THREE: MISSION/VISION

Generally, the parent institution drafts the mission that the units will follow. The mission statement defines what the institution does and whom it serves. The vision statement is where the library describes where it plans to be for the future and how it will reach that destination (Fogg 1994, 10–11). It is important for the library to be mindful that its vision must correspond with the mission of the larger organization.

STEP FOUR: OBJECTIVES

When the team is ready to decide what long-term plans it intends to accomplish, it has reached this fourth step of strategic planning known as Objectives (Fogg 1994). At this level organizations have traditionally listed diversity as a goal. For example, the team may agree that the library should increase the diversity of the staff within three years. It is also at this stage where the Shaper type of posture is significant (Courtney 1997). For example, the library creates a scholarship for minorities to help increase the number of minority library school graduates.

STEP FIVE: STRATEGIES

Once the objectives are set, the library should then formulate how it will accomplish its goals. This step is referred to as Strategies (Fogg 1994). For example, agreeing to advertise available positions on the Black Caucus of the American Library Association (BCALA) listserv would qualify as a strategy for increasing the diversity of the staff if one were seeking more African Americans on staff. If one were seeking to increase the number of applicants who identified as Asian American or Hispanic/Latino American, one could also contact the ALA for such caucuses having identified themselves with such members. Also at this level, the team must be aware of the Adaptor posture as previously discussed by Hugh Courtney in his *Harvard Business Review* article. Adaptors recognize that if the environment changes, the team should be ready to create a new strategy.

STEP SIX: PROGRAM DEVELOPMENT

This is when an action plan is outlined for each strategy (Fogg 1994, 13). The library should determine who, what, timeline, deadlines, funds, etc. It is often at this stage that more action plans are developed than can actually be implemented (Fogg 1994). Therefore, approximately five or six action plans should be selected. The library can determine the best plans by selecting those that support its mission and objectives (Fogg 1994, 13). For example, the team could agree to look at the BCALA Web site to locate information on how to post job announcements to its listserv. It is at this stage that the team can take a Reserve the Right to Play posture (Courtney 1997). For example, the library decides to hire a diversity officer, although it currently has few minority employees.

STEP SEVEN: DELEGATION

Once an action plan has been completed, the facilitator delegates action plans to those persons who have the authority and skill to implement them. Delegation is the seventh step in the strategic planning process (Fogg 1994). For example, the library director selects the head of Technical Services to lead a search committee to hire a new cataloging librarian. The search committee is given the responsibility of screening the applications and referring names to the director for possible interviews. It is at this stage that the team should consider the uncertainties of strategic planning. For example, what happens to the library's plan if all open positions are frozen by the larger institution? Or, if the number of minorities in library schools decreases? Or, a member of the staff files a racial discrimination lawsuit against the library? Each of these variables could impact the library's ability to implement its plan.

STEP EIGHT: ACCOUNTABILITY

During the team-based strategic planning process, the facilitator should periodically check with the coordinator of the action plan to make sure things are progressing as expected. This stage is known as Accountability (Fogg 1994, 14). For example, the director could confirm that a diverse pool of applicants has been selected for interviews and that the search committee has adhered to the suggested timeline.

STEP NINE: REVIEW

The final stage of the process is quite similar to the previous stage. While Accountability is more of a systematic, periodic assessment, Review occurs once the action plan has been completed or on a quarterly basis (Fogg 1994, 215–216). What is the benefit? The benefit of review is that it allows the organization to determine what parts of the plan are effective and which ones are not. If the program development or strategies are not working, they can be reevaluated and changed by the team (Fogg 1994). For example, the library received a number of applications in response to its posting on the BCALA listserv, so the library agrees to participate in the job placement office at the upcoming BCALA national conference. Strategic planning is not a new concept for libraries, but, by using the team-based approach, a library can develop a more effective way to plan for the library's future.

Further Items to Consider When Creating Your Library Team

- What, if any, factors will affect the strategic plan? (outside environment, pending funding, or legislation)
- Are there any members who will not function as team members on this assignment (i.e., are there combinations of staff members who are volatile or combative when placed in the same room for periods of time, and thus nonproductive)?
- Are there staff members who have constructive ideas but their participation may be limited because they can only participate in meetings during their work hours (thus any meetings can only happen during certain hours)?
- Does your staff have flex hours (thus limiting times for meetings)?
- Can a suitable racial composition be achieved?
- How can the religious makeup of the team affect the planning?
- Can one get a marital balance?
- Is there a balance of public and technical service members on this team?
- When is it best to schedule times, places, and dates for team meetings?
- Would it be good for the team to have meetings off site (away from the library), or is there a place in the library where they can meet?
- Depending upon the size of the team, shall the director play a direct role as facilitator, or is it better to hire an outside facilitator?
- If the director is the facilitator, what impact will this have on the staff?
- How are you going to make sure that the team's progress is disseminated to all library personnel?
- How will the final plan be disseminated to all staff members?

SAMPLE LIBRARY STRATEGIC PLAN

You are the library director of a medium-sized library: there are twenty-five people on your staff.

A sample outline of a strategic plan is followed by an existing plan developed by one of this chapter's authors.

Remember to include these items in the development of your plan:

- Library Mission
- Library Vision
- Library Strengths/Weaknesses
- Internal and External Objectives

- Results Anticipated and Required
- Implementation
- Review

SAMPLE LIBRARY STRATEGIC PLAN

Mission

INSERT Library's Mission Statement Here

Vision

INSERT Library's Vision Statement Here

Goals

- What are the Library's goals?
- How do the Library's goals support/promote its University?

Strategies

Questions to Answer:

- Does the Library want more staff training classes?
- Does the Library need to improve its services?
- Does the Library want to produce more publications and programs that benefit the Library patrons?
- Does the Library want to network with librarians at other organizations so as to improve services and encourage development?

Objectives

Internal questions

    Update the Library's collection?
    Storage?
    Periodicals?
    Circulation?

External questions

    Services with other departments?

Values

Internal

How will the Library achieve excellence?

> Professional manner
> Teamwork
> Respect
> Abilities/potentials
> Open communication

External

> To provide excellent customer service

(as developed by Rhea Ballard-Thrower and the Howard University Law Library staff)

The Library's Mission
The mission of the Howard University Law Library is to provide a quality collection of legal materials for the Howard University School of Law, faculty and students. Recognizing that the legal system extends beyond the Howard University School of Law community, the Law Library also provides access to legal materials for the practicing attorney, as well as people of all races, creed and colors.

The Library's Vision
The Law Library's vision is to be a premier legal research library, as well as a major component in the strategic and long-term success of the School of Law and the University.

The Library's Strategies
The goals of the Law Library are to provide access to and maintain a collection of information resources that support law school programs, legal research and the needs of all library users. The Law library will select, organize, preserve, and make available all of its resources as a way to assist those in their pursuit of justice. Recognizing Howard University School of Law's contribution to the field of civil rights, the Law Library shall develop a premier civil rights collection. A collection that is recognized not only for its depth of coverage, but also for its ease of use.

Figure 2-1. Howard University Law Library Strategic Plan (2002–2005)

A. Outreach
    1. Market
        Coordinator:
        Projected Date of Completion:

    2. Become a premier training center
        Coordinator:
        Projected Date of Completion:

    3. Improve relationship with other campus libraries
        Coordinator:
        Projected Date of Completion: ongoing

    4. Develop a library school internship program
        Coordinator:
        Projected Date of Completion:

B. Special Collections
    1. Catalog materials in special collections
        Coordinator:
        Projected Date of Completion:

    2. Integrate materials into special collections
        Coordinator:
        Projected Date of Completion:

C. Legal Research Instruction
    1. Improve legal research training programs
        Coordinator:
        Projected Date of Completion:

D. Staff Development
    1. Assist in offering Academy classes on campus
        Coordinator:
        Projected Date of Completion:

    2. Assist in providing an increased variety of Academy classes
        Coordinator:
        Projected Date of Completion:

    3. Provide staff development opportunities
        Coordinator:
        Projected Date of Completion:

    4. Upgrade staff position and salaries [Note: only the library director may be concerned with this]
        Coordinator:
        Projected Date of Completion:

Figure 2-1. Howard University Law Library Strategic Plan (2002–2005) (*Continued*)

E. Fundraising
- 1. Investigate fundraising opportunities
    Coordinator:
    Projected Date of Completion:

- 2. Identify and apply for grants
    Coordinator:
    Projected Date of Completion:

- 3. Increase book budget
    Coordinator:
    Projected Date of Completion:

F. Technology
- 1. Help IT department to support student's computing needs
    Coordinator:
    Projected Date of Completion:

- 2. Revise library's Web site
    Coordinator:
    Projected Date of Completion:

- 3. Conduct electronic surveys and/or commentaries specific to services and resources
    Coordinator:
    Projected Date of Completion:

- 4. Create a mapped network drive for shipping information and/or working file among librarians
    Coordinator:
    Projected Date of Completion:

- 5. Establish a new (independent) library Web page server with a Uniform Resources Locator that is easily distinguishable and comparable to other law libraries in the area, such as http://library.law.howard.edu
    Coordinator:
    Projected Date of Completion:

- 6. Explore lock down systems for equipment security
    Coordinator:
    Projected Date of Completion:

- 7. Investigate possibilities for digitizing course reserves (electronic reserves)
    Coordinator:
    Projected Date of Completion:

- 8. Provide education and training on information technology and electronic resources (for faculty, staff, and students)
    Coordinator:
    Projected Date of Completion:

Figure 2-1. Howard University Law Library Strategic Plan (2002–2005) (*Continued*)

> 9. Develop a library Intranet to facilitate effective communication and information sharing among librarians and staff
>   Coordinator:
>   Projected Date of Completion:
>
> G. Collection Development
>   1. Improve law library's collection
>   Coordinator:
>   Projected Date of Completion:
>
> [*Author's Note*: The names of existing personnel have been deleted from the following specifics, but the tasks are included to illustrate items that can be included in developing one's strategic plan. The tasks have been divided between public and technical services and librarians and professional staff.]
>
> **Figure 2-1. Howard University Law Library Strategic Plan (2002–2005)** (*Continued*)

CONCLUSION

Whether or not one believes that strategic planning has become too calculating, the idea of planning for the future is still valid. With reduced budgets, changing student populations, technological changes with accompanying rising costs, strategic planning is more important than ever. It is in a library organization's best interest, for its present as well as its future, to create a strategic plan that fits its organization.

In order to remain relevant in a society that increasingly believes everything is on the Internet, libraries must be proactive despite the uncertainties that they face. One certainty, however, is that American society will grow more ethnically diverse each day. Thus, the library workplace must respond to these changes beyond having increasing diversity listed as a goal. It must include diversity at all levels of the strategic planning process from the formation of the team to the final review. Until those steps are taken, diversity in the library will continue to remain on the fringes, and never amount to more than a nice concept for the annual report.

BIBLIOGRAPHY

Carnevale, Anthony Patrick, and Susan Carol Stone. 1995. *The American Mosaic: An In-Depth Report on the Future of Diversity at Work*. New York: McGraw-Hill.

Copley, Frank Barkley. 1923. *Frederick W. Taylor: Father of Scientific Management*. New York: Continuum.

Courtney, Hugh, et al. 1997. "Strategy Under Uncertainty." *Harvard Business Review* 75 (November–December): 67.

Fogg, C. Davis. 1994. *Team-Based Strategic Planning: A Complete Guide to Structuring, Facilitating, and Implementing the Process*. New York: American Management Association.

Goodstein, Leonard, et al. 1993. *Applied Strategic Planning: How to Develop a Plan That Really Works*. New York: McGraw-Hill.

Jacoby, Tamar. 2004. "Defining Assimilation for the 21st Century." In *Reinventing the Melting Pot: The New Immigrants and What It Means to Be American*, edited by Tamar Jacoby. New York: Basic Books.

Kochan, Thomas, et al. November 2002. "The Effects of Diversity on Business Performance: Report of the Diversity Research Network." Cambridge, MA: MIT Sloan School of Management. Available: http://faculty.haas.berkeley.edu/levine/Papers/Diversity%20&%20Performance%20Review.pdf.

Lasch-Quinn, Elisabeth. 2001. *Race Experts: How Racial Etiquette, Sensitivity Training, and New Age Therapy Hijacked the Civil Rights Revolution*. New York: W. W. Norton.

Mintzberg, Henry. 1994. "The Fall and Rise of Strategic Planning." *Harvard Business Review* 72 (January–February): 107.

Mossison, Ann M. 1992. *The New Leaders: Guidelines on Leadership Diversity in America*. San Francisco: Jossey-Bass.

Napier, Rod, et al. 1997. *High Impact Tools and Activities for Strategic Planning: Creative Techniques for Facilitating Your Organization's Planning Process*. New York: McGraw-Hill.

Rea, Peter, and Harold Kerzner. 1997. *Strategic Planning: A Practical Guide*. New York: John Wiley and Sons.

Thomas, R. Roosevelt, Jr. 1991. *Beyond Race and Gender: Unleashing the Power of Your Total Workforce by Managing Diversity*. New York: Amacom Books.

U.S. Census Bureau. 2000. "Diversity Continues to Grow in the U.S." U.S. Census 2000. Available: http://factfinder.census.gov/jsp/saff/SAFFInfo.jsp?_pageId=tp9_race_ethnicity and http://factfinder.census.gov/servlet/QTTable?_bm=y&-geo_id=01000US&-qr_name=DEC_2000_SF1_U_QTP5&_ds_name=DEC_2000_SF1_U&-_lang=en&_sse=on.

U.S. Census Bureau. 2003. Statistical Abstract of the United States: 2003. Available: http://www.census.gov/prod/2004pubs/03statab/pop.pdf.

Webster's New Collegiate Dictionary. 1975. Springfield, MA: G. & C. Merriam Company.

Zangwill, Israel. 1975. *The Melting Pot: Drama in Four Acts*. New York: Arno Press.

3 BEST PRACTICES FOR PLACING DIVERSITY AT THE CENTER OF YOUR LIBRARY

by Tracie D. Hall

> If you're trying to achieve, there will be roadblocks. I've had them; everybody has had them. But obstacles don't have to stop you. If you run into a wall, don't turn around and give up. Figure out how to climb it, go through it, or work around it.
> —Michael Jordan, NBA All-Star

INTRODUCTION

Demographers predict that by the year 2050, the United States will become a "nation of minorities" (U.S. Census Bureau 2000). Population increases among African Americans, Native Americans, and particularly among Asian Pacific Islanders and Latino/Hispanics are projected to result in a society more racially, ethnically, and linguistically diverse than ever before. In light of this fact, many demographers and social scientists have begun to propagate the use of "emergent majorities" as a more descriptive term to define these groups in that it better reflects contemporary social reality. What is clear is that if libraries are to remain relevant to the communities they serve they must make diversity integral to their plan of action.

To be certain, there are some impediments to actualizing diversity in libraries today. Data collected over the last decade indicate that only one out of ten public, academic, and school librarians are nonwhite (ALA Office for Research and Statistics 1994; National Center for Education Statistics 1994). In 1991, racial and ethnic minorities comprised only 9 percent or 344 of the 4,032 graduates receiving accredited MLIS degrees. In 2001, they accounted for less than 13 percent or 504 of the 4,109 MLIS degrees awarded (ALISE Library and Information Science Education Statistical Report), an increase that fails woefully to reflect the combined 152 percent growth increase experienced by these populations between 1990 and 2000 (U.S. Census Bureau 2000). There is also growing evidence that racial and ethnic minorities in the profession seldom find themselves in positions to determine overall service delivery to library users due to limited access to the highest levels of institutional leadership (Jones 2003; Reese and Hawkins 1999).

Race and ethnicity are just two of the many identifiers that contribute to social diversity. Disability, sexual orientation, age, language group, geographic region, and economic status are among the many other markers of difference. Too often those who see the library as a public trust—however that public is defined—particularly those of us within the profession, take for granted the egalitarian and inclusive nature of the library. We believe, often without palpable evidence, in the library's aim and ability to equitably serve each segment of its constituency, but librarianship, however altruistic its intent, is hardly immune to the dominant social discourse. Teresa Neely (1998) observes, "The practice of librarianship, in the aggregate, mirrors the lack of diversity that is reflected nationally, everyday, in media representation, news and sound bites and by major players in the political arena. It reflects the national dominant culture and therefore, has the tendency to share and echo similar ideologies and biases about diversity, race and affirmative action."

To this end those of us concerned with diversity in libraries—whether we be administrators, human resources personnel, members of diversity committees, public service or outreach coordinators, policy makers and planners, or individual advocates—must see ourselves as change agents, as point guards if you will, in the work of advancing diversity as both institutional ideal and outcome. To think that the achievement of true diversity can be attained without considerable action and advocacy is tantamount to believing that an unpracticed, undisciplined team can win a divisional tournament. It could happen, but it's highly unlikely.

This chapter, then, is essentially conceived of as "game talk," the kind of conversation that takes place in literal and figurative locker rooms and at courtside whenever players need motivation, inspiration, or simply to recheck the diagram. Borrowing terms liberally (though not necessarily technically) from basketball, we will consider the following:

> *What steps can be taken to ensure that diversity is not relegated to the sidelines becoming tangential, rather than central to the "real" work of the organization?*
>
> *How can we ensure that diversity becomes a first priority rather than a second thought in daily planning and implementation?*
>
> *How can we change the landscape so that responsibility for diversity work is equitably shared instead of assigned to certain players?*

GET IN THE GAME

Many of us are attracted to diversity work in libraries because of a deep belief in social justice and systemic change. We see the library as playing a central role in the equal access of information and in fostering mutual understanding between groups. All too often, however, we find that while many in decision-making positions are willing to list diversity as a goal of the library, fewer are willing to set aside real resources toward its accomplishment. Indeed in the last few years, diversity as a palpable outcome has generated no small amount of ambivalence. Affirmative action, once considered a cornerstone of civil rights, has been much criticized. As such, programs designed to ensure representative recruitment, hiring, promotion, or service have been pared down or eliminated altogether. As social conservatism prevails at making the discourse of diversity increasingly ambiguous and innocuous, those of us entrusted with this work often find our efforts underfunded, understaffed, underacknowledged, and marginalized. This phenomenon can leave us overextended, overwhelmed, and disillusioned. But before throwing in the towel, it's important to remember why you're playing in the first place. You're working to ensure diversity so that library users and staff from all walks of life can feel validated, supported, and welcomed and find the resources they need to ensure personal growth, social and economic mobility, and lifelong education.

Okay, so now you remember why you suited up in the first place and you want in!

You're tired of lukewarm responses or support for your library's diversity initiatives. You're tired of languishing on the sidelines waiting to be called in. Or if you're called in at all it's only during the last minutes of the game when a win or loss is already inevitable. You know that your ideas are sound and that you can offer critical insights that add real value to your library. You feel that rumble in your stomach. You're hungry for some *real* playing time. That's right, pull off those warm-ups and get off the bench. You're ready to become a STARTER!

But even the most naturally gifted player must invest in some pregame preparation. Before you are deemed worthy of the starting line-up, *you must study your team.* Rerun the video. What are your library's overall strengths and weaknesses? Now think specifically about diversity: what (or who) are your credits and your deficits? When your organization is down and in foul trouble, are you one of the players the team goes to for leadership? Or are you consigned to the bench forced to watch helplessly as the clock runs out? Think about how you answered the question. *What skills and drills do you need to master to stay in the game?*

To be effective, top players must be willing to expand their playing ability. If they tend to favor their left side when shooting or passing, they will have to learn to be just as effective using their right side. If they love the running game, but freeze at the free-throw line, they'll find themselves ineffectual to the team whenever they are fouled. Often a good coach will work with a promising player in identifying and overcoming holes in their game. *What is your relationship to your coach?* There may be multiple coach figures whose support you need for making diversity a priority at your library. The upfront support of the individual to whom you report as well as the director of the institution, if not one and the same, is critical to getting diversity efforts off on solid ground. The lukewarm support of either one can thwart the initiative before it even takes flight. Optimizing your impact often hinges on developing this crucial player-coach relationship. Some players find themselves benched while others with similar or lesser skills enjoy playing time. Sometimes this is simply because the benched players don't realize the importance of asking the coach what they can do to improve their chances of making the lineup. Express intent. Demonstrate to the coach and to the rest of the team that you are ready to play and that you mean business.

Do understand that once you get in the game, the perks will be consistent with the sacrifices. There is always a give and take between greater visibility and greater responsibility, between higher profile and higher scrutiny, between greater resources and greater expectations. This is the duality that comes with all positive action. Great players are able to convert both positive and negative energy into the fuel necessary to optimize their play and realize a higher good for themselves and for their teams. Now that you have mapped your assets and listed your gaps, it's time to *maximize your skills.*

BE A STANDOUT PLAYER

David Garvin's instructions on building organizations also apply to the skills necessary to those seeking team leadership positions. Standout players must:

- Engage in systematic problem solving
- Experiment with and adapt new approaches

- Be able to evaluate and learn from past experiences
- Transfer knowledge throughout the organization

Embodying these qualities is why Kareem Abdul-Jabbar was able to have such an enormous impact as part of the Lakers' championship teams when he was arguably past his prime. Known for his ability to quickly analyze a game, Abdul-Jabbar was able to combine his own time-proven game with the games played by his teammates. His ability to adapt without compromising his style won him the loyalty and admiration of younger players, making it easy for him to pass on tips gained from facing opponents in the past. Abdul-Jabbar's personal commitment to excellence and his willingness to learn from other players and to use their unique skills to build strategy allowed him to quickly pass on to relatively new players the knowledge gained from years of experience.

Those involved in diversity work must be willing to take a holistic look at the institution. The achievement of diversity will not occur in a vacuum. Workplace and service inequities or discriminatory practice may be symptoms of widespread systemic dysfunction. Strategic problem solving might mandate that we put, as Steven Covey would have it, "first things first," meaning that we may have to address issues of poor communication or pervasive low morale before the milieu is healthy enough to begin more specific work. Here again, the library diversity advocate must be willing to experiment with new methodologies and to spread knowledge gained from practice or research to every level of the organization through formal, and even more important, informal channels.

PLAY BY THE RULES

In 1931, Shiyali Ramamrita Ranganathan, considered one of the architects of contemporary library science, developed what have become the five indelible laws of library service:

1. Books are for use.
2. Every reader his or her book.
3. Every book its reader.
4. Save the time of the reader.
5. The Library is a growing organism. (Ranganathan 1931)

For the purpose of this chapter I have adapted Ranganathan's precepts as a template for what I will call the Five Laws of Diversity:

1. *Diversity is for practice.* Idealism is not enough. Diversity recommendations, programs, and services must be practical and practice-able.
2. *Every unit of the library has its own diversity information or training needs.* It is not only the public service areas of the library that have diversity needs. Cataloguing, collection development, information technology, and many other areas benefit from access to the tenets of diversity and inclusion. The library diversity practitioner must strive to weave diversity into the fabric of the organization. Diversity must become as much a priority of the library as intellectual freedom, good

customer service or continuing professional development or it will be unrealized.

3. *Every aspect of diversity is relevant to the library or one of its units.* Some identifiers of diversity may be easier to talk about than others, depending on the workplace. Some individuals may be more comfortable discussing issues pertinent to race and ethnicity than sexual orientation. Where sexual orientation is not a divisive issue, discussion of race, ethnicity, or disability may cause tension. In some regions of the country, religion or religious denomination can be an area of contention. Library diversity practitioners must expand their own comfort zones and cultural competencies to provide information, training, programs, and services that reflect the broad spectrum of diversity.

4. *Save the time of the library.* Oftentimes advocates for diversity in libraries fail to make the business case for diversity. Having fast facts on hand will help an administrator see the need for creating a public library residency for newly graduated Spanish-speaking librarians; or for diverting funds reserved for an underutilized resource to outreach services to home daycares or senior centers. Aggregate, organize, and update information, statistics that speak to the community's shifting demographics and service needs. Your administrator may come to realize that increasing dollars in the area of diversity makes good, sound sense.

5. *Diversity initiatives are growing organisms.* Thankfully, the days of commissioning consultants to craft diversity plans the width of telephone directories are numbered. To be effective, library management and staff must commit at a personal level to the vision, goals, objectives, and action steps outlined in the diversity plan from its inception. Thinking that the existence of an institutional diversity plan alone will ensure the achievement of diversity is similar to believing that the possession of a gym membership will make one physically fit. Diversity is a muscle that must be exercised. Like any long-term fitness plan, the diversity plan must be periodically revisited, adjusted, and evaluated to determine real progress.

OWN YOUR POSITION: CREATE THE SPECIALIST EFFECT

THE SPECIALIST VS. PRACTITIONER

The role of the specialist is to know more about his or her specialty than a general practitioner (Beckwith 1997). Library diversity advocates can create the "specialist effect" by continuously educating themselves and finding effective means of synthesizing and disseminating this knowledge to others. *American Demographics*, *Adult Learning*, *Diversity Inc*, and other periodicals address issues pertinent to various aspects of diversity and offer insights that can and should inspire library policy and service. Oftentimes, making the starting lineup entails honing one's skill in a certain position to the point that entire plays are built around the unique contribution that only you can make. Becoming a subject expert on diversity brings with it the possibility of creating and defining institutional action.

BECOME A MAVEN

In *The Tipping Point: How Little Things Can Make a Big Difference*, author Malcolm Gladwell points to three types of people who have the ability to exert a great amount of influence: "connectors," "mavens," and "salesmen." According to Gladwell, connectors bring people together, salespeople have the charismatic ability to influence people's behavior to their own advantage, and mavens acquire knowledge and use it educate and help others (Gladwell 2000). The term *maven* is Yiddish and describes someone who accumulates knowledge to the point of expertise. While those involved in diversity work best serve themselves and their mission by being well rounded, becoming a diversity maven improves the chance of being able to contribute knowledge or advice that may eventually impact decision making. Gladwell says of a friend who has become the restaurant maven among her group, she "has this incredible influence over how people make up their minds about restaurants. That kind of person, if you think about it, can have an extraordinarily important role in figuring out what kinds of songs or fashion trends take off because they've got the ear of so many of their friends." Being a maven entails more than becoming a walking digest for statistics and trivia. It means being versed enough to find meaning through the connection of seemingly unlike events and to anticipate trends before they crystallize.

One means to ensure ownership of your position is to identify the most frequently asked questions about diversity as well as the most difficult questions to answer and create a personal or organizational "ready reference" tool that is periodically updated and checked for accuracy. Knowing that they can count on you for easy access to demographic information, for instance, may make even the most stubborn "ball-hogger" look to you for assistance. Identifying your strongest service and publicizing it is another way to make sure that you are not permanently relegated to the bench. If you are mavenish about acquiring and disseminating statistics, make that known. If you have the inside scoop on diversity recruitment, share that information. If you have compiled a veritable library of diversity-related research, let the whole organization know that if it was published you probably have it. Creating the specialist effect ensures that you'll be turned to in the clutch. Indeed, becoming a diversity maven allows you to "coach" the organization from your position.

PROJECT, PROTECT, AND RESPECT YOUR BRAND

The contemporary sportswear market is all about signs and signifiers. Playground warriors are lured as much by what a particular product *signifies* about one's athletic ability as they are by whether or not it will actually enhance it. When asked why he was content to spend his birthday windfall on the most expensive basketball shoe, when another seemingly equally attractive and equipped shoe was available, my nephew answered succinctly "because when you show up with these shoes everybody knows you can play." In an era where brands serve as shorthand for quality and performance, it behooves those involved in library diversity work to find ways to distinguish and call attention to ongoing diversity efforts. There are various methods for doing this:

1. *Create a "brand" that will identify diversity work.* Consistently use an original (or stock) logo or phrase to identify diversity programs. Whether it is a multicultural potluck or a bilingual poetry reading, the

consistent use of a logo will place this event in a continuum of services and programs designed to enlighten and enrich.

2. *Create low-cost/high-impact brochures, newsletters, and press releases.* Ensure that diversity work is not the best-kept secret at your library. Utilize a variety of information formats to keep library staff and users up to date with pertinent events and accomplishments.

3. *Publicize diversity work on bulletin boards, near elevators, in the lunchroom, even in bathrooms.* Keep colleagues and customers up to date with diversity programs and initiatives. Simply knowing what's going on can help foster feelings of inclusion and camaraderie.

4. *Establish a Web site presence for library staff and users.* Web sites offer institutions and ideas the opportunity to expand their presence and reach distant or unknown constituencies. Creating a Web site that captures your institution's vision for diversity and inclusion as well as the activities designed to assist in the achievement of that goal may well expand your affinity group and also allow nonparticipants to stay informed. Take steps to make information on your Web site accessible in multiple languages. Your library may have a wealth of services available in Spanish but if all of your advertising is in English, you'll miss much of your target audience.

5. *Create or purchase and disseminate promotional items that reflect your organization's commitment to diversity.* A calendar displaying images of library staff or users in national or cultural attire, a multicultural cookbook, pens or pencils displaying multilingual phrases, posters in the library that include images representative of various backgrounds, physical characteristics, or values all demonstrate an institutional awareness and celebration of diversity.

In addition to physical branding, there are other ways to ensure that your brand commands respect. Library diversity advocates must establish a reputation for walking the talk of diversity. Being exclusive, engaging in or condoning discriminatory practice, or even being silent in the face of injustice can compromise any lasting effects of diversity work. To paraphrase Mahatma Gandhi, we must be the change we want to see in the library. As with the most effective players it is imperative to learn when to press and to pass. Fighting each and every battle just to make a point is unwise and leaves even the strongest individual feeling depleted. While being assertive is key, it is important to pay heed to the overall well-being of the team. Being overly confrontational can result in alienating the very people whose support you need. Being a selfish player, tuning out when you don't have the ball or when the direction drifts away from diversity, puts one at risk of distancing colleagues who resent the "it's only important when it's my issue" attitude. Indeed the best way to win allies for library diversity efforts may come through your participation in a nondiversity endeavor.

Once you have created your brand and begun to put forward your product it is helpful to get to know your fan base. Who most utilizes your services? Who comes to the programs and events? Who calls wanting more of a particular resource? Who has acknowledged the difference the diversity initiative has made in the workplace or even their personal life? Keeping and growing a base of loyal supporters is critical to diversity work. These supporters can be called on to champion current efforts, to proselytize on your behalf, and to provide testimonials should you need to make a case for additional resources.

Identifying the detractors to diversity is also vital to mounting a successful diversity initiative. As the old adage states: "Keep your friends close and your foes closer." Who inside your organization or service community expresses or demonstrates a lack of support for diversity? Who insists that diversity is not a pressing issue in your library or community? Who claims that allocating personnel and financial resources to diversity is just a waste of time and money? Ignoring those who criticize diversity efforts sometimes exacerbates existing schisms. Becoming defensive further serves to break down communication. Whenever possible, invite antagonists to substantiate their arguments either face to face or in writing. Take time to address their issues and concerns one by one. After educating them about the integral role of diversity and cultural competency in building and maintaining a healthy and high-performing institution, ask them for suggestions of how to make the diversity policies, plans, and services more meaningful to them. Though only a few may speak up, detractors to diversity exist at every level of the organization. They may exist in isolation or represent a silent majority. Being willing to uncover and engage criticism is key to the true realization of institutional diversity.

Projecting, protecting, and respecting your brand means playing above the rim. Remember that the best salesperson for diversity in the library is you. As a diversity ambassador you are called on to model inclusive behavior, bring credibility to your brand, and grow diversity stakeholders by serving your fans more of what they want and endeavoring to bring your detractors to the table. Staying out of catfights, crab-buckets, and doghouses frees the best players up to turn on their game. Play like a winner. *Make others want to wear your number.*

PRACTICE THE RIGHT P'S OF MARKETING: RIGHT PLACE, RIGHT PROMOTION, RIGHT PEOPLE, RIGHT POINT IN TIME, RIGHT PRICE

Now that you've created a brand to identify your library's diversity initiatives, demonstrated personal and professional integrity, gained stakeholders, and worked to bring the opposition into alignment, it is time to create a marketing to plan to ensure that diversity stays at center court. Knowing the right areas to place emphasis will help you expand the reach and increase the potency of library diversity activities.

RIGHT PLACE

Make diversity visible and palpable in the workplace. Give it presence. Allocate a physical space, an area of the lunchroom, or a bulletin board in a common room and decorate it with various diversity themes throughout the month. Invite staff to showcase their own diversity affinities through narrated photographs. Make sure whenever possible that trainers are brought to your facility rather than sending employees outside. Have trainers train around actual practices and policies.

RIGHT PROMOTION

Don't just focus on telling your internal or external customers what you do. Tell them what you *could* do. As marketing guru Harry Beckwith opines, "every act is a marketing act." If you promote in the right way you'll answer questions about your programs people didn't even know they had and leave others feeling like stakeholders. The right promotion will not just inform your constituency of your diversity initiative, it will make them feel good about it.

RIGHT PEOPLE

Identify your internal and external customers and peers. While the majority of your focus must be on manifesting diversity within your library, it is important to stay abreast of and participate in library diversity efforts outside your library at the local, regional, and national level. Oftentimes it takes gaining a favorable regional or national profile to enhance one's internal credibility. At the same time, when you expand your external peer and customer network you also expand your leverage and access to information that can in turn expand the level of value and service you are able to provide your internal customers.

RIGHT POINT IN TIME

When it comes to marketing it pays to be proactive. Make people aware of what you do before they need your services. Paying careful attention to trends and bits of news can help you spot potential stakeholders before they form a plan of action. Just found out that your library won a grant to expand bookmobile services? Approach the head of the division about speaking to the bookmobile team about the information needs of the various groups they will be serving. If you are taken up on the offer, prepare a one-page fact sheet combining census information for your town with best practices gleaned from experience and the latest articles on innovative library service.

RIGHT PRICE

To maximize your return on investment, the impact of a purchase must have a value exponential to the investment. One T-shirt emblazoned with the Nike logo has the potential to impact everyone who sees it. A 10-cent-per-unit pencil engraved with the logo "Mt. Rainier Public Library: Diversity Makes Us All Better" may pass through a half-dozen hands at a library and, given the law of transfer, another half-dozen hands outside the library. The costs of hosting a lunch where paper goods and beverages are provided to support a "'Round the World in 60 Minutes" potluck that encourages employees to bring foods from their ethnic, racial, or regional heritage is nominal, but at the end of the hour the diversity committee will have connected with many more people than it may have otherwise.

SWITCH UP YOUR GAME: BE VERSATILE

To ensure that products and services reach the broadest possible consumer base, smart companies strive to provide multiple access points so that customers can access offerings using the mode of communication with which they are most comfortable. Proactive companies embark on multitiered plans that may include several of the following tactics:

- Surveys or questionnaires
- Direct mail
- Focus groups
- Personal interviews
- Email newsblasts
- Formal and informal evaluations

Using these and other means of reaching and engaging library staff and users helps make sure that library diversity work is finding its targets and meeting expectations. You may also use these forums to announce new programs, gauge the audience for a new service, and find out what projects are not working and why. Providing individuals with a variety of ways to access and weigh in on the library's diversity efforts allows you to periodically appraise your progress and, if necessary, to change your game.

MASTER THE TRIPLE THREAT POSITION

Last up on the clipboard is a tip guaranteed to help you make Most Valuable Player. Perfecting this on-court posture allows you to progress the ball down the court and into optimal shooting range. Each direction is followed with a brief explanation of its relevance to library diversity work. But to really make this work you have to get up out of that chair and practice each move.

1. *Stand with your feet shoulder-width apart.* This is what we've been waiting for! You finally have the ball in your hands. Make sure your feet and the floor beneath you are steady.
2. *Stagger your feet slightly, so your left foot fits into the arch of your right foot if you're right-handed.* Now it's time to advance. Make sure that you're off to a good start. As Jim Collins says in *Good to Great* (Collins 2001, 41), getting off to a good start means asking first who, then what. Before you even think about taking a step, ask yourself *who* you want to reach and *who* you need on the team to reach them, then decide what you want to do and where you want to go. If you don't have the right people on the team you're bound to finish last.
3. *Bend your knees and crouch slightly.* Stay limber and loose. Locking one's knees—being inflexible or myopic in thinking or problem-solving approaches—impairs the agility needed to get your ideas down the court and set up for that game-winning play.
4. *Grasp the ball with your left hand on the side of the ball and your right hand on top. Bend both elbows so they're approximately at right angles.* It's all about how you handle the ball. Though he's long retired, former Los Angeles Laker Earvin "Magic" Johnson is still revered for his incredible ball-handling skills. Magic perfected the behind-the-back dribble which allowed him to slow down his defenders while progressing down the court. Perfecting your ball handling means having your diversity, vision, goals, objectives, and action plan in place and creating a

mechanism for review and adjustment when needed. A good support team and a solid plan will give you a firm hold on the ball even while you're running the break.

5. *Survey the court at all times.* The two interchangeable mantras for athletes: "The best offense is a good defense" and conversely "The best defense is a good offense" are indeed words to work by. Keeping your eyes peeled for both problems and progress will keep your diversity efforts in the game.

6. *Decide what the most appropriate maneuver is for your current situation—shooting, passing, or dribbling.* Chapter 12, verse 37, of the recently discovered *Divine Player's Handbook* reads, "There is a time for all things. A time to shoot because you're open, a time to pass when you're double-teamed, and a time for dribbling when you need time to figure out your game plan." Library diversity advocates would do well to heed this edict. When the diversity initiative faces impenetrable opposition, don't risk getting into foul trouble; turn to a teammate for assistance. When the administrators she approached about forming a diversity committee proved unresponsive, one librarian passed the ball to a senior and well-respected colleague whose ideas carried much influence in her library. Having this colleague buy into the proposed diversity plan made all the difference and opened doors that were formerly closed.

CONCLUSION

Well, you've made it! You're in the game. Your diversity initiative or programs are up and running. Your heart's pumping, adrenaline flowing. You've been waiting for this moment for a long time. Now the real work begins. Suddenly the plays you thought you had memorized are getting fuzzy. Your diversity committee teammates, the ones you thought you could turn to in a pinch, are preoccupied with their own workload. One is fretting over a budget; the other is knee-deep in overhauling the library's technology plan. The coach who assured you continued support has been slow to approve any real resources to advance your game. It's down to just you and the ball.

Take a deep breath. Remember the rules, "the five laws of diversity." Now that you've refreshed your memory about diversity's centrality to library performance and service, it's time to create the specialist effect on court. No one can play your position as effectively as you. Don't be afraid to employ all of the tools at your disposal. Playing small won't advance you down the court. Project your brand. Show the opposition that your efforts are part of a larger strategy and that you're playing on behalf of a wide-ranging group of stakeholders. Now is the time to get your fans revved up. Make sure that you are practicing "the right P's." Go on, play to the people in the stands. They are the reason you are in the arena in the first place. When the going gets tough, switch up your game. Remaining flexible will allow you to change directions and elude pitfalls that might land you in foul trouble and back on the bench. And finally, make use of the "triple threat position." Knowing what to do and when to do it can make the difference between sinking that ball at the buzzer or throwing in the towel.

> The following exercise might help build even more muscle in the area of strategy building. Think about how you would handle the situation or make it a group exercise for your library diversity committee or management group:
>
>> You have been named chair of the newly created, Diversity Committee for the Darlington College Libraries. Located in a semirural setting, Darlington College is more than a three-hour drive from a major metropolis. Neither the student body nor the staff makeup at DC has traditionally been very "diverse." Recently however, community demographic data for Darlington indicates that pockets of racial and ethnic minorities are increasingly moving into town in search of better public schools and work opportunities. While statistics for racial and ethnic minorities on campus have only slightly increased over the last four years, the number of students who speak English as a second or third language has notably increased and so has demand for materials written in students' native languages.
>>
>> The committee consists of you and four librarians and library staff members from various library departments. Although the Dean of Libraries at DC has stated her support for diversity, beyond approving the formation of the Diversity Committee she has not set aside any resources for its work. At a staff meeting, when the creation of the Diversity Committee was announced, a long time colleague objected, exclaiming, "What do we need with a diversity committee? We treat everyone the same here. I haven't heard of any complaints. No offense, but this is a waste of personnel time."
>
> **Given this scenario, how do you get diversity into the starting line-up at the Library?**

Figure 3-1. A Scenario Planning Exercise

BIBLIOGRAPHY

American Library Association Office for Research and Statistics/National Center for Education Statistics. 1994. 1993–1994 Report. American Library Association.

Beckwith, Harry. 1997. *Selling the Invisible: A Field Guide to Modern Marketing*. New York: Warner Business Books.

Collins, Jim. 2001. *Good to Great: Why Some Companies Make the Leap and Others Don't*. New York: HarperBusiness.

Covey, Stephen R. 1989. *The 7 Habits of Highly Effective People*. New York: Simon and Schuster.

Garvin, David. 1993. "Building a Learning Organization." *Harvard Business Review* 71, no. 4 (July–August): 78–92.

Gladwell, Malcolm. 2000. *The Tipping Point: How Little Things Can Make a Big Difference.* New York: Little, Brown.

National Center for Education Statistics. 1994. Washington, DC: Institute of Education Sciences, U.S. Dept. of Education.

Neely, Teresa. 1998. "Diversity in Conflict." *Law Library Journal* 90, no. 4: 587–601.

Ranganathan, S. R. 1931. *The Five Laws of Library Science.* Madras, India: Madras Library Association.

Reese, Gregory L., and Ernestine Hawkins. 1999. *Stop Talking, Start Doing, Attracting People of Color to the Library Profession.* Chicago: American Library Association.

U.S. Census Bureau. 2000. *Population of the United States by Age, Race and Hispanic Origin.* Washington, DC: U.S. Census Bureau.

4 PRACTICAL STRATEGIES FOR BUILDING A LIBRARY DIVERSITY PROGRAM

by Molly Royse

INTRODUCTION

Margaret Mead once said that "if we are to achieve a richer culture, rich in contrasting values, we must recognize the whole gamut of human potentialities, and so weave a less arbitrary social fabric, one in which each diverse human gift will find a fitting place" (Mead 1963, 322). Decades later, in today's higher education environment, the value of diversity is recognized on college campuses and seen "as an essential resource for optimizing teaching and learning" (American Council on Education 2000, 1–2). Research indicates that the benefits of diversity for both students and teachers are many. As a result, colleges and universities are being challenged to create and maintain a diverse environment for their students and faculty. Higher education institutions are being encouraged to increase diversity on their campuses so as to offer their students the best education possible.

In the midst of this heightened awareness of the value of diversity in higher education, academic libraries are also being challenged and encouraged to participate in their institutions' diversity initiatives and even develop diversity programs of their own. In my career as an academic librarian, I have had the opportunity to work with diversity initiatives at two universities—Kansas State University and the University of Tennessee (UT), Knoxville. At each institution I had an active role in developing a library diversity program. As I reflect on my experiences, I offer my thoughts and perspectives on some practical strategies for success in building a library diversity program. Though these strategies have a focus on an academic environment, they can be easily modified for other types of libraries.

ORGANIZE AND PLAN

Before a library diversity program is initiated, there are several critical first steps related to organization and planning that need to be accomplished. First, there must be administrative support and commitment within your library for a diversity initiative. This support and commitment should be evident in your organization's planning documents and goals. For example, the UT libraries' strategic plan includes a goal for the libraries to "commit to the value of a broad approach to diversity" and to "set priorities and take action to ensure a diverse library staff, collection, and environment" (UT Libraries 2002–2006, 3).

Second, leadership needs to be established for the initiative within your library staff. This leadership role may be bestowed upon one individual whose full-time responsibilities revolve around diversity, or it may fall to a group of individuals forming a committee or advisory council of interested staff. Regardless, there should be a clear charge from administration and a level of accountability established.

A third important step that needs to occur as part of the organizing and planning stage is to define what your library means by diversity (UT Libraries' Diversity Committee 2003). Diversity can mean different things to different people. It is essential for an organization to come to an agreement on a definition. The process of defining diversity should involve as many people from the organization as possible, for it is important that the staff have the opportunity for input and feel some ownership for the definition. Arriving at a consensus on a definition can take time, but it will prove to be time well spent as your diversity program evolves.

Once a definition for diversity is in place, it is time to develop a mission statement, which will state the purpose and overall goals of your library's diversity program (UT Libraries' Diversity Committee 2001a). Much like the process of defining diversity, creating a good mission statement can take time. It should speak to the purpose of the library's diversity initiative, yet also reflect components of your library's overall mission. As your diversity program evolves and matures, it is important to periodically reexamine both your definition and your mission statement. Revisions may be necessary to more accurately reflect your program's scope and focus.

Setting goals for your diversity program is a final important step in organizing and planning. Develop both long-term and short-term goals, and work to ensure the goals are realistic and attainable. Consult with administration to ensure the goals are compatible with and support the library's goals. Check to make sure the goals reflect a comprehensive diversity program, one which doesn't focus on just a few aspects of diversity but includes a variety of components.

ASSESS AND EVALUATE

As you plan and organize your diversity program, a key question must be asked: "Is my organization ready for a diversity initiative?" Conducting an assessment of the climate of your library organization for a diversity initiative will help answer this question (UT Libraries' Diversity Committee 2001b). The assessment methodology can be formal, such as distributing a survey or questionnaire, or it can be informal, such as conducting focus groups or interviews with staff members. Regardless of the approach taken, the importance of conducting a climate assessment in the development stages of your program cannot be overemphasized. Understanding the unique characteristics, attitudes, and perceptions of your organization's personnel can prove to be most helpful in designing and planning your diversity initiative. Information gathered from an assessment can be used to formulate or revise goals, establish education and training needs, and plan programs. If done early in the planning stages of your program, a climate assessment can provide valuable information to assist in the crafting of a definition for diversity and your program's mission statement. A good assessment can also provide benchmarks against which the progress and success of your diversity program can be measured. It is important to periodically evaluate the success and impact of your program.

In assessing your library's climate for diversity, also take into consideration the climate of your campus and local community in regard to diversity. Are there diversity programs present or initiatives underway outside of your library? If so, learn about these efforts and determine the best role for your library's program.

EDUCATE AND PROGRAM

Appropriate education and training must be provided for the individuals in your organization who are leading your diversity initiative. Reviewing the professional library literature for examples of other diversity programs is a good beginning. The business and industrial psychology literature can also provide good models and advice, which can be adapted for your organization. Take advantage of workshops, online lyceums, and preconferences offered by organizations such as the Association for Research Libraries and the American Library Association's Office of Diversity. Local campus or community expertise can be valuable as well. UT's Office of Equity and Diversity, for example, was most helpful in the early stages of the development of the UT Diversity Committee and conducted a workshop on group facilitation and identity.

Once the leaders of your program have been oriented and educated, expand educational opportunities and diversity-related programming to the rest of the library staff and your users. Staff enrichment and outreach programs can and should be both social and educational. Seek outside funding when possible, and explore opportunities for collaboration with library departments and campus and community groups.

The educational and programming components of your diversity program are most important, for they form the core of your diversity initiative. As the central part, they should consistently reflect your organization's diversity definition, mission statement, the goals of your diversity program, and results of your climate assessment. An effort should also be made for your diversity programming to reflect and complement any campus or community diversity efforts. Timing can be critical to the success of a program. The UT Libraries' Minority Librarian Residency Program, for example, was established in the midst of a university-wide initiative to increase minority faculty and staff (UT Libraries' Diversity Committee 2005b). Establishing a minority residency program was a goal of the libraries' Diversity Committee from the beginning, but it was important to wait until the campus climate was right before setting the wheels in motion. As the program begins its third year, much of its success can be attributed to the university support it has received.

COMMUNICATE AND PUBLICIZE EFFORTS

The practical strategies for success in building a library diversity program outlined thus far are intertwined, each relying on the successful completion of the other. These strategies must all be employed to have a successful diversity program. At each step of the way, it is important for communication and publicity to occur, both within and outside your organization.

Good and consistent communication with your staff will contribute to making your diversity program a library-wide program and not just the effort of one individual or a committee. Keeping campus and community leaders who are involved in diversity-related initiatives informed of your diversity program can result in both partnerships with campus programs and units and participation in campus and community events. When campus diversity initiatives develop, the library should be viewed as a partner and a participant.

It is also important to share your library's diversity program and efforts with others in the library profession and, in the case of academic libraries, with others in the larger higher education community. Attending and participating in state, regional, and national conferences are ways to accomplish this. Contributing to the professional literature and listservs is yet another way to share and publicize your program. In addition, maintaining an up-to-date Web site of your library's diversity program is essential and can assist greatly with communication and publicity (UT Libraries' Diversity Committee 2005a).

CONCLUSION

The academic library has often been referred to as the heart of the university, the center of it all. As the heart of the university, the library is in an ideal position to build a diversity program and support university-wide diversity initiatives. The library is not affiliated with any one particular college or curriculum and thus can be seen as a neutral player with no hidden agendas. The potential for the library to participate in campus-wide diversity efforts or even become a major force or campus leader in such efforts is great. Libraries of all types must seize the opportunity to work with diversity efforts and help make a difference. The rewards will be many for the library organization, its staff, and its community.

BIBLIOGRAPHY

Does Diversity Make a Difference? Three Research Studies on Diversity in College Classrooms. 2000. Washington, DC: American Council on Education and American Association of University Professors.

Mead, Margaret. 1963. *Sex and Temperament in Three Primitive Societies.* New York: William Morrow.

University of Tennessee (UT) Libraries. January 2005. "University Library Plan, 2002–2006." Available: www.lib.utk.edu/plan/plan/plan02-06.pdf.

UT Libraries' Diversity Committee. 2001a. "Mission." (January 2005.) Available: www.lib.utk.edu/diversity/organization/mission.html.

UT Libraries' Diversity Committee. 2001b. "University Libraries Climate Survey." (January 2005.) Available: www.lib.utk.edu/diversity/activities/ClimateSurvey.pdf.

UT Libraries' Diversity Committee. 2003. "What Is Diversity?" (January 2005.) Available: www.lib.utk.edu/diversity/diversity_definition.html.

UT Libraries' Diversity Committee. 2005a. "Diversity Committee." (January 2005.) Available: www.lib.utk.edu/diversity.

UT Libraries' Diversity Committee. 2005b. "Minority Librarian Residency Program." (January 2005.) Available: www.lib.utk.edu/diversity/activities/minorityresidency_position.html.

EXAMPLES AND SAMPLES

UT Libraries' Diversity Committee's Climate Survey
    www.lib.utk.edu/diversity/activities/ClimateSurvey.pdf
UT Libraries' Diversity Committee's Definition of Diversity
    www.lib.utk.edu/diversity/diversity_definition.html (The definition in poster format is available at www.lib.utk.edu/diversity/DiversityPoster.pdf.)
UT Libraries' Diversity Committee's Minority Librarian Residency Program Web Page
    www.lib.utk.edu/diversity/activities/minorityresidency.html
UT Libraries' Diversity Committee's Mission Statement
    www.lib.utk.edu/diversity/organization/mission.html
UT Libraries' Diversity Committee's Web Page
    www.lib.utk.edu/diversity

5 DIVERSITY IN LIBRARIES—A CANADIAN PERSPECTIVE

by Ganga B. Dakshinamurti

INTRODUCTION

What is diversity when applied to people? A review of the usage of the term shows that its meaning is context related and changing and often has a multiplicity of viewpoints. In general, *diversity* as applied to people refers to differences between individuals in terms of their age, gender, race, religion, sexual orientation, disability, and/or social/linguistic/geographic background, thereby denoting a multicultural, multiethnic, multireligious, and/or multilinguistic society. In that context, the concept of diversity naturally is not a new phenomenon, or a passing fad. Neither is it a deficiency that leads to lowering of standards, nor is it divisive or to be feared. Diversity includes all, not just women and minorities, and hence is vital to all instead of being important to just some of us.

A review of organizational and business literature shows that diversity is about adopting an attitude of inclusion and about making people more self-aware so they understand how they impact others. It is about breaking stereotypes and raising expectations and about boosting customer satisfaction, opening up to new markets, and providing a competitive edge. Most important, it is about not letting anything get in the way of recruiting, developing, and retaining talented people in an equitable manner.

DIVERSITY ISSUES IN LIBRARIES: A CANADIAN PERSPECTIVE

The concept of diversity as applied to libraries refers to three distinct areas:

1. Development of collections that reflect the experiences/needs of the diverse community at large
2. Services to diverse library patrons
3. Development of workplace climates that foster and support diversity in staffing/recruitment/retention

Due to its kaleidoscopic population, Canada, and thereby Canadian libraries, offers a unique perspective on diversity issues. The 2001 *Census Canada* reported the Canadian population to be 29,639,035, with diversity varied across the nation. This includes 1,000,890 Native Indians and more than 200 ethnic groups. Immigration to Canada accounted for more than ⅔ of population growth in 2001. In comparison with the United States, which had in the year 2000 11 percent of its population born outside the country, Canada had in the year 2001 18 percent of its population born outside the country. Forty-four percent of Toronto's population is foreign born, as compared to 24 percent in New York City. Within a period of two decades, there has been a threefold increase in visible minorities in Canada, with 13.4 percent in 2001 versus 5 percent in 1981. The majority of the newest immigrants from the 1990s are of working age, with 46 percent in the year 2001 aged 25 to 44, compared to 31 percent of the total population.

Changes and variety of immigrant origin have contributed to a dramatic increase in cultural diversity in Canada. There has been a significant increase in allophone immigrants, with ¾ immigrants in the 1990s versus half in the 1970s. Increasingly immigrants have been coming from Asia. Chinese is the largest visible minority group (3.5 percent of the population, 26 percent of the visible minority), followed by South Asians (3.1 percent of the population, 23 percent of the visible minority). Rapid growth of visible minorities in urban centers as well as the increasing number of intermarriages of visible minorities is changing the face of Canada. *Conference Board of Canada (April 2004)* notes that by 2016, one in five may be a visible minority member in Canada.

Turning to the Province of Manitoba, its population of 1,103,700 includes 12 percent foreign born. The *2001 Census* identifies ninety-two different ethnic groups in Manitoba, which is noted for its multicultural festivals and multiethnic restaurants. Manitoba's capital city, Winnipeg, has a population of 660,000, which is ⅔ of Manitoba's population and includes 12.5 percent visible minorities. The highest proportion is Filipinos, followed by immigrants from India, China, Vietnam, and Poland. More specifically, in the University of Manitoba, aboriginal undergraduate students increased from 2.7 percent in 2001 to 4.3 percent in 2003.

With a changing face in its population mosaic, Canada has accommodated with a variety of policies related to diversity. A commitment to diversity was initiated in 1971, with a policy of multiculturalism within a bilingual framework that represents a distinctive Canadian way of defining diversity. In 1985, the Charter of Rights and Freedoms provided elimination of all forms of discrimination by guaranteeing both equality and fairness to all under the law. The Employment Equity Act (1986) ranks organizations for equitable employment of aboriginal peoples, persons with disabilities, visible minorities, and women. The Multiculturalism Act of 1988 cleared the pathway through active government intervention to promote ethnocultural differences as an integral part of Canadian life.

DIVERSITY ISSUES IN CANADIAN ACADEMIC LIBRARIES

Libraries in Canada reflect the mosaic society at large. Academic libraries are committed to support their respective universities' policies to:

- Comply with government employment equity provisions and antiracism initiatives
- Provide educational equity on improving access, climate, curriculum, and teaching practice

- Respond to equity and diversity issues with fairness and sensitivity as an institutional goal.

For example, the University of Manitoba's Diversity Platform subscribed to by its libraries include:

- Intercultural effectiveness that respects differences and searches for commonalities to serve the diverse university community and the society at large
- Aboriginal focus to provide a welcoming, supportive environment that values and empowers aboriginal people, by graduating the most number of aboriginals
- International focus that supports international students and research activities

The University of Manitoba Diversity/Equity Network includes all the areas that are mandated to attend to diversity issues, such as Aboriginal Student Centre, Disability Services, Equity Services Officer, Faculties of Arts, Education and Social Work, International Centre for students, Libraries, Native Studies, Office of University Accessibility, Student Counseling and Career Centre, and Women's Studies. This Networking Committee has provided a valuable link to all areas concerned with diversity issues in the university.

T. Olsen points out in *Diversity Necklace* (http://www.arl.org/newsltr/188/necklace.html) that Canadian academic libraries illustrate four themes "as colorful beads strung in a necklace":

- The multicultural nature of Canadian population and the contrast between Canadian "mosaic" and American "melting pot" (or "tossed salad")
- Human rights and the focus on antiracism
- Employment equity for four designated groups
- Promotion of the concept of educational equity

Commenting about the Diversity Necklace as "too valuable to be unstrung," T. Olsen points out the following Canadian perspective on equity:

> Focusing on equity has not been at the expense of excellence but rather in the service of excellence. We have been attempting to increase faculty diversity not because of legislation but because we have wanted better institutions. We have focused on career development for administrative staff not only because this will make our "employment equity" numbers look better, but we want to ensure that everyone's full potential is realized.
>
> *Keeping Equity in the Decision-Making Process.* Council of Ontario Universities

As examples of "some very impressive beads for the Diversity Necklace" may be listed the alternative format materials for the sight impaired and the multicultural toolkit from the National Library of Canada (http://www.collectionscanada.ca/8/25/r25-300-e.html) and the multilingual library service offered by the University of Manitoba Libraries as well as its specialized ethnic collections such as the established Slavic collection and the evolving Japanese collection.

DIVERSITY ISSUES IN CANADIAN PUBLIC LIBRARIES

Canadian public libraries are the gateways to its mosaic culture. For instance, through Toronto Public Library's multilingual services, there has been a 9 percent increase in multilingual collection in 2003 and an increase of 15 percent in total circulation. This service offers multilingual children's programs and "dial-a-story"; telephone interpreters; Canadian citizenship preparation assistance; immigrant settlement information; English conversation meetings; and attending to the refugee population's information needs. In Winnipeg, the Public Library has initiated a major planning for diversity services in keeping with building the Millennium Library with expanded space, resources, and programs. Increased attention is being paid to its already varied multicultural collection to suit the changing demographic pattern. Literacy programs for new Canadians are being offered. A new initiative is to partner with community groups for workshops and programs, with the stated goal to have the public library serve as "a civic space to gather and share ideas, socialize and attend programs."

CHALLENGES AND OPPORTUNITIES

Diversity presents both challenges and opportunities. As part of the challenging environment, diversity necessitates librarians to have a solid understanding of the backgrounds, learning styles, and preferences of their diverse group of users; to attend to individual needs without creating unwanted "separateness"; to establish a process to recognize immigrants with professional qualifications and work experiences; and to reduce both the learning recognition gaps and the bureaucratic strictures to handle the huge task.

There are impressive opportunities too. Recruiting community members enables people from the community to feel more comfortable using library resources. Democratization of information occurs through information literacy and empowering people to reach their potential in information society. Equality of opportunities will reduce the widening wage gap (14.5 percent in 2004).

Dealing with diversity enables the community to become upwardly mobile as consumers, as participants in the economy, and in the workings of the information society at large. Canada's prosperity relies on its people, including minorities and immigrants. Today's educational and working worlds call for diverse abilities, ideas, experiences, and viewpoints. Not dealing with the existing reality of diversity would be costly—both economically and socially.

CONCLUSION

Diversity is a process, a journey that develops our diversity consciousness. For Canadian libraries, the journey has begun and can be expected to be ongoing. Diversity is like the five fingers on our hand—each one of us is unique and *uniquely needed* in what we can do,

> "If everybody in the room is the same, you will have a lot fewer arguments and a lot worse answers."
> *Ivan Seidenberg, CEO, Bell Atlantic, 1999*
>
> "Successful modern states make a virtue, not a blood feud, out of ethnic and religious diversity."
> *Bill Clinton, Address to American Society of Newspaper Edition, 1999*
>
> "None of us are as smart as all of us."
> *Japanese Proverb*
>
> "He prayed—it wasn't my religion.
> He ate—it wasn't what I ate.
> He spoke—it wasn't my language.
> He dressed—it wasn't what I wore.
> He took my hand—it wasn't the color of mine.
> But when he laughed—it was how I laughed,
> And when he cried—it was how I cried."
> *Amy Madden, as quoted in* Teaching Tolerance Magazine
>
> "Not to know is bad.
> Not to want to know is worse.
> Not to hope is unthinkable.
> Not to care is unforgivable."
> *Nigerian Proverb*
>
> "Many people want to change the world; only a few want to change themselves."
> *Leo Tolstoy*
>
> "Diversity is, increasingly, the fate of the modern world. The capacity to live with difference is the coming question in the twenty-first century."
> *Stuart Hall*
>
> "In knowledge there is understanding; in understanding there is respect; and where there is respect, growth is possible."
> *Anonymous*

Figure 5-1. Quotable Quotations on Diversity

but we function best when we can work together and yet be distinct. Let us join hands in creating and maintaining an environment that celebrates together the richness of diversity! Canadian perspective on diversity allows for an attitude of inclusiveness without sacrificing distinctiveness. Applied to all types of libraries, this attitude should lead libraries to (1) develop collections that reflect the experiences/needs of the diverse community at large; (2) offer services uniquely suited for diverse library patrons; and (3) take ownership for developing in our workplace climates that will foster, nurture, and support diversity in staffing recruitment and retention.

BIBLIOGRAPHY

2001 Census: Canada's Ethnocultural Portrait: the Changing Mosaic. 2003. Statistics Canada. Available: http://www.statcan.ca/english/census01.

2001 Census of Population. Statistics Canada. Available: http://80-estat-statcan-ca.proxy1.lib.umanitoba.ca/cgi-win.CNSMCGI.EXE.

"Accessibility: Learning and Teaching Perspective." November 2004. *University of Manitoba UTS Newsletter* 13:2.

Antunes, Pedro, Judith MacBride-King, and Julie Swettenham. April 2004. "Making a Visible Difference: the Contribution of Visible Minorities to Canadian Economic Growth." *Conference Board of Canada Briefing.*

Baklid, Bente, et al. 2005. *Business Critical: Maximizing the talents of Visible Minorities—an Employer's Guide.* Conference Board of Canada e-Library.

Bartkiw, Mark. 2004. "Tailoring the Message: in a Multicultural Society, All Ads Are Not Alike." *Canadian Business* (March 29–April 11): 65–66.

Brennan, Patricia. November 14, 1995. "ARL Announces: Canadian Perspective for ARL Diversity Program." Available: http://www/cni.org/Hforums/arl-announce/1995/0017.html.

Bucher, Richard D. 2004. *Diversity Consciousness: Opening Our Minds to People, Cultures, and Opportunities.* 2nd ed. Upper Saddle River, NJ: Pearson/Prentice-Hall.

Dib, Kamal. 2004. "Diversity Works." *Canadian Business* (March 29–April 11): 53–54.

"Diversity in Canada's Arts Labour Force: An Analysis of 2001 Census Data." Updated March 1, 2005. Hill Strategies Research Inc.

Hazen, Mary Ann, and Mary A. Higby. 2005. "Teaching an Issue-based Interdisciplinary Course: Diversity in Management and Marketing." *Journal of Management Education* 29:3 (June): 403–426.

Holloway, Andy, and Raizel Robin. 2004. "Aboriginal Voices." *Canadian Business* (March 29–April 11): 49–51.

Jain, Harish C., and John J. Lawler. 2004. "Visible Minorities Under the Canadian Employment Equity Act, 1987–1999." *RI/IR* 59:3, 585–609.

Kidder, Deborah, et al. 2004. "Backlash toward Diversity Initiatives: Examining the Impact of Diversity Program Justification, Personal and Group Outcomes." *International Journal of Conflict Management* 15:1, 77–102.

Library Instruction for Diverse Populations Bibliography. April 6, 2004. The Instruction for Diverse Populations Committee, Association of College and Research Libraries Instruction Section.

Marchant, Valerie. 2004. "The New Face of Work." *Canadian Business* (March 29–April 11): 37–42.

Multicultural Resources and Services Toolkit. May 22, 2003. Library and Archives Canada. Updated August 15, 2005. Available: http://www.collectionscanada.ca/multicultural.

Nelson, Camille. 1999. "Out of Sync: Reflections on the Culture of Diversity in Private Practice." *Canadian Women's Studies* 19:1/2 (spring/summer): 199.

Olshen, Toni. Updated January 24, 1996. "Diversity and Services in Academic Libraries: A Selective Current Bibliography." Available: http://theta.library.yorku.ca/stff2.tolahen.diversity.htm.

Olshen, Toni. October 1996. "The Diversity Necklace: Reflections on the State of the Art in Canadian Research Libraries." *ARL: A Bimonthly Newsletter of Research Library Issues and actions 188.* Available: http://www.arl.org.newsltr/188/necklace.html.

Rosenthal, Alan. 2004. "Burnett: Diversity Ingrained in the Culture." *Advertising Age* (February 9): D5.
Sanders, Carol. 2004. "U of M Aboriginal Students Honoured: More Doctor, Lawyer, Engineer Grads Than Other Universities in Canada." Winnipeg Free Press (May 2): A1–A2.
Sharpe, Linda. 2005. "The Diversity of Diversity." *Technology Review* (March): M4, M43.
Stule, W. Scot. 2004. "From the Executive Editor: the Best and the Brightest." *Canadian Business* (March 29–April 11).
Tatum, Beverly Daniel. 2004. "Building a Road to a Diverse Society." *Chronicle of Higher Education* 50:30 (April 2): B6.
Thomas, David A. 2004. "Diversity as Strategy." *Harvard Business Review* (September): 98–108.
Tomlinson, Asha. 2002. "The ABCs of Diversity in the Workplace." *Canadian HR Reporter* 15:10 (May 20): 2.
"Update on Cultural Diversity." 2003. *Canadian Social Trends* (autumn): 19–23.
"The Voices of Visible Minorities Speaking Out on Breaking Down Barriers." September 2004. *Conference Board of Canada Briefing*.
Wahl, Andrew. 2004. "Opening Doors: Why Diversity Pays off for Banks." *Canadian Business* (March 29–April 11): 45.
Warner, Matt. 2004. "Why Diversity is the Spice of Working Life." *Accounting & Business* (March): 32–33.
Wilson, Trevor. November 2004. "The Human Equity Advantage." *CMA Management.*
Wright, Patrick, and Chris Brewster. 2003. "Editorial: Learning from Diversity: HRM Is Not Lycra." *International Journal of Human Resource Management* 14:8 (December): 1299–1307.

11 HOW TO RECRUIT AND RETAIN A DIVERSE WORKFORCE

6 CREATING A DIVERSE LIBRARY STAFF

by Hannelore B. Rader

INTRODUCTION

This chapter provides several ideas for diversifying library staff in academic libraries. It describes the creation of a diverse academic library environment for teaching learning and socializing in the twenty-first century; how to recruit a diverse library workforce; and finally how these initiatives can contribute to the academic success of minority students.

A DIVERSE ACADEMIC LIBRARY ENVIRONMENT

In the twenty-first-century academic libraries are undergoing enormous changes in order to stay viable and user-friendly in an ever-changing technology environment. Library professionals are beginning to create a variety of learning laboratories to ensure that students and faculty have appropriate and adequate spaces for interaction in learning and teaching endeavors. Such spaces are being expanded to include a variety of socializing opportunities so that all students representing a variety of ethnic backgrounds can successfully interact while learning and doing research.

As librarians continue their preparations for working in a continually expanding sophisticated technology environment, they face many challenges as well as many opportunities. Most libraries are in better shape than other societal organizations because during the past decade librarians have been on the forefront of technological as well as information developments. Librarians have usually been one of the first groups to computerize their information environment through library system software, hardware, networking, and Web page developments while providing sophisticated assistance to library users. Librarians are also working more closely with diverse groups in their particular libraries and communities to accomplish many information and technology tasks. As professionals they have developed a diverse array of technological skills and information-handling expertise to become leaders in the twenty-first-century information environment.

There are many noteworthy examples in the professional literature regarding how academic librarians are addressing their many professional challenges in higher education, especially the diversification of the profession ("Diversity Now" 2001). Librarians have created many successful scenarios where through a variety of partnerships they have become more involved with the campus diverse teaching and learning community. The described activities involve librarians working with teaching faculty in teaching information skills to a diverse student population. Also described are programs to retain junior faculty of color in order to eventually retain students of color, how to utilize professional development to retain underrepresented academic librarians, challenges people face working in a multicultural environment, cultural diversity and gender roles, and job satisfaction of African American female librarians. Related issues deal with challenges faced by historically black colleges, integrating diversity into the library and information sciences programs, and ethnic and related studies.

An appropriate example of a diverse academic library environment is the University of Louisville Libraries. The University of Louisville is Kentucky's Metropolitan Research University and has ambitious goals for education and research, which are fully supported by the libraries. The university's student population is close to 22,000 students of which approximately one third are graduate and professional students. Louisville has the largest urban area in Kentucky and has the largest African American population. Likewise the University of Louisville has the largest number of African American students in the state. However, there is an acute shortage of librarians, especially African American librarians in the Louisville area.

During the past eight years the university libraries have worked with the school media centers and the public libraries to bring most of the library and information science program headquartered at the University of Kentucky in Lexington to the city of Louisville. Librarians from the University of Louisville and the Louisville Free Public Library teach most of these classes both in the public libraries and in the university libraries. Some classes are taught through video conferencing and online thanks to these partnerships with area libraries. Last year the university libraries were able to establish two minority librarian internships in reference, at the main library, Ekstrom Library, and at the Kornhauser Health Sciences Library. The two African Americans, male and female, work full time as lecturers in the libraries while working on the completion of their master's degree in library and information science from the University of Kentucky.

Some of the initiatives described previously are small, some are large, some are less significant, some are more significant, but all of them have helped libraries become more visible on campus and in the community, more involved in teaching, learning, and research, and ultimately more effective in producing positive learning outcomes for a diverse student population.

ACADEMIC LIBRARIANS' WORK IN THE TWENTY-FIRST CENTURY

Now and in the near future library professionals provide appropriate and necessary diverse information environments on their campuses featuring both print and electronic information formats through utilization of the most efficient and effective user access methodology. They are building, organizing, balancing, digitizing, and preserving collections including a variety of diverse materials for the use of present as well as future academic users. To be successful in these activities academic librarians are partnering with their faculty so that the most appropriate teaching and research materials can be purchased and the best online access to necessary information is offered. They are working with the faculty and the students in distance education programs to ensure the best possible access to information for these programs.

They are creating efficient interlibrary cooperation to address the information needs of the campus community which cannot be met by the existing library collections. This entails using the most current technologies and many partnerships with libraries in the United States and in the international community.

Academic librarians continue to provide effective and successful information services to help and guide their users in their information needs. These services include practical and effective instruction in the use of diverse information in all types of libraries. The instruction can be individualized, in group or classroom settings, or online. Librarians work on providing necessary computer access for diverse groups of society on and off campus through up-to-date computer facilities and the most current software.

Academic librarians provide guidance related to scholarly publications issues from publishing to researching through appropriate information sources, copyright, and licensing expertise through building diverse partnerships and collaborative endeavors within the community they serve. Librarians are also becoming experts in knowledge management, a newly emerging development which brings together faculty members, librarians, and computer experts in the creation of means by which librarians can help scholars and universities retain control of the intellectually generated property that is their most precious and valuable commodity. It is a way of structuring new works as they are created, so that they are maximally accessible, and a way of accessing existing resources to enable the highest level of integration with scholars' work. Through these diverse endeavors librarians can ensure that the library will become the center for information provision and use as well as for teaching and learning.

RECRUITING A DIVERSE LIBRARY WORKFORCE

A diverse population can be defined in the United States as including representatives of various racial and ethnic backgrounds, males and females, people with a variety of international backgrounds, different religious beliefs, and various sexual orientations. Communities throughout the United States are becoming more diverse as demographics are changing, reflecting a changing workforce and a changing population. The community's diversification should be reflected within the educational groups as well as in the libraries.

During the past several years academic librarians have worked together nationally to recruit a more diverse population into their profession to be able to address the growing shortage of professionals due to impending retirements and the need to increase diversity among library professionals to reflect the community composition.

In 2001 the Association of College and Research Libraries (ACRL) and the Association of Research Libraries (ARL) formed a nine-member Task Force on Recruitment.* The task

---

*Members of the Task Force were: Nancy Baker, University of Iowa, Co-Chair Shirley Bake, Washington University, Lois Cherepon, Saint John University, Barbara Dewey, University of Tennessee, Paul Dumont, Dallas County Community College, Emma Perry, Southern University, Co-Chair Hannelore Rader, University of Louisville, Karin Trainer, Princeton University, and Vicki Coleman, University of Virginia.

force's charge was to develop fresh strategies for recruiting and advancing a new generation of talent of the profession of academic librarianship to succeed in the twenty-first century. The following goals were set:

- Compose creative and attractive descriptions of academic librarians' career patterns that serve to highlight the exciting and challenging nature of work in academic libraries today.
- Define and promote academic librarianship in terms of quality of life issues and special opportunities for growth, social contribution, and personal achievement that may appeal to a new generation of talent.
- Inventory and describe available incentives for attracting and keeping talented staff as well as suggesting ways libraries can become more appealing places to work for the new generation of talent.
- Develop case studies of libraries that serve as models for attracting and advancing young and diverse talent.
- List suggestions to recruit highly qualified students on campus for graduate programs in library and information science.
- Identify and describe new sources for recruitment such as students graduating with bachelor's degrees, undergraduate students who minor in Library and Information Science (an increasing trend) for both recruitment to graduate degree work in Library Science programs and for recruitment to academic library positions, where the hiring organization would assume responsibility for further professional development.
- Develop an outline of a promotional plan to recruit individuals to academic librarianship. This might include a strategy to create an attractive national public relations campaign to promote the library profession.
- Suggest appropriate salary structures to attract new professionals.
- This task force should consult with ALA's Office for Human Resource Development and Recruitment and ARL's Office of Leadership and Management Services.

The task force worked from June 2002 to October 2003 and focused on how to attract new talent to the profession. The task force assisted ACRL with the production of a video to recruit people to librarianship. After gathering a significant amount of information the task force provided these recommendations to the governing boards of ACRL and ARL:

1. ACRL and ARL should work together to ensure wide distribution of the recruitment video "Faces of a Profession" to academic libraries, college and university career centers, and schools of library and information science.
    - Announce the availability of the video via email and through Web sites and publications of both associations.
    - Make the video available for downloading and in DVD format.
    - Provide graphical content for printing both the DIV label and box liner.
    - Provide guidelines for its use and for publicity.
    - Provide a form for feedback regarding the use and usefulness of this video.

2. ACRL should develop a recruitment Web page for academic libraries featuring librarians' stories in the form of short vignettes with photographs, building on and going beyond the video "Faces of a Profession."
3. ALISE (Association of Library and Information Science Education) should design a single application form to be used by potential students when applying to multiple institutions similar to many undergraduate admission procedures.
4. ACRL and ARL should work with the subject sections within ACRL to create brief, lively pictorial brochures adaptable for individual subject specialties. These brochures should be made available at academic subject conferences and distributed to career centers at liberal arts colleges. For example, the ACRL Western European Studies Section has developed a powerful flyer which could be expanded into a brochure and could thus serve as an excellent example.
5. There are a number of initiatives in place throughout the United States to address minority recruitment issues and several regional and statewide conferences have been held on this topic during the past several years such as the 2004 National Diversity in Libraries Conference, in Atlanta, GA. (http://www.newyorkdiversitycouncil.com/conf_agenda.html)

The Association of South East Research Libraries (ASERL) has developed professional competencies for academic librarians (www.aserl.org/statements/competencies/competencies.htm). ARL also has developed several SPEC kits related to recruitment and competencies. For a complete list of the SPEC kits go to http://www.arl.org/spec/.

RETAINING A DIVERSE LIBRARY WORKFORCE

Recruiting a diverse librarian population is not an easy undertaking, as explained in the preceding paragraphs. However, retaining diverse academic librarians is yet another difficult endeavor. Academic librarians possess excellent information and technology skills which make them very attractive for recruitment to other professions, particularly those related to information technology such as technology enterprises and business. Since the salary structure in these technology enterprises is often much more attractive than that in academic libraries, the competition is indeed strong. Thus, academic libraries have to ensure that they create stimulating and exciting work environments for their professionals and work on modernizing and restructuring an existing environment to provide what is needed. They must also organize a mentoring program for their new and young professionals and provide appropriate professional development. Such development can serve to encourage promotions and professional advancement on the campus. Other factors that must be addressed by academic libraries concern such matters as why is academic librarianship unique, what does it offer to young professionals not offered by other professions, and what is needed to attract bright, energetic, diverse, and innovative young people into the profession.

ENSURING THE ACADEMIC SUCCESS OF MINORITY STUDENTS

Academic librarians have made many efforts in recent times to ensure that black and other minority students on their campuses can be academically successful. They have partnered with teaching faculty and advisors to create attractive and comfortable learning spaces in the libraries so that students can study and do research in an inviting environment. Academic librarians are teaching students important information and technology skills not only so students can be more successful in doing their research and their class assignments but also so that they can graduate with the necessary skills to be successful in the workforce. Many academic libraries are providing internship opportunities especially for minority students to showcase the exciting information environment of libraries and to attract the students to the library and information profession.

ASSESSING DIVERSITY INITIATIVES IN ACADEMIC LIBRARIES

It is of course most important that the success of any diversity activities in libraries is measured appropriately. There are various factors that will need to be assessed such as the organizational behavior and climate in terms of diversity efforts, whether or not diversity is viewed as a regular part of the organization, successful organizational communication, and the success of diversity initiatives (Love 2001, 73–101). Many universities now have diversity plans in place for all their units and assess these plans on an annual basis to measure the progress they have achieved relative to diversity.

A CASE STUDY

A relevant case study for diversity in academic libraries can be the University of Louisville Libraries. During the past eight years the dean and the Administrative Coordinating Team (ACT) have worked diligently to diversify the library collection, services, and staff. These efforts intensified during the last three years with a new university administration and new major initiatives from Kentucky's Council on Post Secondary Education (CPE), the administrative body of all state-assisted universities in Kentucky. Various initiatives and plans have been developed by the state to accelerate the diversification of the student body, the faculty, and the staff in all state universities. The University of Louisville created the position of Associate Provost for Diversity two years ago and this was followed by a mandate for each academic unit to create a diversity plan. These plans are evaluated and updated on a regular basis.

The libraries have been quite successful in diversifying their collections to ensure that materials are available to represent ethnic minorities, global diversity, many cultures and languages, and particularly minorities present in Kentucky such as the African American community. The university has a strong Pan African Studies Program and the libraries have the very fine Granville A. Bunton Pan African Collection. The Pan African Collection is dedicated to the celebration and presentation of the African American tradition. The collection holds over 4,000 books on Africa and Africans that relate to the history and the study of people of African descent living in the Americas and the Caribbean. Literature, broad anthologies, and works of Pan African and African American literature as well as criticism that cover groups of authors and the body of African and African American literature are found in this collection. Many other related materials are available throughout the libraries (http://library.louisville.edu/ekstrom/tour/panafricancollection.htm).

Another success story concerns the diversifying of the library faculty. Three years ago the library faculty received a mandate based on their diversity plan to have at least two African American library faculty members. When a vacancy occurred, an African American librarian was hired; however, due to national and statewide shortages of African American librarian candidates, it was impossible to fill another vacancy similarly. Thus two faculty librarian reference positions were designated as internships and after internal searches two African American staff persons were selected for these lecturer internships. The three-year internships provide full-time salaries and benefits as well as opportunities to pursue the master's degree in library and information studies at the University of Kentucky. A mentor has been designated for these two lecturers. The library faculty also includes a Hispanic and an Asian American.

To diversify the libraries' student assistant workers, library staff have been working with the university to attract more African American students to work in the libraries, and that has also been a successful endeavor. Furthermore, the libraries have worked with local high school students during the summer to make it possible for African American students to work in the libraries during their summer vacation as part of encouraging them to eventually enroll in the university.

Overall the libraries have been successful in creating a physical environment attractive to all students. More than two million users come to the libraries annually, and these numbers increase substantially each year. Many of the library users are representatives of minority groups including African Americans and many international students. As described earlier, diversification of the library staff has begun and library collections have also been diversified. Throughout the year the libraries offer many diversity exhibits and programs to enhance the multicultural environment on campus.

CONCLUSION

This is not the time for academic librarians to be timid or to wait patiently for new developments. It is the time for academic librarians to be aggressive and dynamic participants in their community's diverse teaching, learning, and information agendas. They must share their enormous information expertise with their various communities and build productive partnerships with other groups to enhance diversity. There are already numerous examples in the nation where librarians have become leaders in their communities in many types of endeavors including diversity activities. There are no limits for librarians as they enter the twenty-first century; there are, however, numerous challenges and endless opportunities.

BIBLIOGRAPHY

Brewer, Julie. 1992. *Internship, Residency and Fellowship Programs in ARL Libraries.* SPEC Kit No. 188. Washington, DC: Association of Research Libraries.

Burrows, Janice, Kriza Jennings, and C. Brigid C. Welch. 1990. *Minority Recruitment and Retention in ARL Libraries.* SPEC Kit No. 167. Washington, DC: Association of Research Libraries.

Cogell, Raquel V., and Cindy A. Gruwell, eds. 2001. *Diversity in Libraries: Academic Residency Programs.* Westport, CT: Greenwood Press.

Diaz, Jose O., and Kristina Starkus. 1994. "Increasing Minority Representation in Academic Libraries: The Minority Library Intern Program at the Ohio State Universities." *College and Research Libraries* 55 (January): 41–46.

Glaviano, Cliff, and Errol R. Lam. 1990. "Academic Libraries and Affirmative Action: Approaching Cultural Diversity in the 1990s." *College and Research Libraries* 51 (November): 513–523.

Jones, Kay F. 1990/1991. "Multicultural Diversity and the Academic Library." *Urban Academic Librarian* 8 (winter): 14–22.

Love, J. B. 2001. "The Assessment of Diversity Initiatives in Academic Libraries." *Journal of Library Administration* 33 (1–2): 73–101.

McCook, Kathleen de la Pena, and Paula Geist. 1993. "Diversity Deferred: Where Are the Minority Librarians?" *Library Journal* 118 (November): 35–38.

Neely, Teresa Y., and Kuang-Hwei Lee Smeltzer, eds. 2002. Diversity Now: People, Collections, and Services in Academic Libraries. Binghamton, NY: Haworth Press.

Peterson, Lorna. 1996. "Alternative Perspectives in Libraries and Information Science Issues of Race." *Journal of Education Library and Information Science* 37 (spring): 163–174.

St. Lifer, Evan, and Corinne O. Nelson. 1997. "Unequal Opportunities: Race Does Matter." *Library Journal* 122 (November): 42–46.

Williams, James F. 1999. "Managing Diversity: Library Management in Light of the Dismantling of Affirmative Action." *Journal of Library Administration* 27 (1–2): 27–48.

Winston, Mark D. 1998. "The Role of Recruitment in Achieving Goals Related to Diversity." *College and Research Libraries* 59 (May): 240–247.

7 FOSTERING DIVERSITY IN RECRUITMENT, STAFFING, AND RETENTION

by Emma Bradford Perry

INTRODUCTION

The 2000 Census estimated that the total number of librarians in the United States was 190,255 and only 11,365 were African Americans (U.S. Bureau of the Census 2000). The census further reported that the number of librarians overall diminished by more than 3 percent (3 percent from 1990 to 2000 but for African Americans the number was nearly 27 percent (26.7 percent). For Native Americans, the drop from 904 to 700 represented a loss of almost 23 percent (22.6 percent) (Grady and Hall 2004). By 2010, nearly 80,000 librarians will reach the age of sixty-five and are expected to leave the profession (Perry 2004, 36). Not only this, but the demographics of America clearly project that there will be more minorities in America within the next decade.

So what does this mean for the library profession? What are the values and benefits of a diverse library staff now and especially for the future? Who will benefit from a diverse library staff? We all do, because a diverse staff improves the organizational culture. It enriches one's professional and educational experiences, promotes personal growth, strengthens the workplace, and enhances America's economic competitiveness. It puts one in tune to other people's backgrounds and different ways of life, and more respect is garnered for people of different races. Diversity promotes a culture wherein all employees, not just specific groups, at all levels are involved and productive. With a diverse staff, contributions from different nationalities, races, genders, ages, styles, and experience will automatically enrich the organization. Without the commitment and support from those at the top of the organization, fostering diversity in staffing will not be successful.

STAFFING

Those in top management must believe in their heart that a diverse staff is right for the organization. There must be a plan of action to increase diversity, one which includes specific goals for developing a diverse staff and specific measurements to gauge the success of all efforts. Diversity in staffing must be woven into every aspect of the organization. If top administrators embrace diversity in staffing, this will certainly send a strong message throughout the organization on the importance of diversity in staffing. Embracing means seeing a diverse staff in the offices of top management. What better way to promote a diverse staff than starting at the very top of the organization.

We must do more than just talk about diversity, because action speaks louder than words. Reese and Hawkins strongly advocate with the title of their book that we should "Stop talking, Start doing." Those in a position to foster diversity in their libraries often only give lip service and very little real committed and sincere action to diversity. At the University of Arizona, more than lip service has been given to diversity because the leader there, Carla Stoffle, has made a commitment to diversity which has resulted in a more diverse staff than any other ARL (Association of Research Libraries) library, with 30 percent of library faculty and 36 percent of classified staff being from underrepresented populations (Weaver-Meyers 2004, 196). Effective leaders engage all stakeholders in the diversity process so that each senses an undeniable and authentic air of inclusiveness. Each library must maintain a focus on staffing patterns which support diversity and inclusion. Having a diverse staff provides more opinions and advice from different perspectives which results in a more informed decision-making process. There is a wealth of talent and knowledge among a diverse staff and it strengthens any organization. Since talent is not gender or race based, we can hire across racial and gender lines without sacrificing quality and exceptional work.

As library leaders, we can send powerful messages to our employees and other librarians about our commitment to diversity by actively recruiting and hiring top-notch minorities and women to work in positions at the top level of management. As the leader of your organization, have you hired a minority to work in your office or to report directly to you? If not, why not?

The key in developing and maintaining a diverse staff is to develop diversity strategies and initiatives in the same way other programs of importance are developed in your library. If you have a diversity officer, does this person report to the dean or director? Is this person at the table where major decisions are made about staffing, recruiting, and retention? What are the symbols and processes used only when something is really important in the library? Are these same symbols and processes used for fostering a diverse staff? If diversity is not at the management table, then you are always positioned to look at decisions previously made. When diversity is at the table, there is a chance to shape decisions and ask others to be accountable for results.

How do you know if you are making progress in your efforts to develop a diverse staff? You must "inspect what you expect," meaning you must measure what you do and gauge your progress. In order to do this, guidelines must be in place for measuring progress. There must be a plan of action, a clear strategy, one which includes specific goals and actions to implement the steps to improve diversity within the culture of the organization. Not only must there be a commitment, but also procedures should be in place and money on the table to fund diversity initiatives and demand accountability.

Fostering and implementing a diverse staff is a moral imperative because of the extraordinary dream of creating a world where everyone has equal opportunity and there is fairness, inclusiveness, and justice for all. The primary reason for a diverse staff is to change and improve the organizational culture wherein all employees, not just specific groups, at all levels are involved and productive. Diversity is not a training program, but it is a strategic process. The strategic process has to be an administrative imperative, meaning those at the top must implement and lead the process.

Because most job descriptions require three or more years of experience with other unrealistic requirements, new library school graduates are often eliminated by these requirements. How can new graduates obtain experience unless more openings are available for them? Recently minted librarians are excited about working and have tons of energy, new ideas, and a real desire to succeed. We must hire these new librarians and provide opportunities for them to succeed, including competitive salaries. Not only this, but fostering diversity in staffing includes valuing the contributions that underrepresented groups can bring to the organization.

RECRUITMENT

In 1997, the American Library Association launched the Spectrum Initiative, a national effort to help curb the pending shortage of librarians and to address the need for a diverse workforce that reflects those who utilize libraries. This initiative alone will not solve the problem libraries face. All librarians must personally do more to recruit and mentor future librarians (Perry 2004, 36).

Recruiting a diverse workforce means reaching out beyond our comfort zone, being more inclusive and embracing a diverse staff. We must actively recruit in a manner which will diversify the staff by including diversity as an integral part of the organization's overall strategic plan. Making recruitment for a diverse workforce a strategic imperative will assist in effective recruiting.

What Can Be Done to Recruit a Diverse Workforce?

1. Actively and personally identify and recruit from diverse, racial, and ethnic groups.
2. Set goals and make a concerted effort to reach these goals.
3. Change the composition of top management, by bringing in a greater number of women and minorities in top management.
4. Improve communication with the minority community and with other major stakeholders.
5. Change the internal cultural, social, and professional environment by assessing the degree to which diversity is promoted and encouraged.
6. Recruit in a manner which will diversify the workplace.
7. Make recruiting for a diverse workforce part of the strategic process of the library.
8. Strongly encourage employees to personally recruit for a diverse workforce.
9. Provide potential candidates contact or mentors to interact with.
10. Provide competitive salaries and any other benefits possible to recruit for a diverse workforce.
11. Discuss diversity and recruitment at library meetings and ask everyone to assist with recruiting.
12. Provide an orientation about library school for student assistants.
13. Furnish shadowing opportunities for those interested in a career in librarianship.
14. Provide recruitment information and assistance which are aimed specifically at current support staff who are interested in a library degree.
15. Display recruitment posters throughout the library and put up exhibits.
16. Meet with career center directors, counselors, and college advisors to talk about opportunities in libraries.
17. Have students to serve on the library advisory committee.
18. Serve as a guest lecturer or adjunct professor in library school.

19. Make sure the library personnel director recruits for a diverse workforce.
20. Recruit with a passion in all venues.

In order to successfully recruit for a diverse workforce you must use effective methods to recruit minority librarians. Often very little emphasis is placed on targeting minority groups, providing staff development, or marketing the library in a way which will attract minority candidates (Edwards 2002, 631).

Recruitment, mentoring, and support for paraprofessionals can be instrumental in implementing a diverse staff. Paraprofessionals are a vital part of the library and these staff should be encouraged to attend library school with adequate support from the library. Our current structure in libraries does little to encourage or facilitate their growth due to a lack of a career development path or advancement strategies for minorities and paraprofessionals (Bonnette 2004, 134). Recruitment is a professional responsibility for each of us in the profession and we should actively recruit for the profession. It has to be a passion and commitment in which one must think "outside the box" on how to effectively recruit for the profession.

A culturally diverse and inclusive environment is its own best marketing tool to recruit and attract others to any organization. If others see inclusion and diversity successfully thriving within the organization, recruitment tends to be easier. One must do more than just talk about recruiting a diverse workforce, as results speak louder than mere words.

There is a wealth of talent in underrepresented groups and these talented librarians should be identified and actively recruited. As leaders of the profession, we can send powerful messages to our employees and other librarians about our commitment to diversity by hiring top-notch and talented minorities and women in top administrative positions.

In Emma Bradford Perry's article "Let Recruitment Begin with Me" in the May issue of *American Libraries*, there are ten recruitment vows for librarians which will help to recruit and increase diversity in libraries.

Promise Yourself To:

1. Make a personal commitment to recruitment and diversity and encourage your colleagues to do the same.
2. Develop a positive vision and think creatively in ways that will excite potential students.
3. Reach out, encourage, coach, and counsel potential students.
4. Provide ongoing professional and emotional support and assistance to library school students.
5. Develop one-on-one relationships with nondegreed library staffers and others. Encourage them to consider librarianship as a career.
6. Provide as much flexibility as possible to accommodate subordinates pursuing the master of library science degree.
7. Encourage and participate in the development and implementation of a first-rate mentoring program in your institution.
8. Get to know and work closely with a library school dean and staff.
9. Branch out from traditional settings to capture the attention of potential library school students.
10. Recruit actively, not passively. (Perry 2004)

Recruitment has many faces, including internships, residency programs, and traditional recruiting methods. Academic libraries are employing other tactics such as identifying and aggressively developing home grown talent. Providing staff with professional opportunities and instituting programs such as tuition assistance and formal mentoring have short-term costs, but the long-term potential for gain is substantial. Identifying talented staff and encouraging careers in academic librarianship are cost-effective ways of recruiting top quality professionals (Raschke 2003, 64). All library professionals need to encourage and promote the profession by recruiting through personal outreach mentoring and with sustained passion.

RETENTION

While you may do reasonably well in recruiting for a diverse workforce, without a culture of inclusion you will end up doing poorly with retention and promotions. Retention of a diverse workforce is just as important as recruiting for a diverse workforce. The following retention strategies can be useful when implemented:

1. First, identify and establish your core values as a library and use this foundation to build a diverse strategy.
2. Once you have developed your strategy, communicate and reinforce the messages and principles constantly to all employees (newsletters, special publications: videos, speech, emails, seminars, workshops, whatever). Keep in mind you are changing the culture of the organization which can be a long and sometimes difficult process.
3. As a senior library administrator, you must champion diversity personally. Embrace it! Celebrate it, like it, talk about it, sing its praises, believe in it. It is a fact that without the administration's commitment, diversity will not take root in your library.
4. Recognize and honor employees who practice diversity. A little praise goes a long way.
5. Measure, measure, measure—you won't know if you are making progress with diversity unless you chart your progress.

Much attention is given to recruiting and hiring for a diverse workforce, but less focus and attention are given to retaining staff. Libraries must make a concerted effort to retain librarians once they are hired. This can be accomplished by providing a nurturing and caring work environment. For new hires, why not assign a mentor or a senior librarian to help with the adjustment of a new job, community, and the new work environment?

Mentoring is a key to retaining staff, but often minority librarians are not afforded the same comfort level as their nonminority peers. There are many who wish to have mentorship and collegial relationships with librarians of color that will allow them to discuss issues that are particular to their minority experience in the profession (Grady and Hall 2004).

Mentoring is beneficial for the mentee as well as the mentor. Mentors serve in various capacities for new staff as they adjust to their new job. Without a mentor, career development opportunities, and management training, librarians often fail. It is a fact that individuals from diverse backgrounds have more barriers to achievement than those from the majority race. Mentoring serves as a means of improving an organization by raising the level of recruitment and retention statistics. Affirmative action, gender equity, and successful mentoring partnerships are combining to break down the barriers and promote equal opportunity. Mentoring is the one shared characteristic of all the people of color who have advanced the furthest because they all shared a strong network or mentors who nurtured their professional development (Bonnette 2004).

What can you do to personally foster the recruitment of a diverse staff and assist with retention?

- Make a personal and professional commitment to foster diversity, recruitment, and retention and encourage your colleagues to do the same.
- Come up with creative ways to attract others to the profession.
- Be a mentor to a newly hired staff member.
- Assist with recruitment by encouraging colleagues and others to apply for positions at your library.
- Volunteer to serve on the library diversity committee.
- Identify and establish core values and use them as a foundation to build a diverse strategy.
- Once you have developed your strategy, communicate and reinforce the messages and principles constantly to all employees.
- Keep in mind you are changing the culture of the organization which can be a long and sometimes difficult process.
- You must be a champion for diversity.
- Recognize and honor employees who practice diversity.
- Chart your progress with diversity.

Diversity requires committed and dedicated leadership operating in a reasoned way. Why not have the library dean or director lead a Diversity Day for top managers of the library? As the leader of your library, it must be crystal clear to everyone in your library that increasing and embracing diversity will be everyone's responsibility. Diversity promotes creativity and innovation, and it fosters problem-solving skills and adds organizational culture and flexibility.

Diversity is more than just equity. It is the whole spectrum of attributes, styles, backgrounds, and experiences. Diversity is complex and as varied as life itself, so it must be thought of in very broad terms. Weaving diversity into the very future of your organization takes time, but patience and persistence are the keys to success. It is an ongoing process—a work in progress. Fostering diversity will significantly improve your organization, but your commitment has to be real. It has to be visible, honest, and embraced at all levels.

CONCLUSION

Recruitment and retention go hand in hand in the overall management of a library. Retention is far less costly than recruitment (Bothmer and LaCroix 2004, 11). Librarians must continue to inspire others to join the profession by providing opportunities, encouraging others to attend library school, mentoring younger librarians, and being active in the recruitment process. Potential library leaders must be identified and nurtured in a way which will provide more librarians for the twenty-first century.

BIBLIOGRAPHY

Bonnette, Ashley. 2004. "Mentoring Minority Librarians Up the Career Ladder." *Library Administration and Management* 18, no. 3 (summer): 134–139.

Bothmer, James A., and Michael LaCroix. 2004. "Recruitment and Retention at the Creighton University Libraries." *Nebraska Library Association Quarterly* 35, no. 2 (summer): 11–13.

Edwards, Ronald. 2002. "Migrating to Public Librarianship: Depart on Time to Ensure a Smooth Flight." *Library Trends* 50, no. 6 (spring): 631–639.

Grady, Jennifer, and Tracie Hall. 2004. "The World Is Changing: Why Aren't We? Recruiting Minorities to Librarianship." *ALA-APA Library Worklife*. Available: www.ala-apa.org.

Hurt, Tara, and Deborah Sunday. 2002. "Career Paths for Paraprofessionals: Your Ladder to Success." *Library Administration and Management* 16, no. 4 (fall): 198–202.

Josey, E. J., ed. 1993. *The Black Librarian in America Revisited*. Metuchen, NJ: Scarecrow Press.

Lynch, Beverly. 2004. "Theory and Practice." *Library Administration and Management* 18, no. 1 (winter): 30–34.

Perry, Emma Bradford. 2004. "Let Recruitment Begin with Me." *American Libraries* 35, no. 5 (May): 36–38.

Raschke, Gregory. 2003. "Hiring and Recruitment Practices in Academic Libraries: Problems and Solutions." *Libraries and the Academy* 3, no. 1: 53–67.

Reese, Gregory, and Ernestine Hawkins. 1999. *Stop Talking, Start Doing: Attracting People of Color to the Library Profession*. Chicago: American Library Association.

U.S. Bureau of the Census. Census 2000. Washington, DC: U.S. Bureau of the Census.

Van Fleet, Connie, and Danny Wallace. 2002. "O Librarian, Where Art Thou?" *References and User Services Quarterly* 41, no. 3 (spring): 215–217.

Weaver-Meyers, Pat. 2004. "Change Masters All—A Series on Librarians Who Steered a Clear Course Toward the Twenty-First Century." *Library Administration and Management* 18, no. 4 (fall): 192–198.

Wilder, Stanley J. 1999. *The Age Demographics of Academic Libraries: A Profession Apart*. New York: Haworth Press.

# DIVERSITY AND RECRUITING PRACTICES: HOW LIS SCHOOLS AND PRACTITIONERS WORK TOGETHER

by Jametoria Burton and W. Michael Havener

INTRODUCTION

Increasing ethnic diversity in the library profession sometimes seems to be like the weather. Everyone talks about it, but no one does anything about it. This perceived state of affairs was reflected by Gregory Reese and Ernestine Hawkins when they chose the title of their 1999 book on recruiting people of color into our profession. The book's title is *Stop Talking, Start Doing!* That title was a challenge that some within the profession have taken.

Many are doing and not just talking. This chapter describes some concrete ways in which individuals and groups within the library and information professions can work together in successful recruitment efforts. The focus of the chapter is on recruitment, but we will also cover some retention strategies, because if we cannot retain and promote the people of color whom we attract to librarianship, our recruitment efforts will be meaningless.

One of the authors of this chapter is a practicing librarian who completed her Master of Library and Information Science (MLIS) degree in 2002; the other is the director of an ALA (American Library Association) accredited master's program. One of us is white; one of us is black. One of us is female; one of us is male. One of us has experienced what it is like to be part of a targeted recruitment program and later to be selected for a minority residency program; the other has experienced the challenges that an educator and administrator faces in trying to make the ideal of ethnic diversity a reality.

Our personal experiences have shaped our beliefs about how practitioners, libraries, professional organizations, and library and information science (LIS) graduate programs can successfully work together to recruit and retain a more ethnically diverse library work force. We believe that our experiences also illustrate many of the recommendations that we make in this chapter, and we therefore want to tell you something about those experiences before we make those recommendations.

JAMIE'S STORY

I received my MLIS degree in 2002, but my journey into the field of librarianship began back in 1996 after talking with a good friend who was a practicing librarian. At that point in my life, I was looking for a career change from social service work to a career where I could continue to utilize my helping skills and love for working with people. Until then, I had never considered becoming a librarian though I possessed all of the trappings of an information professional. Looking back, I realized that people came to me for all sorts of information and I would always seem to find the answer for them. As a former teacher with a thirst for knowledge, it was only natural for me to gravitate to librarianship. But the biggest influence came from my good friend who saw my potential and took the initiative to personally guide and mentor me into the profession. I can never thank a wonderful librarian and dear friend, Joia Dinkins, enough for seeing something in me that I could not see in myself. She knew I would flourish as a librarian and at the time, she helped me get started in a new career which has turned out to be a perfect match for my personality and professional interests. As illustrated, never underestimate the power of a mentor, for mentoring remains a key factor into the success of any recruitment effort undertaken particularly in regard to persons from underrepresented groups.

Although my convictions were definite in my quest to become a librarian, there were a few barriers that kept me from immediately pursuing my dream. As a military wife, I was limited by geographical location to having access to a library education program. During the mid-1990s, only one ALA-accredited distance education existed. However, lack of financial resources and the untimely death of my sister put everything on hold for several more years. After being transferred to Rhode Island with the Navy, I finally realized my opportunity had finally come to attend library school at the University of Rhode Island with the inception of the newly established Prism Fellowship Program at the University of Rhode Island Graduate School of Library and Information Studies. Being selected as one of the Prism Fellows propelled me into what has become the most exciting period of my entire professional life.

I was a Prism Fellow from 2000 to 2002. The Prism Program was funded by the Institute of Museum and Library Services (IMLS) in conjunction with the University of Rhode Island Graduate School of Library and Information Studies under the directorship of Dr. W. Michael Havener, the principal investigator for the project. Under his leadership, seven graduate students from underrepresented groups successfully graduated after two years of full-time study complemented with graduate assistantships and travel funds for conference attendance and presentation opportunities. This was the first major library diversity education initiative housed at the library school which took the combined efforts of the library school and university library partnering together. This dynamic cohort consisted of four long-time library support staff and three individuals with no library background. All of the participants took full-time class loads while working part-time at the university library. A few also maintained part-time work schedules at other libraries in addition to their work at the university library. The program provided for conference support (ALA, International Federation of Library Associations [IFLA], state, and regional), memberships to professional library organizations, part-time work experience as reference assistants, stipend, and graduate teaching opportunities within the library.

The program encompassed many of the components mentioned in more detail in the following pages. Important elements were a substantial financial support package, caring mentors, diverse and supportive faculty, issues of diversity woven throughout the curriculum, being a part of a cohort group, and myriad other benefits along with the added exposure and responsibility to participate in conference presentations in a variety of state and national settings. To me, the combination of elements noted above greatly added to the overall graduate educational experience. With all of these elements in place along with our own sheer determination to excel and succeed, there was no possible way we could fail. But most of all, we were all supportive of each other in various ways. Being a part of a cohort helped us to bond together as friends, giving us a valuable internal support among ourselves. Because of the Prism Fellowship Program, a total of seven more librarians of color have entered the profession. Each of us has since landed meaningful employment in her respective area. Prism opened up a whole new world to me by further extending my circle of librarian mentors and opening up new professional opportunities for me. Immediately following graduation, given my interest in pursuing a career in academic libraries, I was blessed to be selected as the Resident Librarian at the University of Iowa Libraries and continued to enhance my skills as a librarian with one of the nation's leading research libraries. Clearly, being a part of the Prism program at the University of Rhode Island put me on the road to success for the next two years and for years to come. My experience as a resident librarian gave me the additional confidence and professional library experience needed to further advance my career in academic librarianship with an opportunity to extend into a permanent position. While there, I was mentored by Janice Simmons-Welburn and other librarians who felt strongly about the success of this program. But most of all, I was regarded as an equal and vital part of the staff. No doubt, having those crucial first two years of professional experience has indeed given me an edge in attaining future employment at the conclusion of my residency.

Another benefit of the residency centered around my acceptance and participation in the Institute for Early Career Librarians sponsored by the University of Minnesota for new librarians from underrepresented groups (http://sdt.lib.umn.edu/institute). The only program of its kind, this program is designed for librarians from racial and ethnic groups that are traditionally underrepresented in the library profession. And unlike many library leadership development programs, which focus on midcareer professionals, this institute gives librarians in the first three years of their careers hands-on professional training and professional networking opportunities.

As a librarian with a strong leadership orientation in the area of information literacy, my journey also took me to the halls of the University of Washington in Seattle, where I participated in the Institute for Information Literacy Immersion Program sponsored by ACRL (Association of College and Research Libraries). This annual four-and-a-half-day program provided intensive information literacy training and education for instruction librarians. The institute was taught by a faculty of nationally recognized librarians, and participation is limited to ninety persons to ensure an environment that fostered group interaction and active participation (http://www.ala.org/ala/acrl/acrlissues/acrlinfolit/professactivity/iil/welcome.htm). Again, my perspective of libraries expanded to an even greater level of understanding. Out of ninety librarians, only five were from diverse backgrounds, which let me see how much recruiting work still needs to be done. I was thankful for having the chance to participate in this unique program while vowing to strengthen my resolve in playing a greater role to increase those numbers for future immersion classes.

As a graduate of the first cohort and a new librarian, I am grateful to have had the opportunity to be a part of all of these marvelous professional training opportunities. Indeed, having started under the Prism Fellowship at University of Rhode Island proved to be a wonderful initiative, for it was where my new career was launched and nurtured. But moreover, it was where my love of librarianship and commitment to diversity developed. Right away, I saw the need for increased diversity in this profession, sensing the struggle of those individuals who blazed the trail for me and other underrepresented individuals in the profession. I soon recognized the burden for me to further work in this area where I was a beneficiary and to do my part to carry the torch in helping new librarians. Recruitment became my passion and recruiting other diverse applicants became a personal mission.

MIKE'S STORY

Recruiting for ethnic diversity requires commitment and passion, and most of us can remember seminal experiences that energized that commitment. For me, one such experience came during the 1999 ACRL National Conference in Detroit, Michigan. During that conference, I attended a session on recruitment and heard a speaker say that a major reason for the lack of ethnic diversity in the library profession was apathy (or worse) on the part of the administrators at ALA-accredited MLIS programs. He stated that the attitudes and behaviors of approximately fifty white male deans and directors were largely responsible for the lack of people of color in the library profession.

As a white male in my first semester as the director of an ALA-accredited master's program, I was furious. As a faculty member, I had recruited and mentored on a one-on-one basis. I had also helped write and administer multiple Title II-B grants to support students of color. As a new director, I had come to the presentation to get more ideas on how I could work with practitioners to recruit more librarians of color; instead, I was told that I was the problem.

All of us who are deans and directors of master's programs can and should do more to recruit librarians of color, but LIS faculty, library directors, library department heads, and frontline librarians all can and should do more. It is unrealistic to think that the men and women who head accredited programs can change the complexion of our profession by themselves. There are fewer than sixty ALA-accredited master's programs in North America, but there are more than 117,000 libraries in the United States. The practitioners should hold LIS programs and their leaders accountable, but they also need to work with our educational programs in recruiting efforts. IMLS has recognized this by encouraging partnerships in grant applications.

I know that practitioners, both administrators and line librarians, also often feel limited in their ability to facilitate change. However, each of us can make a difference, and we can accomplish much more when we work together. Ecclesiastes 4:9 tells us, "Two are better off than one, because together they can work more effectively" (Good News Version). This chapter is dedicated to partnership and the belief that we need to work together to diversify the profession of librarianship.

THE EVOLUTION OF RECRUITMENT

Our personal experiences and beliefs are reflected in this chapter, but the inspiration and ideas that we have received from many others are also central to the recommendations that we make. It is said that "a dwarf standing on the shoulders of a giant may see farther than a giant himself," and we are indebted to those who have gone before us in the development of recruitment programs and to the many others who are working on recruitment today.

Our profession has made some major strides in the area of diversity. We can tout the very successful Spectrum Initiative and other institutional programs within the ALA and some its divisions such as the ARL Initiative to Recruit a Diverse Workforce. The ALA has awarded over 270 Spectrum Scholarships since the initiative began in 1998, and support from an IMLS grant will increase the number of scholarships awarded over the next few years. No doubt, we will see considerable difference as a result of ALA programs and other viable programs, like the IMLS-funded Knowledge River program at the University of Arizona. Residency programs and other initiatives have been growing steadily in a variety of libraries all across the country.

We hope that momentum has finally caught on to make recruitment of underrepresented groups a priority issue within our library organizations in every aspect of the ALA and our sister organizations, such as the Medical Library Association (MLA) and the Special Library Association (SLA), as well as our five major ethnic caucuses. However, we still have a long way to go. If we look at the ethnic composition of the United States as reflected in the 2000 Census, we are actually losing ground in our attempt to reflect the ethic diversity of our library users in the composition of our profession.

This is nothing new. Going back fifteen to twenty years ago and even farther, a fair amount of literature was being written about the declining numbers of minorities in librarianship. Some of the key figures and change agents who made long and sacrificial efforts to help promote, push, and propel the diversity movement include Dr. E. J. Josey, Dr. Arnulfo D. Trejo, Elisabeth Martinez, John Ayala, Marva DeLoach, Dr. Lotsee Patterson, and Dr. Em Clair Knowles, to name just a few.

Many of the strategies that they recommended and implemented are still as viable today as when they were originally recommended. For example, in 1989, Dr. Josey, founder of the Black Caucus of ALA, teacher, mentor, former ALA president, professor emeritus at the University of Pittsburgh School of Library and Information Science, and an inspiration to a generation of black librarians across this country, wrote and published an article entitled "Minority Representation in Library and Information Science Programs." In this article, he stated, "When one examines the totality of students in LIS programs, we can conclude the minorities are grossly underrepresented. Therefore the schools of library and information science should reaffirm their commitment to increasing minority access to the library profession by adopting a comprehensive program for the recruitment of minorities." He further went on to present specific strategies for action to redress this issue regarding what LIS programs could and should do as a part of an overall comprehensive and coordinated plan of attack for both effective recruitment and retention, not a watered down feel-good approach with no real long-term impact.

Dr. Josey laid out a structured strategic framework that advocated specific steps to take in four major areas of recruitment: (1) awareness programs, (2) funding, (3) working with large urban public libraries and major research libraries, and (4) recruitment and retention of minority students. His detailed and practical recommendations will still work today. He recommended:

- Develop ethnically centered promotional brochures for LIS to market LIS opportunities to potential minority students.
- Make visits to high schools to begin awareness programs.
- Make visits to colleges that have large minority enrollments to recruit students.
- Use the help of minority alumni to identify potential minority students.
- When promotional literature is available, distribute through minority organizations such as the Urban League and the NAACP, etc.
- Make contact with minority organizations to participate on their programs to promote library and information science.
- Work with the ALA Black Caucus, the Association to Promote Library and Information Services to Latinos and the Spanish speaking (REFORMA), the Chinese American Librarians Association (CALA), and the Asia/Pacific American Librarians Association (APALA), and the American Indian Library Association (AILA) associations in establishing a nationwide recruitment drive of minorities to the profession.
- Library school faculty should initiate informal contacts with Black Studies and other Ethnic Studies faculty to seek their help in the recruitment of minority students to library and information science programs.

Regarding funding because of the lack financial support at that time, Josey advocated for the implementation of the following:

- Commit funding to initiate a comprehensive and targeted recruitment program.
- Fund participation in graduate career days at HBCUs (historically black colleges and universities) and other institutions.
- Tap resources from foundations, corporations, and alumni, particularly from ethnic groups.
- Ensure the adequacy of stipends for students who may be married and have family responsibilities.
- Ask alumni to make contributions to support this special thrust; a special mailing could be made for this purpose.
- Establish a minority weekend. Minority alumni would be made aware of the critical need to contribute to the alumni fund for scholarships as well as aid in the recruitment of minorities.
- Stimulate legislative and policy initiatives to obtain state and federal funding for the education of minorities. Build upon the legislative hearings held on higher education and promote increased funding at the federal level.

In working with public urban libraries and research libraries, Dr. Josey advocated for:

- Urging both types of libraries to establish a tuition support program for minority staff who attend library school with a promise to work for a minimum of two years after graduation
- Establishing formal mechanisms with the large public libraries and the large research academic libraries to seek the development of liaison programs for minority recruitment
- Sending representatives to large urban public libraries, major research libraries, and others to contact minorities by addressing associations and library unions and by participating in continuing education programs

It is not enough to recruit those from underrepresented groups to LIS programs; adequate support mechanisms must be incorporated as essential elements for their successful retention. Regarding retention, he also recommended:

- Hiring additional faculty members from underrepresented groups who can serve as role models and who understand the challenges faced by minority students
- Inviting outside speakers from underrepresented groups to address colloquia and serve as adjunct professors
- Establishing a counseling support service program to help avoid a revolving door admission program

The comprehensive recommendations for action outlined by Dr. Josey are complemented by recommendations developed by Dr. Em Clair Knowles and others who served on the ACRL Task Force on Recruitment of Underrepresented Minorities. Their work began in 1989, the same year Josey's article was published. After one and a half years of intense work between the ALA's midwinter conference in 1989 and the ALA annual conference in 1990, the task force developed a comprehensive report outlining and detailing specific recommendations to eliminate barriers and create tangible and measurable opportunities. That report was adopted by the ACRL Executive Board. Their 1990 article, "Recruiting the Underrepresented to

Academic Libraries," provided the catalyst for specific, tangible, and deliberate actions taken by then ACRL president Barbara Ford to push this effort forward.

The key targets for change identified by the task force were (a) barriers to institutional commitment to change and accountability, (b) barriers of personal and institutional accountability, and (c) barriers to advancement and retention. At their conference in November 1990, the ACRL board took specific and decisive action on the final report by voting to establish an ACRL standing committee on racial and ethnic diversity with the following charge: to *initiate*, *advise*, and *mobilize* support for immediate and appropriate action based on the recommendation of the report. The executive board also endorsed position statements included in the report, which affirmed ACRL's continuing commitment to the elimination of barriers for recruitment and retention. Lastly, the report was sent to all ACRL units with a request for consideration and *immediate* action. Among recruitment strategies were improvements in:

- Position announcements
- Advertising
- Soliciting of information on résumés
- Interview processes
- Networking
- Skill development training
- Assessment and evaluation and needs assessments of entry-level trainee internships
- Management apprenticeships and exchange programs
- Opportunities for career outreach training
- Career outreach for paraprofessional library staff and students
- Regard for the importance of mentoring, role modeling, and other support efforts
- Regard for participation inclusion in library school programs, curriculum, and recruitment
- Efforts by library schools to recruit and provide financial assistance, mentoring, and faculty from underrepresented groups
- Regard for participation in youth programs to arouse interest in librarianship at an early age

The recommendations of this report served as the foundation and plan of action for:

- Position statements
- Committee and coalition appointments
- Training and future conference programs
- Survey and data collection
- Publicity, awards, and funding

These are just two examples of some of the most strategic efforts in the advancement of this issue. But how far have we come since that time?

For instance, some of the programs cited in this report were identified as models that could be utilized and replicated. One of the programs identified at that time was the REFORMA/UCLA Mentor Program, considered a model effort by a library school and professional organization to provide mentoring, role models, and support by a group of underrepresented librarians for a group of underrepresented students in the library school.

Another collaborative model program cited in the report was the Teenage Library Association of Texas (TALA), which provided extracurricular activities for youngsters in high school and middle school, involving them in local library activities. This was an example of how academic librarians saw the need to participate with the colleagues from school and public libraries in youth programs to arouse their interest in librarianship. Included in this initiative was an awarding of a $1,000 scholarship every other year to former members of the group attending library school.

Another collaborative example of a program designed to attract youth was a program by the Special Libraries Associations' Affirmative Action Subcommittees where discussions were held with school principals to have teams invited to individual school to give talks about librarianship.

An example of addressing the issue of training needs for career outreach in attracting paraprofessional library staff and students from underrepresented groups to librarianship was another model endeavor sponsored by the California Librarians Recruitment Project. Within their programs, they held an informational program at a state library conference which included a series of recruitment and training workshops, and they produced a handbook describing recruitment techniques and a career information brochure that highlighted various aspects of the information profession, including two key brochures, entitled "Career Opportunities for Minorities for Librarianship" and "Careers in College and University Libraries." The project's success was attributed to the partnership of the state's three library schools, combined with the efforts of practitioners from various types of library and information settings along with the representation of underrepresented librarians.

A strong example of that kind of library staff development continuing education was a daylong workshop for librarians and staff at the University of California (UC) on cultural diversity in the UC Libraries. Participants took part in a workshop, which concentrated on an issue paper regarding recruitment and advancement of racial and ethnic minorities as well as better hiring practices. Equally as effective were sessions and discussions on Bibliographic Access to Ethnic Collections within the UC, Reference Services and Bibliographic Instruction for Resources on Cultural Diversity in UC Libraries, and Collection Development for Culturally Diverse Materials in UC Libraries. They even created effective exhibits throughout their libraries' system such as a popular Ethnic Heritage Map. The map geographically represented the diverse range of countries and cultures in the ethnic backgrounds of both UC Libraries staff and students. Both of the efforts were highly successful in raising the awareness of cultural presence in the campus community as well as in-house training for the library personnel.

A great example of a successful LIS initiative in the late 1980s was the Minority Internship/Scholarship in MLIS program through the State University of New York library system whereby minority undergraduate students were recruited for a year-long paid internship during their senior year. Students were then encouraged to attend library school following graduation. Full fiscal support for tuition and stipend was provided by the SUNY system; however, students could attend any accredited MLS program in New York. In 1991, a similar program was initiated between the Northern Illinois library systems and LIS schools in the area in collaboration with contacts through campus placement directors. The library project directors set a specific goal to recruit 25 percent of the interns. The interns were then encouraged to refer names of others who might be interested in library careers.

Another major initiative was the work of Dr. Arnulfo D. Trejo. Dr. Trejo, founder of REFORMA, established the Graduate Library Institute for Spanish-Speaking Americans (GLISA) at the University of Arizona in 1975. His persistence and perseverance in creating GLISA to recruit and train librarians to serve the growing Spanish-speaking community in the United States has had a profound impact on the number of Hispanic/Latino librarians. During its four-year run, approximately sixty students earned their MLS (Master of Library Science) degrees, substantially increasing the percentage of bilingual and bicultural librarians.

RECRUITMENT AND RETENTION TODAY

Many of today's most successful programs have much in common with the earlier programs described previously. As we have already mentioned, the Spectrum Initiative has given tremendous financial support, mentoring, and access to over 270 participants to date; and, with the help of the IMLS grant it received this year, the number of annual participants will increase.

The Knowledge River Program from the University of Arizona School of Library and Information Science has been touted by John Berry in his March 2004 *Library Journal* editorial as one of the most promising diversity library recruitment models currently in place. Knowledge River has already recruited three cohort groups of Native American and Latino students. Elements contributing to the success of this program include cohort recruitment, an ethnocentric curriculum where the Native American and Latino perspective is an integral part of the curriculum via a special area of concentration, exposure to national library leaders of color, a substantial financial package including full tuition, stipend, travel, and conference registration support in addition to other support counseling services, and even help with child care, housing, registration, technology, and parking.

An exciting new program from Tracie D. Hall, the new director of the ALA's Office of Diversity, is the "Grow Your Own" campaign. The Grow Your Own campaign was launched in the fall of 2003 and aimed at promoting librarianship to students and support staff working at HBCUs (historically black colleges and universities) and HBIs (historically black institutions). It addresses those issues of awareness of the profession and a milieu of funding opportunities, exposure to underrepresented professionals, and mentoring. I personally believe this program has the potential to be one of the most successful diversity recruiting initiatives as it opens a groundswell of interest from many potential LIS recruits. Through consistent marketing efforts showcasing the success of this initiative, we will begin to see larger numbers of LIS recruits from these institutions indeed creating a domino effect.

PRACTICAL SUGGESTIONS

How can we translate what we have learned from these recruitment efforts and our own experiences into concrete and meaningful actions? Here are some practical suggestions, first for recruitment activities and then for retention activities.

WHAT CAN WE DO? AWARENESS AND RECRUITMENT STRATEGIES

Practitioners Can:

1. Encourage staff in their libraries to pursue an MLIS degree.
    Many library staff were encouraged to pursue a library career because of the encouragement of fellow librarians and other interested persons. This type of recruiting is the basis for the campaigns such as Grow Your Own and other initiatives which both encourage and support library staff desiring to attain the MLIS degree in library science.

2. Promote librarianship as a potential career to individuals known through churches, schools, civic organizations, etc.

   Librarians are involved in the community through all sorts of civic organizations and should therefore take advantage of these venues to promote the profession and actively recruit people with whom they interact on a regular basis. Talking to a class of high school and middle school students or presenting a career day program at a church are great ways to raise the interest level of students who may never have considered a career in librarianship otherwise.

3. Mentor LIS students and potential students.

   Librarians particularly in the academic arena have the unique advantage to interact with library students on a regular basis since library schools work closely with their campus library. Librarians can take opportunities with students, teach and coach them to attain on-the-job training, and encourage conference participation. The mentoring approach can not only serve as a valuable recruitment tool but also play an important role in early retention of new students and graduates.

4. Serve on advisory groups for LIS programs.

   Librarians can positively effect change in diversity recruiting effort by serving on advisory boards for library schools. These groups are also comprised of individuals from the professional and corporate community which can influence funding and diversity efforts.

LIS Educators Can:

1. Work with alumni (especially minority alumni) to identify potential minority students
2. Provide financial assistance
3. Provide both full-time and part-time options to study
4. Schedule classes to accommodate working students
5. Work with library organizations and others to develop mentoring programs
6. Publicize availability and deadlines for all scholarships (not just those offered the program)
7. Sponsor recruitment programming
8. Create recruitment brochures and/or Web sites
9. Participate in career days or job information fairs
10. Recruit minority faculty and staff
11. Incorporate multicultural issues throughout the curriculum
12. Try to recruit cohort groups so students can support each other
13. Assess success of current programs

Financial assistance is usually one of the first factors mentioned when discussing the needs of students of color. Many potential students are not aware of possible funding sources. In addition to publicizing a program's own scholarships, fellowships, and assistantships, LIS programs should also publicize support available through the ALA and other professional organizations. Applicants, especially those new to the field of librarianship, are unfamiliar with the myriad scholarships offered and the availability of matching scholarships, such as those the New England Library Association offers to those individuals accepted into the Spectrum program.

Designing programs that allow students to choose either part-time or full-time status is also a critical factor. To give just one example, many of the potential applicants who contacted the University of Rhode Island about the Prism Program could not consider full-time status as a viable option because they already had full-time jobs with benefits. However, due to the strong interest in the program, full-time status appealed to those individuals between jobs and some even took a leave of absence to pursue the full-time program requirement.

When scheduling class times, LIS programs need to address the sometimes rigid work scheduling needs of library staff with full-time jobs. One approach might be a master's program with a set-up similar to that of the Executive MBA program or weekend college with a distance learning component built in. This type of scheduling allows a student to keep his or her full-time job which maintains current income and health care benefits. (This is an area where libraries can help by allowing flexible scheduling or release time for support staff who are pursuing MLIS degrees.)

Libraries Can:

1. Encourage staff to pursue MLIS degrees
2. Give staff release time and/or flexible schedules so they can attend classes
3. Provide financial assistance to help pay for tuition, fees, etc.
4. Market librarianship by using ALA and other recruitment materials, such as posters, pencils, and the video "Me, a Librarian?"
5. Support residency programs
6. Develop marketing strategies to increase minority librarians and staff in your employment pool
7. Communicate with the SLIS program about potential minority library school student
8. Work with functional teams to identify appropriate developmental work

Libraries should think creatively. Look at your own support staff as a potential applicant pool for MLIS programs. Talk to staff about the opportunities within our field and encourage them to seek professional degrees.

If you are considering establishing a residency program, a mentoring program, or any other initiative, talk to those who already have such programs. Make site visits to see how the programs work. Study the literature for associate, residency, and mentoring programs. Since the 1980s, there have been numerous articles and books written on the experiences of individuals involved in residency programs based at some of the nation's leading academic libraries. Personal stories of actual residents along with useful information from library directors who instituted them on their respective campuses provide rich accounts describing their development through post-placement in many cases. These tools are invaluable for any institution looking for guidance and potential residents desiring to apply to them.

Professional Organizations Can:

1. Sponsor awareness and recruitment programs
2. Provide scholarships

3. Develop mentoring programs
4. Create recruitment brochures and/or Web sites
5. Visit schools to raise awareness of libraries and librarianship

WHAT CAN WE DO? RETENTION STRATEGIES

Practitioners Can:

1. Mentor new librarians.

    Librarians regardless of their years in the profession should commit to mentoring at least one person, whether they are a student or new librarian. Because people enter the profession with an array of experiences, everyone has something valuable to share that will enhance their chances for success.

2. Create or join state and regional ethnic caucuses and involve ethnic paraprofessional library staff.

    Librarians can develop and participate in regional or state chapters of ethnic library organizations. These organizations give librarians opportunities to participate in a professional organization in a more cost-effective way without having to incur extra travel expenses in addition to networking with other professionals practicing in their geographical area.

3. Attend conferences such as the NDIL (National Diversity in Libraries) Conference or others with similar themes and support librarians who attend.

    This conference is one of the greatest to ways to interact with other professionals who passionately share the tenets of diversity work. It also offers opportunities for librarians to make a conference presentation.

4. Sponsor or be a part of Multicultural Day symposiums by including a multicultural library workshop. For example, sponsor sessions such as "Diversity on the Internet" led by librarians of color.

    Take advantage of these special days on your campus to be part of the diversity discussion, symposiums and workshops, and other special events in highlighting the contributions of librarians while promoting librarianship to a targeted diverse audience. Lead a workshop sponsored by the librarians on campus to attract potential students of color from campus to the profession.

LIS Educators Can:

1. Establish a counseling support service program to help avoid a revolving door admission program and to eliminate low expectations of minority students.

    LIS educators who believe in diversity can establish both informal and formal support networks to assist LIS students through the graduate program. Diverse students can benefit through networking with each other and LIS professors in addition to the general student body for positive support.

2. Faculty should be more sensitive to the needs of minority students and make a special effort to make personal contact with them especially during the orientation period.

   Diverse students comprise a small percentage of library students across the country, which can be an isolating experience for some students of color. Faculty can offer support to students by reaching out to them in a special way through discussions and informal mentoring gatherings.
3. Support minority student organizations.

   Educators can also show support by sponsoring and consulting graduate student organizations who support efforts that emphasize diversity.

Libraries Can:

1. Conduct climate surveys to assess and identify the extent to which diversity issues are regarded within the institution.

   Climate surveys are a wonderful way in which to gauge an institution's level of receptiveness and participation in issues related to diversity and provide valuable insight for those individuals (administrators, directors) as to how best to introduce and maintain diversity efforts in libraries.
2. Help to provide an atmosphere to support through professional development opportunities in multicultural training issues.

   For example, libraries play an important role in offering and supporting professional development education where diversity is the key focus. Ideally, library administrators should lead the way in setting the tone and requirement for training all staff in public services as well as technical services areas.

Professional Organizations Can:

1. Provide leadership training institutes for librarians at the state and national levels.

   For example, an exciting new trend has begun to spread across the country with the development of leadership institutes offered via national, regional, and state library organizations. The primary purpose of these meetings are to encourage and coach and oftentimes train new librarians to the profession. Embedded within the goals of these meetings is the importance of achieving diversity by offering increased programmatic and scholarship opportunities for librarians from diverse groups. Aimed at retention and building the next generation of librarians, leadership institutes offer relevant training and mentoring to the new library professional.
2. Make diversity a thematic track in conference programs and strategic planning as part of an overall and ongoing diversity goal.

   For example, taking cues from the ALA, many of the professional library organizations have now given diversity a prominent place within conference thematic tracks for available programming to its members. Because of this change in approach to diversity, topics specifically related to this theme can easily be tracked in one category rather than randomly scattered and lacking cohesiveness. This change gives increased credence and emphasis to issues, topics, problems, and solutions related to diversity work within all aspects of the library profession.

CONCLUSION

Over the last several decades, significant improvement has been made in developing effective recruitment and retention strategies, but much more can still be done in recruiting and retaining librarians from diverse backgrounds. It will continue to take concerted effort among all members of the library profession, including library educators, administrators, activist librarians, and new recruits themselves, to continue this campaign. Many courageous individuals have laid the foundation and path before us. Now it will be up to the new generation to carry on the torch, to guide our efforts for the future as we set the pace for another new generation of diverse librarians. It is crucial to our existence to duplicate ourselves and not rest on our laurels. Each one must indeed reach out to keep this movement alive and viable for potential librarians coming after us. The future is here and the future is now for us to capitalize on the interest to diversify our profession by real talk and real action. We can no longer afford to simply talk about diversity. Rather, each of us must do our part to make diversity happen in very deliberate and concentrated ways. This is the challenge laid before us.

BIBLIOGRAPHY

Adkins, Denice, and Isabel Espinal. 1994. "The Diversity Mandate." *Library Journal,* June 16. Available: http://www.libraryjournal.com/article/CA408334.

Alire, Camila A. 1996. "Recruitment and Retention of Librarians of Color." In *Creating the Future: Essays on Librarianship in an Age of Great Change*, edited by Sally Gardner Reed. Jefferson, NC: McFarland. 126–143.

Berry, III, John. 2004. "Knowledge River." *Library Journal,* April 15. Available: http://www.libraryjournal.com/article/CA408335.

Black, William K., and Joan M. Leysen. 2003. "Fostering Success: The Socialization of Entry-Level Librarians in ARL Libraries." *Journal of Library Administration* vol. 36(4): 3–27.

Buttlar, Lois, and William Caynon. 1992. "Recruitment of Librarians into the Profession: The Minority Perspective." *Library and Information Science Research* 14 (September): 259–280.

Grady, Jennifer, and Traci D. Hall. April 2004. "The World Is Changing: Why Aren't We? Recruiting Minorities to Librarianship." ALA/APA Worklife e-newsletter, vol. 1(4). Available: http://www.ala-apa.org/newsletter/vol1no4/recruitment.html.

Hall, Traci D. January 2004. "Grow Your Own." Bulletin of the Office for Diversity of the American Library Association. VERSED. Special Midwinter Meeting 2004 Issue, e-newsletter. Available: http://www.ala.org/ala/diversity/versed/versed2004/backissjan2004/growingown.htm.

Josey, E. J. 1991. "E. J. Josey Recommends Recruitment Strategy." *Library Personnel News* 5, no. 1(1): 54–57.

Josey, E. J. 1999. "Minority Representation in Library and Information Science Programs." *The Bookmark* 55 (fall).

"Recruiting the Underrepresented to Academic Libraries." 1990. A Task Force Report with Edith M. Fisher et al. *College and Research Libraries News* (December): 159–163.

Reese, Gregory L., and Ernestine Hawkins. 1999. *Stop Talking, Start Doing: Attracting People of Color to the Library Profession*. Chicago: American Library Association.

EXISTING AND EMERGING RESOURCES*

ALA Office for Diversity, Traci Hall, Director. http://www.ala.org/ala/diversity.htm

   a. Provides consultant services, speaking and training services to your organization
   b. Provides resources and materials solely dedicated to the advancement of diversity within librarianship; ex) pamphlets on financial aid information, brochures, etc.
   c. A new Web site featuring VERSED, an online newsletter published five times a year
   d. Harnesses the efforts of the Council of Diversity and the new list of ethnic library organizations compiled by Tiffeni Fontno
   e. Features recently published literature and a leading academic library journal dedicated to the furtherance and promotion of diversity and diversity-related issues

ARL Program Officer for Training and Diversity, Jerome Offord, Jr., Director

   a. Features initiative to Recruit a Diverse Workforce
   b. Features compilation of Library Residency programs

ALA/APA Worklife Web site. http://www.ala-apa.org/

   a. ALA/APA newsletter: http://www.ala-apa.org/newsletter/newsletter.html

First Joint Librarians of Color Conference in Dallas, Texas, 2006
Existing ALA Diversity Resources

   a. Support and participate in the Diversity Fair at the ALA Annual Conference.
   b. Promote and utilize Spectrum Initiative to influence potential minority LIS students.

---

*Originally compiled by Jametoria Burton for the 2004 National Diversity in Libraries Conference in Atlanta, Georgia.

c. Utilize Recruitment Toolkit from the ALA Office for Human Resources.
d. Support and participate in Public Library Association (PLA) Job Shadow Day http://www.pla.org/projects/jobshadow.
e. Support and participate in the ALA Recruitment Assembly.

Other Initiatives Forming outside ALA

a. HBCU Alliance and other ethnic university alliance organizations
b. African American Read-In by the Black Caucus of National Council of Teachers of English

Both venues offer the target audience and easier means for concentrated dialogue of recruitment efforts and planning among diverse library leaders and early exposure to potential students.

Potential Projects

a. Compile a list of LIS programs around the country with active recruitment initiatives.
b. Write or edit a book chronicling the history of diversity initiatives.
c. Utilize the power of ethnic media outlets and influential ethnic media personalities to support and promote the "diversity mandate."
1. BET, Black Entertainment Television—Youth Summit Show
2. PBS, Tavis Smiley and Tavis Smiley Speaks and Juan Williams of National Public Radio
3. Oprah Winfrey and the Oprah Winfrey Show
4. Tom Joyner and the Tom Joyner Morning Show/Foundation
5. De Colores

Additional Resources

a. Clearinghouse of conference proceedings from NDIL and other ethnic caucus conferences
b. Multicultural centers
c. Ethnic student campus groups
d. Community groups such as churches, college alumni chapters, alumni Greek organizations
e. Other professional groups or meetings
f. Venues for second professionals such as career fairs and job expos
g. Office for International Programs
h. High school guidance counselors
i. Community colleges
j. Public libraries: Library programs
   Children and youth librarians: Reading clubs and computer clubs
k. Teachers from underrepresented groups
l. Career Days: Both high school and college settings
m. Ethnic celebrations and festivals

n. Book talks
o. Author visits
p. Library-sponsored computer training workshops
q. Listservs
r. Support for conferences and other types of professional development
s. Cohort recruiting

9 DIVERSITY AND RESEARCH LIBRARIES: THE CIRLA FELLOWS PROGRAM

by Irene M. Hoffman

INTRODUCTION

What we have to learn to do, we learn by doing.

—*Aristotle*

Making the decision to become a librarian is the first step toward a promising career. However, given the complexities of the profession and the abundant opportunities that lie ahead, how does a new librarian choose from among the many possible career directions available? The Chesapeake Information and Research Library Alliance (CIRLA) program provides a select group of competitively recruited individuals the chance to explore, sample, and learn about the wealth of potential career opportunities that exist within the world of research libraries.

In October 2004, eleven library school students were inaugurated into the first cohort of the CIRLA Fellows. This new two-year program, funded in part by a grant from the Institute of Museum and Library Services (IMLS), offers students enrolled in an ALA (American Library Association) accredited library school program the chance to obtain hands-on learning experiences that integrate academic study with practical and comprehensive work experience at some of the nation's most prestigious research institutions.

BACKGROUND ON DEMOGRAPHICS

Between 1995 and 2001 nearly 25 percent of all library placements, approximately 400 per year, were made in academic libraries (ACRL 2002). More academic librarians are retiring now due to the graying of the profession, and the recruitment pools are small (Kaufman 2002). According to Association of Research Libraries (ARL) statistics, the greatest hiring increases between 1985 and 2000 were in functional specialties (196 percent), subject specialties (61 percent), and reference (50 percent) (Wilder 2002). Among research libraries, these retirements will result in the loss of functional specialists in languages, area studies, preservation, government information, cataloging and metadata, multimedia applications, research and instruction, digital initiatives, systems, scholarly communication, and more.

Additionally, among U.S. research libraries, there is a very low percentage of librarians representing underserved populations, only 12.4 percent (ARL 2003). Therefore, the real management issue resulting from retirements is replacements: how can librarianship recruit new entrants to the profession in sufficient numbers, quality, and expertise to replace its retirees? (Wilder 2002). What can we do to attract a pool of diverse (in both experience and ethnicity) new librarians? And, how can we prepare them both for the rigors and the variety of types of work in a research library environment?

CIRLA FELLOWS PROGRAM HIGHLIGHTS

The CIRLA Fellows Program (Figure 9-1) outlines a complete pathway: from recruitment, to education, employment and training, all the way to launching professional careers at the completion of the fellowship. Funded in part through an IMLS *Recruiting and Educating Librarians for the 21st Century* grant opportunity, Georgetown University initiated the grant on behalf of CIRLA. CIRLA is a not-for-profit organization of educational and research institutions in Delaware, the District of Columbia, and Maryland, committed to education and research through the collaborative development of library collections, service programs, and expanded use of information technology. The participating partner institutions are Georgetown University, George Washington University, Howard University, Johns Hopkins University, the Library of Congress, the National Agricultural Library, the Smithsonian Institution Libraries, the University of Delaware, and the University of Maryland.

Awarded in October 2003, the grant addresses the most compelling needs of research libraries: accelerating the increase in qualified librarians entering research librarianship, particularly from underrepresented populations, and successfully launching them into a research library career.

The grant provides funding for eleven fellows, competitively recruited to fill the numerous anticipated vacancies, who demonstrate through the application process their ability to contribute to the diversity of the profession and desire to be trained in the functional specialties needed by research libraries. Six of these fellows were recruited from within the ranks of the CIRLA member libraries. These six "internal" fellows are full-time employees at one of the CIRLA libraries and are pursuing their library degree on a part-time basis. The other five, the "external" fellows, were recruited from library schools where they are enrolled full-time. Their appointment to the fellowship includes a paid, 20-hour-per-week pre-professional position at the member library of their choice.

The grant funding provides the stipends, release time for the internal fellows and mentors, and professional development support for fellows to attend at least one national conference. The grant requires that each fellow attend library school with the intent of receiving the library degree within two years, work in close collaboration with a mentor, and participate in what we call a work curriculum designed to provide a comprehensive introduction to career possibilities while developing the necessary skills to work in the complex arena of research libraries.

Working to Learn; Learning to Work

> One must learn by doing the thing. For though you think you know it, you have no certainty until you try.
>
> —Sophocles

Central to the program is the work curriculum designed to provide each fellow with extensive workplace-related training in critically needed functional areas within research libraries. Fellows are exposed to a work environment that has been shaped to provide them with hands-on training in areas well matched to the future needs of research libraries and their own professional interests.

The curriculum is designed to provide broad-based experiential work for each fellow over the course of their two-year fellowships. Their curriculum is made up of four work rotations and two elective (or customized) rotations, each lasting for a four-month period. These rotations expose fellows to a variety of meaningful projects and professional library work settings, and ensure that fellows experience the variety of career possibilities within research librarianship. Shaped and guided by the mentor, the rotations align work experience with academic study and individual interests.

The core rotations include Reference/Public Services, Cataloging/Metadata/Technical Services, Acquisitions/Collection Development, and Digital Initiatives/Technology/Systems. Within each rotation, fellows will gain a basic understanding of the routine operations and career possibilities within those functional areas. Upon completion of these core rotations, the fellow will develop two elective rotations to provide them with specific and individualized work experiences that can form the foundation for their future career objectives. These custom rotations will be designed to have a slightly more professional slant to them to assist the fellow in building their portfolio of experience. Examples of elective rotations might include specific work assignments within Archives, Special Collections, Preservation, Scholarly Communication, Teaching and Learning with Technology, Language or Subject Collection Development, Licensing and Copyright, etc. Another important feature of these elective rotations is that fellows are free to explore this customized approach at any of the member libraries.

Mentors

> A teacher's purpose is not to create students in his own image, but to develop students who can create their own image.
>
> —Author Unknown

A critical factor in the effectiveness and success of the fellowship is in the development of a strong and trusting relationship between fellows and mentors. Each fellow is assigned a primary mentor who serves as a resource guide and coach for the duration of the fellowship. To ensure that these relationships are successful, one of the grant partners, the ARL, provided a day-long training session for fellows and mentors to help them learn how to be effective in these new roles, and establish how they can work together to develop a supportive and professional relationship for ongoing support and feedback.

Mentors are asked to commit to working with their protégés for a minimum of 4 hours per week. They meet with each other on a regular schedule to talk about issues pertaining to their studies, their work, or their careers. The mentors also serve as the point-persons for managing the specific work activities working with the various internal departments to make appropriate arrangements for the work. The mentors also help navigate the often overwhelming waters of professional development, networking, and stress that might surface from juggling work, school, and careers.

The mentor also plays a critical role in shaping the work experiences of the fellows by assisting in identifying areas of interest within the core work curriculum as well as assisting with the customized, elective portion of the work activities. The mentor works with the fellow to help identify those specific areas of the profession where the fellow is most interested in learning more, and assists them in identifying which of the CIRLA libraries might be best suited for gaining that experience.

Competencies

> Give the pupils something to do, not something to learn; and the doing is of such a nature as to demand thinking; learning naturally results.
>
> —John Dewey

To ensure that all the fellows receive the same basic skills within each rotation, we developed a list of core competencies and goals for each of the work curriculum areas. For the elective portion of the work curriculum, competencies and learning outcomes will be crafted based fellows' specific learning objectives.

Through the work curriculum, CIRLA fellows will develop a sense of commitment to the values and principles of librarianship. The "Core Competencies and Learning Outcomes Statement" (see Figure 9-1) helps to articulate the skills, knowledge, abilities, behaviors, and attitudes that all CIRLA fellows should have or will attain as they matriculate through their formal course work, utilize their mentoring relationship, and work at a CIRLA institution.

Professional Development and Networking

> To acquire knowledge, one must study; but to acquire wisdom, one must observe.
>
> —Marilyn vos Savant

With the help of their mentors, fellows will also be exposed to the profession at large and learn how to navigate through the complicated waters of conference attendance, professional contributions, faculty status, and career networking. As part of this process, the grant provides funds for all fellows to attend at least one national professional conference (of their choice) to see how their work and studies fit within the larger professional landscape.

Fellows will also have access to a variety of professional training and development opportunities. The ARL will provide mentoring in multiculturalism and in the issues critical to the future of research libraries. Fellows will also receive assistance in their personal career development including résumé advising, job search and interviewing techniques, and other types of professional development opportunities. They will also be given numerous opportunities to network with highly respected and influential leaders in research libraries.

Career Boost

> Don't just learn the tricks of the trade. Learn the trade.
>
> —James Bennis

Armed with their graduate degree and completion of the work curriculum rotations, fellows will be given a head start in their professional career development. The CIRLA libraries, with their own funds, have made a commitment to provide one-year full-time, paid, post-MLS positions so that each fellow can enhance his or her portfolio for the future. This is a win-win opportunity for both the libraries and the fellows: the libraries will be able to capitalize on the rich experiences fellows have gained through the program, while the fellows will be able to put their new skills into practice.

These competitive positions will provide CIRLA fellows with valuable professional-level experience in a research library environment to jump-start their careers. They will be able to enter the workforce with an extra year of substantive professional experience, tailored to their areas of interest, preparing them for midlevel leadership positions in research libraries.

CONCLUSION

What I hear, I forget. What I see, I remember. What I do, I understand.

—Confucius

The CIRLA fellows program is one of replenishment and rejuvenation. By linking the growing recruitment needs of research libraries with a cadre of well-prepared professionals to invigorate the workforce, the profession can begin to tackle the looming dearth of librarians.

The professional experience offered through the program is a valuable complement to the formal education that the fellows receive. These deep and rich experiences suggest that when fellows launch their careers they will be able enter the workforce at a more experienced level, thus contributing quickly to the expertise of the library. Adding staff with more than entry-level experience is a boon to research libraries, especially since they have workplace-related training in critically needed functional areas.

This program, which is designed for easy replication, will create an ongoing number of well-qualified candidates for the profession after only three years. The individuals will be able to enter the workforce with an extra year of substantive professional experience, tailored to their areas of interest, preparing them for midlevel leadership positions in research libraries. This will lead to the enhancement of the profession with a cohort of well-trained, experienced, and diverse librarians who can readily assume important positions in research libraries or other types of libraries in the near future.

BIBLIOGRAPHY

Association of College and Research Libraries (ACRL). Ad Hoc Task Force on Retention and Recruitment Issues. 2002. *Recruitment, Retention, and Restructuring: Human Resources in Academic Libraries.* Chicago: Association of College and Research Libraries.

Association of Research Libraries (ARL). 2003. *Annual Salary Survey for 2002–03.* Washington, DC: Association of Research Libraries.

Kaufman, P. T. April 2002. "Where Do the Next 'We' Come From? Recruiting, Retaining, and Developing Your Successors." *ARL: A Bimonthly Report on Research Library Issues and Actions from ARL, CNI, and SPARC, 221.* Washington, DC: Association of Research Libraries. Available: http://www.arl.org/newsltr/221/recruit.html.

Wilder, S. J. April 2002. "New Hires in Research Libraries: Demographic Trends and Hiring Policies." *ARL: A Bimonthly Report on Research Library Issues and Actions from ARL, CNI, and SPARC, 32.* Washington, DC: Association of Research Libraries. Available: http://www.arl.org/newsltr/221/newhires.html.

Chesapeake Information and Research Library Alliance
CIRLA FELLOWS PROGRAM

Recruiting for Diversity: Careers in Librarianship

**Program Information
and
Application**

**Application deadline:
July 1, 2004**

CIRLA FELLOWS Program
Georgetown University Library
37th & O Streets, NW
Washington D.C. 20057
(202) 687-1601
(202) 687-7501 (fax)
http://CIRLAFELLOWS.georgetown.edu

Figure 9-1. CIRLA Fellows Program Brochure

The **CIRLA FELLOWS PROGRAM** is the result of an Institute of Museum and Library Services (IMLS) grant to Georgetown University on behalf of the Chesapeake Information and Research Library Alliance (CIRLA). The Program is designed to:

- Increase the diversity of the library profession, particularly among academic libraries;
- Recruit the next generation of librarians to fill the numerous anticipated vacancies over the next 10 years; and
- Train and educate new librarians in functional specialties needed by research libraries.

CIRLA Fellows are a select group of individuals competitively recruited for a unique and valuable opportunity to obtain mentoring and professional work experience in research libraries while pursuing a Master's degree in Library Science.

CIRLA is a not-for-profit organization of educational and research institutions in Delaware, the District of Columbia, and Maryland, committed to education and research through the collaborative development of library collections, service programs, and expanded use of information technology.

The participating partner institutions are:
- Georgetown University
- George Washington University
- Howard University
- Johns Hopkins University
- Library of Congress
- National Agricultural Library
- Smithsonian Institution Libraries
- University of Delaware
- University of Maryland
- Association of Research Libraries (ARL)

WHO CAN BECOME A CIRLA FELLOW?
CIRLA Fellowships will be awarded to applicants who demonstrate an ability to contribute to the diversity of the library profession, either because they are a member of a traditionally underserved ethnic or racial group, or because they can otherwise demonstrate contributions to diversity based on background or experiences.

Successful applicants must have been accepted at, or have recently enrolled in, an ALA-accredited Master's program in Library Science. Fellows can be **full-time students** who will receive part-time employment, or **part-time students** who are currently employed in the CIRLA libraries.

Full-time students will be given a 20-hour per week pre-professional position in one of the CIRLA libraries. These positions will include a $14.00 per hour stipend, paid bi-weekly.

Part-time students will continue their full-time employment in a CIRLA library. Depending on their institutions, these Fellows might receive one of more of the following: tuition assistance, release time to attend classes, or other types of support.

THE BENEFITS:
Fellows benefit through
- Active participation with a group of peers attending library schools and working in CIRLA libraries.
- Broad-based work experiences that complement study for the MLS degree through the "work-curriculum".
- Customized training in areas of research librarianship that match their interests.
- Financial support to attend one national professional conference.
- Opportunities to network with highly respected and influential leaders in research libraries.
- On-the-job, professional and educational coaching, mentoring and networking with experienced professionals and library leaders.
- ARL training on diversity and other issues affecting research libraries.
- Career and job-seeking counseling and interview skills development.
- A career "jump-start" with placement in a one-year, paid, post-MLS professional position in a CIRLA library.

Figure 9-1. CIRLA Fellows Program Brochure (*Continued*)

WHAT IS THE "WORK CURRICULUM"?
The work curriculum is designed to provide a broad-based experiential work environment. The curriculum is structured to expose Fellows to a variety of meaningful projects and professional library work settings, matching Fellows' interests to library needs. The Fellowship includes 4 core rotations (approximately 4 months each), followed by 2 elective work experiences appropriate for the library and the Fellows' career objectives.

Core Employment Curriculum:
- Reference/Public Services
- Cataloging/Metadata/Technical Services
- Acquisitions/Collection Development
- Digital initiatives/Technology/Systems

Elective Employment Curriculum:
Upon completion of the core curriculum, Fellows, working with their Mentors, will be able to create custom work experiences in different areas of librarianship at the CIRLA Library of their choice.

Examples of the elective curriculum may include: Archives, Special Collections, Preservation, Scholarly Communication, Teaching & Learning with Technology, Language or Subject Collection Development, Licensing and Copyright, etc.

APPLICATION PROCESS AND CRITERIA:
Applicants must complete all five (5) sections of the application form (attached) and will be judged on the following:

1. Demonstrated ability to contribute to the diversity of the library profession.

2. Acceptance to an ALA-accredited Master's program and ability to graduate from the program within 2-3 years.

3. Ability to commit to a 2-year part-time position while attending graduate school (for full-time library school students), or ability to commit to continued full-time employment while attending graduate school on a part-time basis (for applicants currently working in a CIRLA library).

4. Demonstrated interest, commitment and willingness to contribute to the library profession.

5. Demonstrated interest in being mentored.

6. Commitment to obtaining full-time employment as a librarian in a U.S. academic or research library upon completion of the program.

7. Prior library work experience.

NEED MORE INFORMATION?
If you would like more information on the CIRLA Fellows program, the application process, the work curriculum or any portion of this program, please contact:

Irene Hoffman
E-mail: cirlafellows@georgetown.edu
(202) 687-1601

CIRLA Fellows Program
Georgetown University Library
37th & O Streets, NW
Washington, D. C. 20057

Or visit the CIRLA Fellows website:
CIRLAFELLOWS.georgetown.edu

Figure 9-1. CIRLA Fellows Program Brochure (*Continued*)

Application Form

CIRLA FELLOWS PROGRAM
Recruiting for Diversity: Careers in Librarianship

DEADLINE: JULY 1, 2004

PART 1: PERSONAL INFORMATION

Name:_____

Address:_____
_____
_____

Phone: (H)_____ (W)_____

E-mail:_____

Ethnic Identity:

☐ American Indian or Alaskan Native
☐ Black or African American
☐ Native Hawaiian or other Pacific Islander
☐ Asian
☐ Hispanic or Latino
☐ White or Caucasian

Part II: GRADUATE SCHOOL INFORMATION

☐ I have been accepted to **OR** ☐ I am enrolled in an accredited Master's program.

University:_____

Program beginning date: _____

Expected graduation date: _____

PART III: NARRATIVE

Write a 1-3 page letter expressing:

1. What influenced your decision to attend library school;
2. What you hope to contribute to academic or research librarianship;
3. How this fellowship will help you in your career objectives as a librarian in a U.S. academic or research library;
4. How you believe you can contribute to the diversity of the library profession.

PART IV: RESUME AND LETTERS OF RECOMMENDATION

Include a current resume and two (2) letters of recommendation with your application.

PART V: FELLOWSHIP PLACEMENT REQUEST

☐ I am currently employed full-time at a CIRLA Library *(indicate below)*.

OR

☐ I am NOT employed at a CIRLA Library, and I am interested in a Fellowship at the library indicated below. (*Indicate in order of preference, $1=1^{st}$ choice, etc. Every attempt will be made to match Fellows with their placement preference.*)*

__ Howard University
__ Georgetown University
__ Smithsonian Institution Libraries
__ George Washington University
__ University of Delaware
__ University of Maryland (College Park)
__ Johns Hopkins University

*The Library of Congress and the National Agricultural Library will participate in the electives portion of the work curriculum later in the program.

Timetable

July 1, 2004	Application Deadline
July 2 - 7, 2004	Application Review
July 8 - 15, 2004	Personal Interviews
July 26, 2004	Fellowships Awarded
August 15, 2004	First Fellowships Begin

Submit completed application to:

CIRLA FELLOWS PROGRAM
Georgetown University Library
37th & O Streets, NW
Washington D.C. 20057
(202) 687.1601

Figure 9-1. CIRLA Fellows Program Brochure (*Continued*)

10 REACHING HIGH SCHOOL STUDENTS: SOWING THE SEEDS OF LIBRARIANSHIP

by Jessica Kayongo, LeRoy LaFleur, and Ira Revels

INTRODUCTION

Libraries seeking to recruit a diverse and inclusive staff must look beyond traditional means of identifying candidates from underrepresented minority communities. This chapter discusses two separate initiatives designed in the summer of 2002 to recruit high school students from underrepresented minority communities to the library profession. The background, structure, and philosophical approaches of each program will be discussed, compared, and contrasted. Lastly, recommendations for initiating a high school recruitment program will be provided.

Recruitment and diversity are two areas of interest that have increasingly taken the spotlight within academic libraries. As a growing number of librarians move closer to retirement, attracting a pool of next-generation practitioners to carry on their work is of the utmost importance to the profession. Additionally, as college and university campuses continue to attract and recruit an increasingly diverse body of students and faculty, librarians must take an active role in identifying candidates who are representative of those served.

Statistics on the number of minority library professionals in the field would seem to confirm these concerns. Data collected in 1998 by the American Library Association (ALA) Office for Research and Statistics indicated that minority librarians accounted for roughly 13 percent of academic librarians working in the United States. Additionally, according to a 2003 Association of Library and Information Science Education (ALISE) Statistical Report, minority librarians made up approximately 491 of 4,923 ALA-accredited MLIS (Master of Library and Information Science) degree recipients.

Over the past few decades, a number of university library initiatives geared toward addressing these issues by targeting the recruitment of professionals from underrepresented minority groups have been developed.

In addition to minority residencies and fellowships, hosted by many academic libraries, programs like the ALA Spectrum Initiative, which provides funding and support for library school students of color, have made great strides toward the recruitment and development of minority library and information professionals. Likewise, the University of Minnesota's Training Program, which specifically targets new professionals from underrepresented backgrounds, is geared not only toward retention, but also toward moving librarians of color into administrative and leadership positions.

Proactive recruiters within the profession are increasingly looking for innovative ways to identify potential candidates from nontraditional areas and groups including undergraduates, PhDs, and more recently from high school students. In an article entitled "The World Is

Changing: Why Aren't We?" by Jennifer Grady and Tracie Hall, the authors identify a number of initiatives geared toward exposing high school students to the world of librarianship. Two notable programs, both run by public libraries, include one coordinated by the Chicago Multi-type Library System in conjunction with Junior Achievement to host a Job Shadow day for minority high school students and another by the Philadelphia Free Library which trains and pays teenagers to assist with an area after-school program. Likewise, two videos entitled "Looking for Leaders in the Information Age" and "Me? A Librarian?" were produced by the Ohio Library Council to reach out to youth and teenage audiences. Additionally, the more recent waves of grants from the Institute of Museum and Library Services (IMLS) Librarians for the 21st Century Program have included the recruitment of high school students among their list of funding priorities.

High school students represent a unique group for a number of reasons. Unlike some other potential candidates, high school students often have had recent interactions with librarians in leadership roles in the form of school media specialists. They also tend to be open-minded about their career choices which are usually still a number of years away. Lastly, high school students increasingly have the technological savvy, curiosity, and skills that are generally prized by the library profession. But high school students as a group also pose a number of recruitment challenges. Like many other potential candidate groups, teenagers often have little knowledge of the actual library profession and what librarians do. Traditional stereotypes about the profession also have little appeal to high school students who are often most attracted to professions deemed as "cool" by popular society. Furthermore, many high school students, particularly minority students, often do not have access to the personal contacts that can highlight exciting aspects of the profession and encourage interest. Most important, perhaps, is the fact that high school students still have a great number of years of education ahead of them before attaining the MLIS degree that is often required to attain professional positions within the field. It is, however, important to get the idea into place now to have access to these students down the road.

During the summer of 2002, two academic library systems, Cornell University Library and the University Libraries of Notre Dame, developed summer work and recruitment initiatives aimed at introducing high school students of color to academic libraries and librarianship. While different in their origin, structure, and design, both programs recruited from among area high schools and offered students a paid work experience and training on issues related to librarianship as a profession.

CORNELL UNIVERSITY LIBRARY JUNIOR FELLOWS PROGRAM

The Cornell University Library Junior Fellows Program was a 6-week program designed as an expansion of the existing Cornell Library Fellows program, which recruits recent MLS graduates from underrepresented minority groups. The summer program was started as a grassroots initiative by one of the resident librarians in the Library Fellowship program and was developed to support the academic achievement of minority high school students through involvement in research and technology training opportunities.

Among its many goals, the program sought to expose young people of color to the profession of academic librarianship; to address challenges associated with the digital divide through the provision of library, information literacy, and technology training opportunities; to provide college preparatory and admissions counseling; to provide opportunities to interact

Week 1—Sample Day	Activity
9:00 A.M.–10:30 A.M.	Locating print resources using the online library catalog
10:30 A.M.–11:45 A.M.	Tour of Mann Library
12:00 noon–1:00 P.M.	Lunch
1:00 P.M.–2:00 P.M.	Introduction to Library of Congress Classification
2:00 P.M.–3:00 P.M.	Research Project Discussion / Brainstorming
Week 2—Sample Day	
9:00 A.M.–10:30 A.M.	Popular vs. Scholarly Literature
10:30 A.M.–11:45 A.M.	Technology Training: Scanning/Graphics
12:00 noon–1:00 P.M.	Lunch
1:00 P.M.–2:00 P.M.	Introduction to Archival Research: Primary Sources
2:00 P.M.–3:00 P.M.	Tour: University Archives
Week 5—Sample Day	
9:00 A.M.–10:30 A.M.	Research Project Development
10:45 A.M.–12:00 noon	CAVE/Server Farm Tour[1]
12:00 noon–1:00 P.M.	Lunch
1:00 P.M.–1:45 P.M.	Tour: Engineering & Physical Sciences Library
2:00 P.M.–3:00 P.M.	Digital Libraries & Information Technologies/Desktop Services Tour
Week 6—Sample Day	
9:00 A.M.–10:30 A.M.	Research Project Development
10:30 A.M.–12:00 noon	College Preparation Information and Discussion
12:00 noon–1:00 P.M.	Lunch
1:00 P.M.–3:00 P.M.	Research Project Development and Presentation Test Run

[1] Cornell Theory Center's CAVE provides a three-dimensional, stereo immersive virtual reality environment for viewing scientific, engineering, architectural and art applications.

Figure 10-1. Sample Schedule—Cornell University Library's Junior Fellows Summer Program 2002

with academic faculty and staff; and to showcase the university as a welcoming environment for young people of color. The program also sought to help bridge the division between the university and city populations by working closely with the local school district and community-based organizations.

In addition to payment for employment with the library, the Cornell students also received a number of other benefits including a summer bus pass for transportation to and from work, free lunch until their first paycheck, and a free refurbished computer upon successful completion of the program.

Recruitment and publicity was undertaken by Cornell librarians who served on a program advisory committee, and included an informational pizza party for students at the main high school and participation in a high school career fair. Interested students submitted essays and filled out applications that had been distributed by staff at area high schools and local community centers. Student finalists were interviewed at an area high school and eight were selected to participate in the program.

The summer program kickoff occurred in early July with an opening reception hosted by the University Librarian. The junior fellows, as program participants were called, worked a weekly Monday through Thursday schedule, from 9:00 A.M. to 3:00 P.M. Instead of performing one consistent job or work function, however, the students were provided with a wide array of introductory and skill-building experiences. The program curriculum was designed to introduce the students to careers in academic librarianship and to familiarize them with the principles and methods of academic library research and project development. Information literacy instruction was provided on how to use the library catalog and databases, evaluating content on Web sites, and evaluating print sources. Additionally, students participated in a number of tours both on and off campus including trips to an alternative special

Gender	
Male	2
Female	6
High School	
Alternative Community School	2
Ithaca High School	6
Grade Level	
Entering Sophomore	2
Entering Junior	4
Entering Senior	2
Race/Ethnicity*	
African American	4
Afro Caribbean	1
Muslim American	1
Cambodian Émigré	1
Kenyan Émigré	1
*self-reported	

Figure 10-2. Demographic Characteristics of 2002 Cornell University Library Junior Fellows

library, a local historical society, the former home of Harriet Tubman, and the CAVE virtual reality laboratory at Cornell. In order to ensure that students gained an awareness and appreciation for the library profession, all instruction sessions and tours were led by Cornell University librarians and library staff who were encouraged to share information about their duties and experiences in libraries. Students also were assigned time over the course of the program to "shadow" library staff on the job. Some opportunities for job shadowing were provided by librarians and staff in Access Services and Preservation and Conservation. Likewise, junior fellows participated in college preparation and career exploration activities with a librarian experienced in college admissions, who also led discussions on the growing need for librarians of color. As part of their employment responsibilities, the junior fellows were also required to develop and work on a research project of their choice to be completed at the end of the program. During their final week of service, a showcase was held for the students to present their research to an audience of library staff and family members. Students were provided with laptops, projectors, and display materials and asked to give an overview of their research to visitors who cycled through the session. Research topics were both diverse and unique, covering a range of subjects from the experience of Cambodian refugees to the role of women in rap videos to a history of African American fashion.

Both during and at the end of the summer program, evaluation surveys were given to the high school students as well as participating staff. Survey responses were varied, but generally indicated support on the behalf of library community and enjoyment, learning, and interest on the part of the junior fellows. At this point in time Cornell University Library is no longer holding the Summer junior fellows Program for a variety of reasons; however, librarians at the university remain active in community programs geared toward outreach with area youth of color, and there are hopes to revive the program sometime in the future.

UNIVERSITY OF NOTRE DAME LIBRARIES' SUMMER PROGRAM

The Summer Program of the University of Notre Dame Libraries, now in its fourth year, was also developed to recruit minority high school students, from the South Bend metropolitan area. This recruitment initiative was implemented in the summer of 2002. The impetus for its creation was the 2002 Library Administration and Management Association (LAMA) *Cultural Diversity Grant*. The Diversity Committee secured funding for the program, through library administration, in the event the proposal was not accepted. Although the LAMA grant proposal was successful, the award was shared with another co-winner and was not enough to fully cover the expenses, so the previously secured funding was still utilized.

The winning proposal contained the following key elements. Notre Dame Libraries would hire four college-bound high school students to work in both University Libraries and Kresge Law Library as library student assistants. The students would work for 40 hours per week for 10 weeks during the summer in different departments throughout the libraries. The Diversity Committee would schedule extra programming over the duration of the program and create a Web site about the program. Finally, the students would receive a memento of the experience, an engraved plaque with their photograph on it.

The ultimate goal of the program was to attract young people to academic librarianship earlier through meaningful work experiences in various departments within the libraries. In the short term, perhaps students would continue to work in academic libraries while they attended college, maintaining their interest and building experience. Ideally, they would enter library school immediately after graduation from college and join the profession, addressing both the issues of shortage of librarians and lack of diversity in librarianship.

The Summer Program provided full-time summer employment in campus libraries to area high school students. The first step in the process, after securing funding, was to make a library-wide call, via the library listserv, for work proposals for the upcoming program. Interested department heads and unit supervisors were asked to provide a description of projects they would need assistance with and an estimate of how many hours they could use a student's help. Based on the work available and the amount of funding available, the committee chose to offer the program to students from the public schools in South Bend.

High school guidance counselors were contacted with a letter advertising the position and requesting their assistance in gathering interested candidates for an onsite interview. The counselors were very willing to help and very useful in identifying qualified students. Committee members then conducted short, 20 to 30 minutes per student, interviews at each high school. The makeup of the librarians conducting the interview varied based on availability; however, there was at least one librarian who attended every interview in the event there was a tie in the hiring decision between candidates that only one set of interviewers had seen. After all interviews were completed, the committee met to discuss the various candidates and to make the decision about which candidates would be offered a job. Letters, both rejection and acceptance, were sent out to the interviewees. In addition, guidance counselors were sent letters informing them, if appropriate, that the committee had chosen one of their students, and thanking them for their assistance in the process. Small tokens of appreciation were also inserted in the guidance counselors' mailings (library bookmarks, library pens, etc.).

Employment for the students began very shortly after the end of the school year. Since several departments showed an interest in hiring these students, the students had some variation. Each student was assigned to work the first half of the program in one set of departments and then the second half of the program in another set of departments. All the departments were covered for the duration of the program by scheduling one set of students to one set of departments and the other set of students to the other set of departments, and then swapping the groups midway through. Students were assigned to a variety of projects as they rotated through departments, but standard student assistant work (shelving and filing) was avoided as much as possible. Again, this program was supposed to attract people to the profession. The students did data entry, database corrections, catalog searching, and Internet searching. They helped with the replacement of computers in the libraries. They also learned to make several preservation tools—boxes, pam binders, etc.

In addition to the regular work duties, extra programming was provided. The programming was scheduled during work hours and the students were still paid while they attended these functions. Programming included the following: demonstrations about government documents online and on electronic resources, presentations on library preservation and on librarianship as a career, tours of other campus libraries and of campus, and lunches with diversity committee members and library directors.

At the end of the program, exit interviews were conducted with each student individually. The responses were overwhelmingly positive. The students particularly enjoyed the work in the preservation department and in the computing department, but, as anticipated, were not fond of the more monotonous tasks such as searching for missing microfiche or labeling. They were pleased with the overall process of the program—interviewing, work rotations, and extra programming—and would recommend it to others. They even felt they had learned things about libraries they were not aware of and other skills that would be useful to them in the future.

There were some differences between the first year (2002) of the program and subsequent years (2003, 2004) of the program. The first year of the program, the students worked

School: _____

G.P.A. _____

Name: _____

1. Could you please share your goals/plans after you complete high school?

2. Why would you like to work for the ND library during the summer?

3. To what extent have you used libraries? (school, public, academic)

4. What skills do you possess that a library might find useful?

5. Do you have any limitations in working this summer?

6. Describe your familiarity with libraries and with what librarians do.

Figure 10-3. Notre Dame High School Summer Program Interview Questionnaire

WORK SCHEDULE
June 16–July 11
Toni

	MONDAY	TUESDAY	WEDNESDAY	THURSDAY	FRIDAY
8 A.M.–10 A.M.	Gov Docs	Reference	Reference	Reference	Reference
10 A.M.–12 P.M.	CADM	CADM	CADM	CADM	CADM
1 P.M.–3 P.M.	Current Per.	Current Per.	Current Per.	Current Per.	Current Per.
3 P.M.–5 P.M.	Reserve	Reserve	Reserve	Reserve	Reserve

July 14–August 8
Toni

	MONDAY	TUESDAY	WEDNESDAY	THURSDAY	FRIDAY
8 A.M.–10 A.M.	Preservation	Law	Preservation	Law	CADM
10 A.M.–12 P.M.	Preservation	CADM	Preservation	CADM	CADM
1 P.M.–3 P.M.	Gov Docs	Gov Docs	Gov Docs	Gov Docs	Gov Docs
3 P.M.–5 P.M.	Current Per.	Current Per.	Current Per.	Current Per.	Current Per.

Figure 10-4. Notre Dame Summer Program Sample Work Schedule

---

1. What did you like best about your experience as a summer student assistant at the University Libraries and the Law Library? Why?

DCNS; because of the computer aspect; had fun with it

Moving around a lot helps with monotony; not stuck doing one thing all day; also, getting out to Law and Preservation

Preservation; because it was hands-on; had a variety of things to do

2. What did you like least about your experience as a summer student assistant at the University Libraries and the Law Library? Why?

Gov Docs; boring, dragged on; particularly when checking for missing microfiche

Reserve Book Rm; people were nice, but the work was so boring; wouldn't want future summer students to have to do that work (labeling, pulling cards); if continue with Reserve Book Rm, should find a more interesting project; didn't get anything out of it

Reserve Book Rm; boring; one project all week

3. What did you think of the extra programming that we provided for you? Was it worthwhile? Do you have any ideas for future programming?

Liked it; got to know more besides library work; the amount of programming was enough

Figure 10-5. Notre Dame Summer Program Exit Interview Responses

Programming was good; maybe do more of it, like on a weekly basis

Liked it; interesting; enough programming; maybe tour of other campus libraries for future programming

4. What did you learn about library resources that will be useful to you in your future?

Most library work is done through computers; in the future, maybe I can make better computer programs to make the work easier

Call numbers; what's available in the library; microfiche/film collections of old newspapers would be helpful in research

How to research and find stuff in catalog; how to look for certain call numbers; Microsoft Access (used in Microtext)

5. What did you find interesting about academic libraries?

How much goes on behind the scenes; surprisingly, very busy

A lot of things were new; how many things are in the library; not aware of all the stuff that's available in government documents

Different duties that librarians take on; librarians do actually have to work, not just sit around as they do on TV

6. How would you change this program and why?

Wouldn't change

Reserve Book Rm and helping with the move (to the basement) were a real turnoff; it's understandable that those things have to be done sometimes, but that kind of work defeats the purpose of the program (to attract people to librarianship); keep an eye on the supervisors and find out what they're having the students work on, whether the students are learning anything; be on the students' side (in making sure supervisors are providing projects that are useful)

Programming is fine; maybe get the students parking passes for closer parking

7. Should we continue this program in the future? Would you recommend it to your friends?

Yes, yes

Yes, yes—really good job for high school student

Yes, yes

8. Is it necessary for us to visit high schools and interview for this program in order to get applicants? Would you have applied if, for example, we had simply sent a flyer to your school announcing the program and asking you to send a written application to Notre Dame?

Keep doing interviews; will be able to see who's really interested in the job

Face to face interviews really help; student can ask questions to see if they're really interested; also, it's good experience to do interviews and become more comfortable with that process

Interviews are better; can get a better idea of who the person is

Figure 10-5. Notre Dame Summer Program Exit Interview Responses (*Continued*)

for 30 hours a week for 10 weeks. The second and third years of the program, the hours per week were increased to 40 and the duration was scaled back to 8 weeks. The reason for this change was to allow the students enough time at the end of the summer to make their college preparations. In 2002, there were forty students interviewed and five students hired—four juniors (female) and one senior (male). In 2003, there were twenty students interviewed and three students hired—all seniors, two male and one female. The reason for the difference in the number of students hired was driven by funding. In 2002, five students were hired, one from each area high school. In the interim, one of those high schools closed, and by 2003, there were four high schools to choose from, but only enough funding for three students. So, a difficult decision-making process was made even harder because one school would not be represented. In 2004, the Diversity Committee had enough funding to hire four students. Twenty-three students were interviewed and the four seniors hired were three females and one male.

As the program goes forward, the Diversity Committee intends to explore other funding sources to maintain, or even expand, the program. Other funding sources could be grants or local business financing. University Libraries recently secured an IMLS (Institute of Museum and Library Services) grant for this recruitment program. In addition, the committee will attempt to track the program participants' movements through voluntary communications. Contact information and permission are collected during exit interviews for that purpose. The committee plans to monitor whether students continue to work in libraries during their college years, by working at their campus libraries or by returning to work in the Notre Dame libraries during the summers, and whether they attend library school and join the profession. Ultimately, it will be interesting to see if the Summer Program accomplished its goal of attracting a young and diverse group of people to academic librarianship.

CONCLUSION

There are a number of notable similarities and differences in the two high school recruitment initiatives. One similarity is that library fellows or residents at each institution played a key coordinating effort in both. However, while the Notre Dame Libraries have a Diversity Committee who helped to administer and support the program there, Cornell has no such formal body.

Both programs used library staff to expose student workers to the profession; however, the development and approaches of each varied. The Notre Dame program recruited students who had previously expressed interest in attending college. The Cornell initiative, however, focused on targeting some students who while not planning to go to college could possibly be encouraged to do so through participation in the program.

In terms of their work assignments, the students at Notre Dame were employed to work 40-hour weeks with time set aside for additional programming. Students who participated in the Cornell program did not work in a traditional capacity, but spent much of their 24-hour work week developing research projects and in a variety of hands-on sessions including job shadowing, tours, and information literacy training.

Program funding for each initiative also differed. Funding for the Cornell program was contributed from a number of units on campus including the library, the office of the vice provost for Diversity, and the Office of Workforce Diversity. Two students were funded through a community youth employment service. At Notre Dame, the program initially was funded partially through a grant from the LAMA, but is now fully funded internally.

Overall both programs represent successful experiments for introducing high school students to the profession of librarianship; however, the full impact may take a number of years to ascertain. As both summer programs were developed to recruit future library professionals, the looming question as to whether the students will go on to pursue graduate degrees in library science remains to be answered. Effective means for tracking the activities and progress of students after they have completed such programs have yet to be developed, and it can be difficult to follow up with the students once they moved on into other areas of their lives. Concerns of this nature highlight the importance of conducting program evaluations while the students are still involved in the program. The use of surveys and focus groups can aid in determining student worker reactions and attitudes toward program activities, work experiences, and perceptions of librarianship as a career. Furthermore, methods of keeping in touch with students beyond high school graduation should be explored.

There are a number of questions that administrators should consider addressing before starting a library high school recruitment program. Questions such as "How many students should be hosted by the program?" and "How will the program be funded?" are two that will need to be answered early on. Other questions regarding desirable characteristics for student participants should also be considered. Ages and grade levels of potential candidates as well as academic achievement status and plans to pursue higher education may have different effects on program outcomes. Additionally, questions about funding, program staffing, and management will need to be addressed. Such programs can be both costly to run and expensive in terms of staff time and commitment.

Implementation of the program presents more questions. Will your program focus more on educational aspects of the library or on job skills training or both? Feedback from both student and staff participants in the Cornell program indicated that clear expectations and day-to-day scheduling are key to a successful program. Follow-up from the Notre Dame program showed students' desires to be presented with challenging and nonmundane tasks. Some recommendations are to have written job descriptions, performance contracts, and clearly defined objectives for instruction and training components.

BIBLIOGRAPHY

American Library Association, Office for Research and Statistics. 1998. "Racial and Ethnic Diversity Among Librarians: A Status Report." Available: http://www.ala.org/ala/ors/reports/racialethnic.htm.

Bayard, Laura. 2002a. "Diversity Committee Adds New Program." *Access: News from the University Libraries of Notre Dame.* No. 80, spring. Available: http://www.nd.edu/~ladvance/access/issues/2002/Spring/diversityprogram.htm.

Bayard, Laura. 2002b. "A Diversity Success Story: Summer Program '02." *Access: News from the University Libraries of Notre Dame.* No. 81, fall. Available: http://www.nd.edu/~ladvance/access/issues/2002/Fall/Summer.htm.

Crawford, Franklin. 2002. "Junior Library Program Exposes Minority High Schoolers to New Worlds, Careers." *Cornell Chronicle*, July 25. Available: http://www.news.cornell.edu/Chronicle/02/7.25.02/jr_library_fellows.html.

Grady, Jennifer, and Tracie Hall. 2004. "The World Is Changing: Why Aren't We?" *Library Worklife* vol. 1, no. 4. Available: http://www.ala-apa.org/newsletter/vol1no4/recruitment.html.

Revels, Ira, and Kornelia Tancheva. April 2002. "CUL Junior Library Fellows Program." *Kaleidoscope* vol. 10, no. 9. Available: http://www.library.cornell.edu/staffweb/Kaleidoscope/april02.pdf.

Revels, Ira, LeRoy J. LaFleur, and Ida Martinez. 2003. "Taking Library Recruitment a Step Closer: Recruiting the Next Generation of Librarians." *Reference Librarian.* No. 82: 157–169.

PROGRAM WEB SITES

Cornell Library Junior Fellows Program, Cornell University Library. http://www.library.cornell.edu/diversity/jrfellows/

Summer Diversity Program, University Libraries, University of Notre Dame. http://www.library.nd.edu/diversity/summer/index.shtml

III HOW TO IMPROVE DIVERSITY THROUGH SERVICES, COLLECTIONS, AND COLLABORATIONS

11 DIVERSITY AND THE DIGITAL DIVIDE AT AN HBCU: THE UNIVERSITY OF MARYLAND EASTERN SHORE

by Sharon D. Brooks, Marvella Rounds, Theodosia F. Shields, and Teri B. Weil

INTRODUCTION

Today, nestled on the eastern shore of Maryland sits the University of Maryland Eastern Shore, which dates back to 1886, with humble beginnings including only nine students and one faculty member. The institution with its rich religious foundation, the Delaware Conference Academy, was established for the purpose of providing a land grant institution for people of color because the Maryland Agriculture College Park doors were not open to African Americans.

Since those early days, the university has undergone many name changes and affiliations to become the only research and doctoral degree–granting institution on the Eastern Shore. It is now affiliated with the thirteen member institutions called the University System of Maryland (USM). The Fredrick Douglass Library is the only library and information center for the university. It is our goal to provide resources and services to support the university's program.

In this chapter, we wish to share with you the role technology has played in servicing the students, faculty, and staff at the University of Maryland Eastern Shore. Every aspect of service delivered is affected by technology. We have selected several key service functions to illustrate and also demonstrate the role of technology in the library. These service functions include distance education, the integrated library system, and training and instruction.

IMPACT OF TECHNOLOGY IN OUR LIBRARY

One of the most significant ways that technology has had an impact is through the implementation of our new automated library system. In January 2003, the USMAI (University System of Maryland and Affiliated Institutions) launched our new library system Aleph 500, from ExLibris. According to the ExLibris contract, the Aleph system has been described as a "generalized, fully integrated, comprehensive library system." The modules included in this system are OPAC, Cataloging, Acquisitions, Circulation, Items, Serials' control, Users' control, Administration, Tasks Manager, and Inter Library Loan. These modules all share the same database. The system is uniquely arranged and designed in a manner such that all USM schools and affiliated institutions share one common database.

Some new features include requests on multivolume series, Chinese/Japanese/Korean character support, limiting by location and collection, the ability to save searches and items in a personalized folder, online renewals, a separate journals catalog, and reserves checkout.

One of the immediate changes in the library was the purchase of new equipment for the staff and patrons. The Aleph 500 is an online real-time system and is accessible via the Internet; therefore, each staff member and all patron terminals needed computers with Internet access. All staff received new Gateway E-6000 series computers, including 17-inch LCD flat panel screen display monitors, with much excitement. Additionally, our student research laboratory received twenty Gateway E-6100 series computers. Two scanners and three additional printers were purchased to support patron use.

As the staff became acquainted with the new technology, it was necessary to provide instruction and training to our patrons and campus community. A media campaign was presented to the campus community regarding our new system along with mini workshops and campus presentations.

DIGITAL DIVIDE

Our presentation will discuss the digital divide as it relates to the libraries' resources which include a multiplicity of resources including print, nonprint, electronic media, the integrated library system, distance education, and staff training. The Frederick Douglass Library has the resources, technology, and personnel to develop and implement this approach.

The digital divide is the phrase used to explain about those who have access to technology and those who do not. According to the Digital Divide Network, the digital divide is defined as a

> gap between those who can effectively use new information and communication tools, such as the Internet, and those who cannot. While a consensus does not exist on the extent of the divide (and whether the divide is growing or narrowing), researchers are nearly unanimous in acknowledging that some sort of divide exists at this point in time.

For the purpose of this presentation, the digital divide will be defined as those who do not have access to the computers and/or the Internet.

HISTORY OF TECHNOLOGY

The Frederick Douglass Library has been involved with technology since 1981 with the implementation of the OCLC (Online Computer Library Center) system. It was one of the few libraries to begin using the system for cataloging and interlibrary loan. In 1988, the library installed computers that were dedicated for the CD-ROM databases such as ERIC and InfoTrac. The first Integrated Library system was installed in 1990, which was the GEAC System from Colorado. This system contained cataloging and circulation modules. In 1990, the library implemented the CARL system (online catalog) which clearly automated acquisitions and serials and updated the cataloging and circulation departments.

The Interactive Video Network system was first instituted in 1992 which now links over fifty sites to allow for course instruction and academic meetings in the University System of Maryland. In 1998, the library installed the multimedia classroom that contained twenty-two computers and an LCD projector. Also during this time, a computer room was designed exclusively for accessing databases online. Email was also accessible at this time. During the academic year 2002–2003 the entire library became a wireless environment.

In 2003, ExLibris, the current integrated library system, was implemented. It was also during this time that approximately 255 laptops were purchased for student distribution. Thirty of those were placed in the library for student in-house use. These laptops contain the latest software and have full Internet access in a wireless environment. In addition to the laptops, the library has fifty-three workstations for library users to conduct their research, one of which has been designated for the visually impaired.

With the increase in technology the role of the librarian has changed. Over the course of time, librarians have had to become computer literate. Cross-training in other areas and on new systems is no longer an option, but a requirement. It is a necessity that librarians attend various types of technology workshops including Web page development, word processing, and database management.

In addition to the changes in the role of the librarian, services at the Frederick Douglass Library have also changed. These changes include extended operating hours, access to information 24 hours a day 7 days a week, and more focus placed on the subscription of online resources.

DISTANCE EDUCATION

In 1992, the Interactive Video Network system (IVN) went online. Initially linking four campuses, over fifty sites are now connected. Due to the popularity of IVN, some campuses have multiple sites because one system cannot accommodate the needs of an entire campus. The University of Maryland Eastern Shore is one of those campuses with sites located in the library, the Department of Agricultural Sciences, the Department of Engineering and Aviation Sciences, and the Department of Natural Sciences.

According to the University System Academic Telecommunications System 2, IVN is described as follows:

> The two-way, multi-site cameras and television monitors make it possible to carry real time discussions, transmit photographs and illustrations, and even show video footage. Both picture and video are transmitted in real time through digital telephone lines. Instructors and students can simultaneously see, hear and interact with each other in the classroom. IVN has added a great deal of flexibility to broadening the availability of coursework to more students and has become a valuable way of linking faculty and students throughout the University System of Maryland. It provides another technological capability for the development of distance learning.

University of Maryland Eastern Shore students have received courses via IVN in Social Work, Biology, Marine Estuarine Environmental Science, Principles of Accounting, and Technical Writing. IVN courses taught by University of Maryland Eastern Shore faculty and received by other institutions include Fish Physiology and Curriculum and Instruction in Technology. Although the IVN is set up to link institutions in USM (the University System of Maryland), it has the capability to be used outside of the state and country. Most recently, a University of Maryland Eastern Shore Jazz History class received lectures from Rutgers University in New Jersey. Past linkages with IVN outside of the country have been from Norway, Sweden, and South Africa. Students from the Department of English and Modern Languages were enrolled in a Zulu Language course that was linked from the University of Witswatersrand in Johannesburg, South Africa, then to Indiana University and bridged to the University of Maryland Eastern Shore.

There is a policy from the University of Maryland Academics Telecommunications System (UMATS) which states that the initiating university campus is responsible for costs incurred when connecting outside of the university system. This is the policy regardless of whether using services provided by UMATS or arranging such connections independently.

IVN classes are usually small in size and for each course offered; an average of four other sites can be connected to receive instruction.

The advantages of IVN include:

- Students have accessibility to course offerings on other campuses.
- Courses are shared when there is a shortage of instructors.
- Students become familiar with other faculty members and students in the system.
- Administrators network with colleagues in meetings.
- The need for extensive travel to other campuses is eliminated.

Some challenges of IVN include:

- Instructors must remain within the scheduled class time frame.
- Students must call or email the instructor if further discussion is needed before the next class meeting.
- Some users say distance learning is impersonal, therefore preferring the traditional method of instruction.
- Technical problems can occur.

The use of IVN throughout the USM for academic and administrative purposes has been successful and continues to increase.

For additional information on IVN, please refer to the USM, Interactive Video Network Web site at http://www.umats.ums.edu/IVN.

In addition to the IVN system, the University of Maryland Eastern Shore is currently offering a bachelor's degree program in Early Childhood Development and an Educational Doctorate in Leadership (EdD) at the satellite location of Chesapeake Community College in Wye Mills, Maryland.

INTEGRATED LIBRARY SYSTEM

The Frederick Douglass Library currently uses Aleph the software of the ExLibris system. There are sixteen institutions of higher education in the university system of Maryland

(USMAI), sharing one bibliographic database. The catalog contains books, journals, and nonprint materials. Faculty and students are able to request books from any of the University of Maryland libraries through a multicampus request search.

A typical work flow starts in the acquisition department where the materials are ordered, received, and then sent to cataloging. In cataloging the bibliographic record is searched and the item and holdings records are created. A bibliographic record is required and can be obtained in any of the following three ways: (1) using an existing record from the system, (2) creating a short record in the bibliographic module (either from Acquisitions or Circulation), or (3) importing a record from an external file. To use an existing record, the user may search the database using one of the key searches, author, title, ISBN (International Standard Book Number), and many others. Once a record is found, the bibliographic record is cataloged, items are added, and the record is linked in the system. If a short record is used, the user must complete the cataloging process by overlay and then export from an external file.

The Aleph PAC (Public Access Catalog) is available through a Web browser over the Internet (see http://www.catalog.umd.edu). Faculty and students search the catalog through the library home page. On-campus users as well as off-campus users *should* type the university identification number and enter the last name to access the system. Entering the identification number allows students to request books, put a hold on books, access the system remotely, save items, and check circulation records.

Faculty and students can request books from other catalogs within the consortium using the following methods. Once a record is found, click the "availability" to see if the book is checked out. Then click the title to get the call number. If a book is needed from another school, click other catalogs. Search the catalog and place a hold on the book by clicking the word "request."

There are challenges in the Aleph system. When the Internet is down, library users are unable to use the online catalog or databases. The solution is the good memory of the librarians of the Library of Congress Classification System to point students in the direction for finding their books. There is traveling involved to attend committee meetings of the different task forces. Since improvements within the system are always forthcoming, this necessitates continued testing and training with new software. Other challenges to the system involve incoming staff members becoming familiar to the consortia environment and ensuring institutions within the system have a voice on consortia committee.

LAPTOPS AND THE WIRELESS ENVIRONMENT

In June 2001, the Information Technology (IT) Department began to implement a wireless campus-wide environment. A wireless environment was one component mandated in the University System of Maryland's Board of Regents Minimum Information Technology Standards policy of 2001. The campus Information Technology staff began preparing many campus facilities, including the library, to support a wireless environment.

In support of the Minimum IT Standard policy and a grant initiative to eliminate the digital divide on the system's HBCUs, the University of Maryland Eastern Shore received 255 Gateway laptops for students. Two hundred and twenty-five laptops were distributed to students for the semester. Currently, there are thirty laptops in the circulation department for in-house use to further accommodate the demand.

Prior to the distribution of any laptops, the library and IT staff prepared an extensive policy on laptop use and distribution. The circulation staff assisted the IT department in the distribution of laptops by registering all prospective recipients in our system and barcoding all laptops. A collaborative effort proved to be most beneficial. Circulation of the laptops began in January 2003. This effort was well received by students. As this afforded students the opportunity to go beyond using the library for research and study, students now have access to various software applications including the full Microsoft Office Suite, Visual Basic, and C++.

Some challenges were faced with having the laptops. Initially there was some reluctance from some staff members. There was a concern as to whether they would have to address equipment problems and questions. The staff was informed that at no times were they expected to address problems of this nature. All questions and equipment were to be referred to the IT department. If there was a problem with the laptop, the student just returned it and received another one. The laptop was simply sent to IT for repair. Since this, the library's automation department has been very much involved in solving technical problems.

One challenge for us has been providing adequate support at the circulation desk. Because the circulation desk was already one busy service station before this practice, it has been necessary to place additional support at the desk. This is especially problematic during peak evening hours. It has been necessary to seek assistance from other departments in the library.

Overall, it is our opinion that the laptop program has been very successful. We have been able to address a need and provide a beneficial service to our patrons. The library is now a more popular place on campus and attendance has significantly increased. It is exciting to see students throughout the library taking advantage of this service.

ONLINE RESOURCES

To further assist our users, the Frederick Douglass Library provides access to a wide variety of online resources. Working with the University System of Maryland Electronic Resources Committee (USMERC) and PALINET (a mid-Atlantic library cooperative), the library is able to provide access to approximately 120 online databases, 40 of which either contain or are full text. These databases cover subjects ranging from agriculture to technology. In addition, users have the added tool SFX (known as "find it"). SFX, or find it, provides links from a citation in a database to the full text of that article, where available, and to other helpful resources and services such as Inter Library Loan (ILL) and ask a librarian. ILL provides access to journal articles not available in the library. The department also requests books that are in the collection, or any of the other USM libraries.

Furthermore, remote access to the library's online resources is provided via MetaLib (software that enables searching across catalogs and databases): a gateway and authentication tool called Research Port. Research Port is a gateway to the electronic resources held by the Frederick Douglass Library. It allows users to access the library's databases, search the library catalog, and find links to articles in other databases using SFX.

When users log on to Research Port, users can save and later access their favorite databases ("my databases"), access online journals ("my e-journals"), store searches ("my searches"), or create folders to save articles for later use ("my items").

With all the rich online resources available in the Frederick Douglass Library, we are still faced with challenges to continue to provide access to quality sources. Some of these challenges include:

- Budget constraints
- Changes made to databases by vendors
- Technical difficulties

TRAINING AND INSTRUCTION

To prepare library clientele to use the library services and resources, eight online tutorials, one general and seven subject based, have been developed. These tutorials are designed to assist library users to:

- Recognize a need for information
- Locate materials in the library (books, periodicals, special collections, etc.)
- Find and retrieve information
- Evaluate the information retrieved
- Process and use information
- Develop lifelong learning skills

As the users progress through the tutorials, they learn:

- How to begin their research, which includes information on how to formulate a thesis statement
- How to find information, which discusses various reference tools
- How to select resources, which includes types of resources like abstracts and indexes
- How to use online resources
- How to evaluate the Internet
- What to do after the research is completed (social and ethical responsibilities)

Each subject-based tutorial includes a bibliography of relevant print and online resources available.

These tutorials have been invaluable in assisting library users in learning the research process and about library services. However, there are several challenges faced in creating the tutorials. Some challenges to creating tutorials include:

- Training on how to create a Web page or site
- Changes to database search screens
- Time constraints

The library is a major component of the academic program through an organized structure. Faculty and staff of the University of Maryland Eastern Shore recognize the responsibility of the library to support the teaching function of the institution. The Frederick

Douglass Library offers library instruction sessions to support the university's curriculum and to support the research needs of faculty, staff, and students.

The purpose of this program is to:

- Prepare faculty, staff, and students to make effective use of the library and its resources
- Teach faculty, staff, and students to do research independently by introducing them to the various types (print and nonprint media) sources and services available in the library

Library instruction sessions are held in the library classroom. The library classroom has twenty-one workstations (one for the instructor). This allows librarians to provide hands-on instruction to library users. As well as the library classroom there is a research lab available for users. In the research lab, users have access to the library databases and the Internet. There are currently nineteen workstations available in the research lab.

Some challenges to providing library instruction include:

- Staffing shortages
- Instructors not understanding the need for library instruction
- Technical difficulties
- Limited facilities—some classes are too large to fit into the library classroom and there is only one room available

CONCLUSION

Have we conquered the digital divide?

The Frederick Douglass Library is working diligently to conquer the digital divide. It is an ongoing process. This process is evidenced through the technological advancement made through recent years. These advances include but are not limited to:

- Dedicated terminals to access CD-ROMs
- Upgrades in integrated library systems
- Interactive Video Network (IVN)
- The creation of online tutorials
- The development of a hands-on library classroom
- Access to a wide variety of electronic resources

With these technological advances, we still face the challenge of maintaining and expanding library services. Coupled with this is the fact that budgets are being reduced or cut as prices and the demand for services continue to escalate.

In responding to the question "Have we conquered the digital divide," we have determined that the digital divide is not something to be conquered, but an ongoing challenge to be met.

BIBLIOGRAPHY

Brooks, Sharon, et al. 2004. Divide and Conquer: The Digital Divide at an HBCU. PowerPoint, National Diversity in Libraries Conference (May 5).

Digital Divide Network. Available: http://www.digitaldividenetwork.org/content/sections/index.cfm.

Loghry, Patricia A. 2001. "The Aleph Serials Control Application." *Serials Review*. Online March 9, 2004. Available: Academic Search Premier. http://search.epnet.com/direct.asp?an=4356825&db=aph.

National Telecommunications and Information Administration. October 2000. *Falling Through the Net: Toward Digital Inclusion*. Online, Internet, June 11, 2002. Available: http://www.ntia.doc.gov/ntiahome/net2/falling.html.

Newburger, Eric C., and the U.S. Census Bureau. September 2001. "Home Computers and Internet Use in the United States: August 2000." *Current Population Reports*. Online July 15, 2002. Available: http://www.census.gov/prod/2001pubs/p23-207.pdf.

University System Academic Telecommunications System 2. Available: http://www.umats.ums.edu/IVN.

University System of Maryland, Board of Regents Information Technology Committee. August 10, 2001. *Minimum IT Standard Responses*. Online, Internet, March 30, 2004. Available: http://www.usmd.edu/Leadership/USMOffice/AdminFinance//ITPlan/MinITStds.html.

12 DEVELOPING APPROACHES FOR WORKING WITH DIVERSE USER POPULATIONS

by Deloice G. Holliday

INTRODUCTION

This chapter will outline some challenges and positive experiences I have encountered as the multicultural outreach librarian for Indiana University Libraries. Techniques for fostering student engagement and learning and other activities that have been implemented or tested will also be discussed.

CHALLENGES PROVIDING SERVICES TO DIVERSE STUDENT POPULATIONS

The user groups with whom I work are explicitly directors of the major culture centers and their constituents. Collaborating with the directors for the most part has been easy because they, like librarians, are engaged in outreach to students. Outreach for them includes recruiting students from the overall student base who use and participate in programs and services they provide. Outreach for librarians includes collaborating with already established programs and program directors as well as developing new innovative programs.

The multicultural outreach librarian faces a major factor or obstacle in whether services created will be embraced by the students and faculty. Progress has been slow with student involvement, but this is not a deterrent or detriment because students do know that library programs exist and that they can get information to further their knowledge quest there. Some techniques employed since the inception of the multicultural outreach librarian position include designing visual displays in the main library lobby that include collections that the libraries own which support cultural specific topics. For example, we have developed displays on topics and events such as Asian Pacific Heritage Month, Hispanic Heritage Month, the Martin Luther King, Jr. Holiday celebration, and Juneteenth and to commemorate the *Brown v. Board of Education* of Topeka, Kansas. This special display was designed to educate all who visit the Main Library about this historic landmark Supreme Court decision.

Other techniques used to pique student interest in the libraries have been developing both bibliographies and Webliographies of the libraries' collections on and about the cultures of traditional underrepresented groups. By participating in activities that students support such as the annual Multicultural Orientation which is held at the beginning of the fall semester, we have been able to reach hundreds if not thousands of students. This annual festival introduces new students to the campus and programs and services that will enable them to successfully complete the first four years of education. We have participated in the annual Festival Latino since its inception more than three years ago which introduces students as well as the local community to programs and services geared toward this specific student group and those who would like to learn more about Latino culture. My involvement includes introducing participants and attendees to library resources and services in the form of handouts and a visual display that is portable, meaning that we can take it outside the library. I have also developed yearly programs that are devoted to topics such as higher education in Indiana, a look at racism in Indiana in the context of lynching during the twentieth century, and the *Brown v. Board of Education* commemoration lecture.

As the multicultural outreach librarian for Indiana University, I have a targeted audience in mind, and the groups I serve are first-generation undergraduate students and students from underrepresented populations. It was necessary to conduct a literature review to ascertain what others around the country are doing with outreach services in academic libraries. While reviewing the literature, a couple of things stood out more than others. The first was what avenue others have taken in terms of multicultural, diversity, and outreach programs to undergraduate and international students. Second, it was also necessary to find out whether students felt that the current level of library services was meeting their information needs. And lastly, it is very important to know what kinds of services this audience felt they needed and how to best meet those needs.

MULTICULTURAL OUTREACH LIBRARIAN: FOUR ASPECTS OF THE JOB

The position description for the multicultural outreach librarian has two major components: (1) The librarian develops educational and collection-specific programs and activities to promote library services to underrepresented populations on the Indiana University Bloomington campus. The librarian also serves as a liaison to the Office of Multicultural Affairs and participates in initiatives to recruit or retain minority students. (2) The librarian participates in all programs of the Information Commons, sharing responsibility for general reference service, orientation activities, development of Web resources, and the selection of materials for the core collection.

LEARNING CURVE (LOW)

The learning curve for reference and formal library instruction was low. Working at the reference desk and providing formal library instruction for a number of years permitted me the confidence to provide these services unfettered. The part of the job that is new is minority outreach. Minority outreach is where I have concentrated much time and energy. Getting to know the people in the Office of Multicultural Affairs and the culture centers and to learn the kinds of programs and services this department and the centers wanted the libraries to partner with them on by far has been the steepest learning curve.

WORKING WITH ADMINISTRATORS AND DIFFERENT MINORITY GROUPS (STEEP)

The learning curve for working with diverse populations and administrators has been steep. First of all to meet with so many different people and to ascertain students' library information needs is challenging. Not having a mechanism to measure student information needs available to me, I relied heavily on the culture center directors' advice for developing programs. In the beginning, none of the programs offered piqued the interest of students. However, during the course of nearly four years students have begun to come to programs sponsored by the multicultural outreach librarian. I'm uncertain what changed the attitudes of the targeted student groups; currently most programs are well attended and received.

CHALLENGES FOR THE FUTURE (TIME)

Finding time to complete tasks and remaining on par with developing this position so that it is what library administrators envisioned it to be is most challenging. Managing time effectively comes into play when trying to develop and produce high-quality educational programs, and providing services to engage and promote student learning is also a challenge. But the most challenging aspect of the job is developing an instrument to measure the effectiveness of multicultural programs in terms of student satisfaction with programs and services currently offered to them. What seems to be working and what students would like to see changed are questions that remain to be answered.

SUPPORT FROM COLLEAGUES AND ADMINISTRATORS: ASSESSING MULTICULTURAL PROGRAMS

The strategic goal is to conduct periodic assessment of the needs of minority faculty, students, and staff for library collections and services. The operational goal is to encourage staff to participate in diversity programs on campus and at national conferences. Some form of measurement (survey, interview, questionnaires, observation) is needed to provide better library services and programs. Designing the measurement tool(s) and implementing a delivery system for the tool whether that format is paper, electronic delivery, database-backed Web page, or email is required. Plans are in progress to design such a tool for assessing multicultural programs. We could measure the success of a program by conducting head counts, but a more definitive tool is needed so that student information needs can be met in consistent and more systematic ways.

WAYS IN WHICH LIBRARIANS CAN PROMOTE OUTREACH SERVICES TO DIVERSE POPULATIONS

EMPHASIS ON WAYS TO SERVE ALL SEGMENTS OF A LIBRARY'S COMMUNITY

The primary way to serve all segments of a library's community is by promoting services through channels with which most users are familiar. These channels include Web-based services such as blogs, instant messaging, and email, or more traditional means of getting the word out such as flyers or bookmarks. Many library users are familiar with one or more of these information delivery systems. Library personnel just need to find a seamless way of reaching their users through systems that are contemporary and easy to use.

DEMOGRAPHIC TOOLS AND SURVEY METHODS

By creating demographic-specific tools and survey methods that show a more accurate picture of the current library users, librarians may be able to reach greater numbers of their customer or patron base. There may still be library users who are not fully comfortable with their level of knowledge of computer software, databases and indexes, or search engines. For these library users, the librarian could create a tool covering a set of skills for relatively new users of library resources in a workshop format. The new library user could tell us during those workshops of their information and technological needs, at which point the librarian could offer to patrons more effective workshops based on patron input.

CHANGING PERCEPTIONS OF THE ROLE OF LIBRARIES AND EDUCATION IN VARIOUS ETHNIC CULTURES

The library and its role differ from culture to culture. Find techniques for building or adapting library services to reach a greater number of culturally diverse customers. Acquire techniques to create or adapt library programs, services, and collections so that people in various cultures find those programs and services valuable to them, and so that the library is a more useful and welcoming place for them.

A few perceptions that ought to be changed right away are: (1) librarians can sit and read all day, and (2) the librarian position is an obsolete one because everything can be found on the Web. To build or adapt library services to reach a greater number of culturally diverse customers is the most challenging obstacle or question to answer. What can librarians do to change the perceptions or attitudes of the traditionally underrepresented library users? How can these perceptions be changed? Providing a welcoming environment is one way that will change the perceptions of library users from culturally diverse groups. With so many different cultures being represented in American communities nowadays, it would be wise for librarians to devise ways of planning, teaching, and coordinating library programs and services that are general enough to reach all library users, but specific enough that culturally diverse groups can participate as well.

METHODS FOR RECRUITING AND RETAINING A CULTURALLY DIVERSE WORKFORCE

Some methods that have been used to recruit and retain a culturally diverse workforce are through firsthand contact via formal presentations from staff and administrators, whose libraries serve diverse populations. Learning from those who have produced successful programs would be the first step. Polling the patrons who frequent your library to ascertain their information and technology needs is another way. Do they feel overwhelmed when visiting the library by the number of resources available? If there is that overwhelming feeling, it could be the reason some would-be library users don't take advantage of what the library offers. Some sort of outreach program is essential to bridging barriers between those who know and those who would like to know. Exposing library programs and services to diverse cultures is necessary to live and become successful in our global community. Library employees need to understand, value, and embrace these diverse cultures. Many library employees may have never encountered other cultures; it is with these employees that diversity outreach programs can have the most impact.

Some major reasons to market outreach activities in academic libraries are:

To inform users about the collection and services of the library

To improve the image of the library on campus

To make the library more user friendly

To gain support for library programs

To generate funding during a period of budget cutbacks

Outreach services that need to be promoted to diverse student groups are:

Online services (ask a librarian, live or virtual chat)

Bibliographic instruction (promote new resources through Bibliographic Instruction)

Development of special collection (divert funds from other areas to promote new products and services)

As a model for future programs and services, I look to Kansas State University Libraries, whose diversity program has been in existence since the mid-1970s. According to Kansas State University's 2000–2001 Annual Report, some of the programs they have developed include post-MLS residency, internship, climate survey, staff development and education, outreach, and participation in Tilford Focus Groups and the Tilford Conference. The Tilford Group is a Kansas State University research and development group consisting of inter-disciplinary faculty, administrators, and students who are developing a multicultural curriculum model to facilitate the total student experience.

Lastly, it is important to have a good working definition of diversity and how to apply that definition to programs, services, and the people who use them. Diversity cannot be viewed as different cultures forced into getting along with each other, but rather it is a common fact that need not be forced upon anyone. All who respect cultural heritage, social justice, and rights of humanity should never feel forced into accepting diversity. Diversity should be accepted as freely as the air we breathe, but as we all know there is still much work to be done before diversity is accepted, respected, and embraced by all.

Best Practices for Multicultural Programming at Indiana University Libraries

Work to ensure that the libraries' facilities, exhibits, publications, and staffing at public service desks reflect the diversity of the community we serve.

Create and fill a multicultural librarian position to provide outreach to diversity programs at IU.

Appoint and charge a diversity committee to work with the libraries' Human Resources on diversity initiatives.

Create a Web site.

Host diversity staff luncheons.

Conduct a diversity climate assessment.

Collaborate with other campus departments to sponsor cultural programs and events.

Participate in national conferences.

Acquire grant monies.

Have representatives of the committee periodically meet with units throughout the libraries and with library users to discuss and evaluate the libraries' diversity program.

Direct the committee to develop a goals document to be shared with the libraries' administration and staff in August of each year.

Diversity Programs Hosted Annually

Martin Luther King, Jr. holiday celebrations

Juneteenth celebrations

Asian American Pacific Islander Heritage Month celebrations

Latino American Heritage Month celebrations

Black History Month celebrations

Discussions/literary readings/academic-centered programs

Diversity education programs

Best Practices National Programs and Resources

ALA Diversity Fair http://www.ala.org/

National Conference on Diversity in Academic Libraries, co-sponsored by the Committee on Institutional Cooperation (CIC) and the Association of Research Libraries (ARL). This conference is hosted biannually. In 2002 the third annual conference was held at the University of Iowa, Iowa City, Iowa.

ALA Diversity Brochure http://www.ala.org/

ALA Spectrum Initiative http://www.ala.org/

Office of Literacy and Outreach library outreach to underserved populations http://www.ala.org/Template.cfm?Section=Outreach_Resources

State of Diversity on the Bloomington Campus
http://www.iub-chancellor.indiana.edu/diversity/

ARL Programs/Projects http://www.arl.org/arl/programs.html

Office of Women's Affairs Report on the Status of Women
http://www.indiana.edu/~owa/

CONNECTING CULTURES: PROMOTING DIVERSITY ACROSS CAMPUS THROUGH OUTREACH PROGRAMS

Because Indiana University is a global community serving more than 4,400 international students throughout the state, Indiana University Libraries have initiated programs designed to attract students, faculty, and staff, as well as members of the local community to visit the libraries and learn more about the many international collections that are housed here.

There are nineteen libraries throughout the Bloomington campus which house our great collections with more than twenty subject and area collections specialists covering collections on Central Eurasian studies, Chicano-Riqueno studies, East Asian studies, Germanic studies, Global studies, India studies, Latin American and Caribbean studies, Middle Eastern studies, Tibetan, Uralic, and Altaic, and many more areas of global and language-specific interests.

Diversity and multicultural initiatives have sprung up all over campus, and at Indiana University Libraries matters regarding diversity programs are as commonplace and as important as research and teaching initiatives on campus. Libraries are essential in promoting and sustaining the higher education students of today. We highlight the collections, and through panel discussion on relevant and current events students are participating and using the libraries more effectively.

OUTREACH SERVICES IN ACADEMIC LIBRARIES

In the August 2001 issue of *American Libraries*, Elaina Norlin from the University of Arizona writes, "The secret is [to] start by understanding a given group's needs and interests" (Norlin 2001, 60). Cultural administrators felt that students needed more time and hands-on instruction than the traditional library instruction courses offer. They requested additional instruction sessions prior to midterm exams. These midterm refresher courses would better prepare students for retrieving materials from the various databases and locating those materials in the event that they were not full text.

Like the University of Arizona, Indiana University's library outreach initiatives are directed toward targeted campus communities. We felt that it was important to promote already existing library programs and services by developing a Web page that showcased these programs and services so that students could easily find out what is already in place. Knowing students can find information from a remote location when they visit the physical setting, it was our hope that they would feel welcomed because of familiarity with a Web page that was especially designed with them in mind.

Resources offered to minority students include online library resources, reference resources, Internet resources, and videos. Services for instructors, directors, and coordinators of the culture centers are available from the multicultural outreach programs and services page so they can collaborate with librarians to design specific programs and services for minority students. The Undergraduate Library Services department personnel wrote a mission and service statement to ensure that specialized programs and services for minority students would be embedded in the library's mission and would be done in collaboration with the culture centers. This questionnaire was developed to gather from students what information they felt pertinent.

Sample Questionnaire

What are you interested in learning about the library? (**Write your response in the space provided below**)

How often do you visit the Indiana University Main Library?

Circle one   daily   weekly   monthly   yearly   never

Do you feel comfortable asking questions at the reference desk?

Circle one   Yes   No

Do you know what IUCAT is? If yes, how often do you use it?

Circle one   daily   weekly   monthly   yearly   never

How often do you use the Web to find information for classes?

Circle one   daily   weekly   monthly   yearly   never

Students were asked to complete the online questionnaire or bring the completed paper questionnaire to class with them.

This basic questionnaire was developed in September 2001. Information gathered is to be used in developing future programs for diverse student populations. The workshops were designed to go hand-in-hand with the questionnaire. In other words, the workshops were designed for anticipated student responses. The information covered in the workshops was geared toward first semester freshmen with little or no familiarity with the Indiana University, Bloomington (IUB) libraries. Electronic, print, Internet resources, and a tour of the undergraduate stacks were part of the workshops. The following topics were covered in the two-day workshops:

> Information is Power.
>
> Find it at the Undergraduate Library.
>
> The Undergraduate Library is offering workshops to help you find the resources to meet your academic and personal information needs.
>
> Get acquainted with the Main Library.
>
> Locating information that you can use.
>
> Learn online searching techniques.
>
> Moving beyond the mainstream press—finding alternative points of view.
>
> Find information for your papers and projects.
>
> Learn to find reliable info from your home or on campus.

The target audiences were people who frequent the main cultural centers. The venue for them by which they received the invitation was listserv. The attendance for these workshops was poor, prompting me to scale down the workshops and to reevaluate what the students want to know about the library as opposed to what the directors felt they wanted to know. My question now is, what are the ten most important things freshmen and new students should know about the library? Ideally, a portable workshop that all librarians can promote to incoming students would be the most advantageous way to reach more students. This program could be designed for use through the Web or by PowerPoint presentation software. After such a dismal showing during the first attempt, I am left wondering, if I build it, will they come?

> *Ideas for the Proposed 30-Minute Multicultural Outreach Class Presentations*
>
> Librarians would extend formal library instruction to students involved with the following centers:
>
> Neal Marshall Black Culture Center http://www.indiana.edu/~nmbcc/
>
> Asian Culture Center http://www.indiana.edu/~acc/
>
> La Casa Latino Cultural Center http://www.indiana.edu/~lacasa/
>
> Gay, Lesbian, Bisexual and Transgender Student Support Services http://www.iub.edu/~glbt/
>
> Design Web page that showcases or identifies existing library services http://www.indiana.edu/~libweb/mainlib.html
>
> IUCAT (locate a book; locate a journal or journal article) http://iucat.iu.edu/
>
> Databases—conduct a simple search; keyword, author, title [displaying search] results and printing http://www.libraries.iub.edu/index.php?pageId=16 [select a database from the IUB Libraries alphabetical listing that is universal such as Academic Search Premier]

Media and Reserve Departments
http://www.indiana.edu/~libreser/index.html (see feature film list)

Document Delivery Services http://www.indiana.edu/~libfind/ [what to do when you cannot find a book]

CIC (Big Ten) Virtual Catalog http://www.indiana.edu/~libcic/

Guides for Citing Sources http://www.indiana.edu/~libinstr/cite/

Workshops/Updates http://www.indiana.edu/~libfind/

Remote Access http://www.indiana.edu/~libfind/access.html

These ten items will help students learn to use the library more effectively when a librarian is not present. All sites can be reached remotely, giving students the added advantage of accessing resources when the library is closed. The library's catalog is a key resource that all students should learn how to use as soon as they set foot on campus, as it will allow students to find information quickly by author, title, and location. The library's electronic databases and indexes are valuable resources that students should learn to use during their initial library orientation, as these resources will allow students access to information remotely and in many cases the full-text articles are available. Resources that are little used by undergraduate students but very important to their overall education are the media and document delivery services. While all ten points are valid for incoming freshmen, one of the most crucial is citing information correctly using a specific style manual. Students could easily unwittingly or unknowingly plagiarize the work of others without this essential tool.

BIBLIOGRAPHY

Balderrama, S. 2000. "This Trend Called Diversity." *Library Trends* 49:1 (summer 2000): 194–214.

Bonvillain, Nancy. 2000. *Language, Culture, and Communication: The Meaning of Messages.* Upper Saddle River, NJ: Prentice Hall.

Bonvillain, Nancy. 2003. *Language, Culture, and Communication: The Meaning of Messages.* Upper Saddle River, NJ: Prentice Hall.

Brand, Myles. 1999. *The Chronicle of Higher Education.* April 2.

Bronski, Michael. 1984. *Culture Clash: The Making of Gay Sensibility.* Boston, MA: South End Press.

Brooks, David. 2003. "People Like Us." *Atlantic Monthly* 292:2 (September 2003): 29, 3p.

DeMott, Benjamin. 2002. *You Don't Say: Modern American Inhibitions.* New Brunswick, NJ: Transaction Publishers.

Hill, Katherine Hoover, ed. 1994. *Diversity and Multiculturalism in Libraries.* Greenwich, CT: JAI Press.

Indiana University Homepage. Available: http://www.libraries.iub.edu/index.php?pageId=3.

Internationalizing the Campus: Profiles of Success at Colleges and Universities. Available: http://www.nafsa.org/content/professionalandeducationalresources/publications/campusreport2003.pdf.

Jackson, Ronald L. 2004. *African American Communication and Identities: Essential Readings.* Thousand Oaks, CA: Sage.

Kansas State University. 2000–2001. Annual Report.

Kita, Sotaro. 2003. *Pointing: Where Language, Culture, and Cognition Meet.* Mahwah, NJ: L. Erlbaum Associates.

Kohls, Robert, and John Knight. 1994. *Developing Intercultural Awareness.* Yarmouth, MN: Intercultural Press.

Kuh, George D., and Robert M. Gonyea. 2003. "The Role of the Academic Library in Promoting Students Engagement in Learning." *College and Research Libraries* 64:4 (July): 256–282.

Lie, Rico. 2003. *Spaces of Intercultural Communication: An Interdisciplinary Introduction to Communication, Culture, and Globalizing/Localizing Identities.* Creskill, NJ: Hampton Press.

Liu, Mengxiong. 1995. "Ethnicity and Information Seeking." *Reference Librarian* 5: 49/50, 123, 12p.

Nelms, Charlie. 1998. *20/20: A Vision for Achieving Equity and Excellence at IU Bloomington.*

Norlin, Elaina. 2001. "University Goes Back to Basics to Reach Minority Students." *American Libraries* 32: 60–62.

Pigford, Aretha B. 1996. "Celebrating Diversity." *Educational Leadership* 53:7 (April): 86, 2p.

Seelye, Ned, and Alan Seelye-Jones. 1995. *Culture Clash: Managing in a Multicultural World.* Lincolnwood, IL: NTC Publishing Group.

Smith, Diane H. 1993. "Management of Government Information Resources in Libraries." In *Outreach, Promotion, and Bibliographic Instruction*, edited by Susan Anthes. Englewood, CO: Libraries Unlimited. 173–182.

Souza, Yvonne de. 1996. "Reference Work with International Students." *Reference Services Review* (winter): 41–48.

Stoffle, C., B. Allen, J. Fore, and E. R. Mobley. 2000. "Predicting the Future: What Does Academic Librarianship Hold in Store?" *College and Research Libraries News* 61:10 (November): 894.

Storti, Graig. 1999. *Figuring Foreigners Out.* Yarmouth, MN: Intercultural Press.

Ting-Toomey, Stella. 1999. *Communicating across Cultures.* New York: Guilford Press.

Torchinsky, Alberto. 1999. "Facing the Challenge of Achieving Minority Equity in Faculty Representation." Indiana University, Strategic Hiring and Support. Available: http://www.indiana.edu/~shs/reports.html.

Tripp, Harvey. 2002. *Culture Shock! Success Secrets to Maximize Business in the United Arab Emirates.* Portland, OR: Graphic Arts Center Publishing Company.

Vega, Garcia. 2000. "Racial and Ethnic Diversity in Academic Library Collections." *Journal of Academic Librarianship* 26:5 (September): 311, 12p.

Vega Garcia, Susan A. 2000. "Racial and Ethnic Diversity in Academic Library Collections: Ownership and Access of African American and U.S. Latino Periodical Literature." *Journal of Academic Librarianship* 26:5 (September): 311. Available: Academic Search AN: 3671966.

Wierzbicka, Anna. 1999. *Emotions across Languages and Cultures: Diversity and Universals.* Cambridge: Cambridge University Press.

13 TIPS AND PRACTICES FOR QUALITY LIBRARY USER SERVICES IN A DIVERSE ENVIRONMENT

by Justina O. Osa

INTRODUCTION

Libraries have always taken pride in their philosophy of providing equitable services to all users. They also claim that the needs of their patrons always drive all their activities. As the U.S. population becomes more diverse, library patrons continue to present increasingly diverse characteristics such as background, age, special needs, educational specialties, cultural and ethnic heritage, information culture, language, intellectual ability, and socioeconomic status. Furthermore, the student body includes individuals with disabilities, scholars in the university honors programs, distance education students, and students at the undergraduate, graduate, and postgraduate levels. The reality of the diversity of patron population has created practical challenges in terms of library resources and services. Patrons from different geographic, cultural, and social backgrounds and age groups face various challenges in addition to adjusting to a new academic environment and reality. Individuals with disabilities, university honors program scholars, and distance education students form part of the user groups to be served by the library.

SERVING DIVERSITY

There is a lot of talk about serving diversity. But what does this really mean? There is a dire need for libraries to have a clear understanding of what serving diversity means because recognizing and responding to diversity is a distinct characteristic of the twenty-first century. What is needed is a thoughtful, informed, imaginative, and exciting approach to providing resources and services to diverse users. It is also necessary to create a library environment and ethos that are welcoming to and representative of diversity. Understandably, this is a huge challenge to the library.

It is a huge misconception for the library to believe that when it provides equal access to library resources and services to all students it is providing equitable service to all students. Equal access does not necessarily mean equitable access or equitable services. For all students to take full advantage of the library, certain resources, services, practices, facilities, and a certain library climate must be in place. The library cannot support and meet the information needs of all patrons the same way. To make diversity in the library real we need to respond to the needs of all our users and not only to the needs of the majority user groups.

ADDRESSING DIVERSITY ISSUES IN LIBRARIES

Supporting the success of all our patrons should be our mission. The only way the library can fulfill this mission is to be mindful of the diverse characteristics and needs of its patrons. Because patron needs vary, strategies to meet these needs will of necessity vary. The library has to realize and respond to the reality that one size does not fit all its users.

If the library is to adequately address the issue of diversity, the library has to go beyond mere lip service to diversity and has to develop plans and initiatives that go beyond tokenism. Meaningful diversity initiatives must consciously plan to include people of diverse characteristics into library plans and activities that will culminate in real diversity that will be reflected in:

1. Collections
2. Services
3. Facilities
4. Staffing
5. Culture and Climate

Then and only then will all library users enjoy the invitation to cross boundaries and go beyond what they know and what they are familiar with.

NEEDS ASSESSMENT

Needs assessment is the first step in creating and maintaining a library that has the potential of meeting the information needs of all patrons, equipping patrons against the odds against them, and enhancing their academic success. "Needs assessment serves as a systematic diagnostic tool to carefully and to cautiously identify what the clienteles need, what the thrust of the collection should be, which services and facilities should be provided, and what the librarians should be doing to effectively and efficiently meet all patrons' needs" (Osa 2003, 134). Understanding who library users are, what they do, and the type of information they need should be some of the critical components in the needs assessment. This knowledge would foster the potential of the library to effectively assess the resources and services with the goal of verifying if there are discrepancies between the existing resources and services and the ideal resources and services that should exist.

HOW TO DO A NEEDS ASSESSMENT

There are three primary information collection methods that are often used to gather necessary information before launching into planning and action. The techniques and methods used to obtain user and task information may range from formal to informal methodologies that collect quantitative and qualitative data. Some of the methodologies include the use of surveys, observational methodologies, focus groups, and structured and unstructured interviews. Each has its advantages and disadvantages. Whatever the research or information gathering tool used, it is significant that the information gathered includes:

- Who the patrons are
- Programs the library is supposed to support
- The resources, services, and facilities patrons need
- How well the existing resources, services, and facilities are meeting patrons' needs
- Who is using the resources, services, and facilities
- Which group of users are underserved or "ignored"
- Areas and issues of concern
- How different user groups feel about the library climate

It is crucial that the library designs an adequate needs assessment report template. It would enable the library to report the findings in a clear, concise, and easily understandable manner. This would also facilitate making decisions based on the findings and recommendations derived from the needs assessment tools.

COLLECTIONS

The mission of most libraries is to acquire and provide access to information resources that support the curriculum, research, and service needs of the faculty, students, and the immediate and extended university community. The needs and interest of intended library users should drive the collection development policy and should determine what is acquired and the level of emphasis in areas of selection. Meeting the needs of diverse users and not just the mainstream users should be a criterion as the library decides to select materials for areas at the comprehensive, research, advanced study, initial study, basic information, or minimal levels.

In terms of collection, the library should design a research instrument that will enable the library to know:

- Programs the collection is to support
- Who will use the collection
- How the collection will be used
- When to solicit assistance from faculty and patrons
- Available budget
- Collection adequacy and currency
- Gaps and areas of needs in the current collection based on deficiency

SERVICES

Library services comprise everything that librarians do which is intended to be helpful and useful for the library users. These activities are quite diverse and they call for different sorts of skills. They are likely to attract different sorts of people with different sorts of interests and characteristics. The research tools should gather information to answer the following questions:

- Are services relevant and current?
- Who uses them?
- Who is not covered or whose needs are not being met?
- What services do the underserved and "the ignored" need?
- How will the library provide these services for them?
- Does the library have the resources, human and material, to provide the needed services?

FACILITIES

Library facilities promote easy access to and use of the resources libraries provide. They may include space and equipment. Some of the questions to seek answers to in terms of facilities should include:

- Are all user groups aware of available facilities?
- Who is using the facilities?
- Who is not using the facilities?
- Why are they not using the facilities?
- What special facilities do patrons need?
- Is the library providing what patrons need?
- How will the library provide the lacking facilities?

STAFFING

Employees are the single most important resource of the library. It is through the employees that the library does and achieves everything. The library should design instruments to find answers to the following questions:

- Do the current library employees reflect the student body in terms of their diverse characteristics?
- Do library employees have the knowledge and skills needed to adequately meet the needs of the diverse groups of users?
- Do library employees possess the right dispositions to provide services to all user groups?

LIBRARY CLIMATE

Library climate is a significant environmental variable that is associated with a high level of user satisfaction. When the library climate is positive and nondiscriminatory, a healthy rapport is established and maintained between library employees and users. Therefore, patrons keep coming back to use the library resources. The items on the research instrument used to collect data on library climate should include:

- How do patrons feel about the library?
- How do employees feel about the library?
- What type of relationship exists between the patrons and the employees?
- Does the library environment show sensitivity to diversity in the broad sense?
- What else can the library do to make it more welcoming to all users?

TIPS AND PRACTICES THAT WORK

It is often easy to identify and discuss problems. The difficult issue in most cases is that solutions are not offered or suggested. The second part of this chapter focuses on identifying, suggesting, and discussing tips and practices that have the potential to boost quality service to library users when one size does not fit all users because of their uniqueness.

COLLECTION

The library that is committed to building useful, meaningful, and adequate collections must build collections that contain a very broad range of materials such as books, serials, manuscripts, archives, photographs, recordings, movies, kits, flash cards, posters, models, dioramas, test materials, and much more. There are tips that have proved helpful in building and maintaining library collections that reflect the diverse qualities of all library users and meet their needs. The library that is eager to pay attention to diversity and to meeting the needs of all users should:

- Know all the programs on campus
- Set up a committee to focus on the globalization of the collections
- Evaluate the collections to verify if they adequately support all the programs both at the undergraduate and graduate levels
- Identify and use the services of relevant publishers and vendors, including small press publishers, and distributors
- Seek input from liaisons and patrons from as many programs and student groups as possible
- Conduct professional evaluation of collection and candidate items
- Collect materials representing a broad range of viewpoints
- Have a diversity selection criterion—to include materials presenting different views and representing the broadest diversity of human thought and creativity—not just materials that represent dominant societal viewpoints
- Have a diversity acquisition code—it will make it easy for the library to know what percentage of the acquisition budget is spent on acquiring diversity-related materials

- Consult locating and verifying tools such as catalogs, bibliographies, Web sites, databases, and publication announcements
- Consult reviewing sources—to know what is worth acquiring, especially in subject areas and disciplines in which librarians lack adequate knowledge and expertise
- Take advantage of publication announcement and selection tools provided by professional associations and committees
- Know when to request copies for preview
- Know when to solicit expert opinion from faculty and senior colleagues on the quality and appropriateness of the item being considered for acquisition
- Compare collection with comparable libraries
- Seek special funding to acquire needed items

The collection development policy should encourage the acquisition of materials that have special features and accompanying materials that make information and knowledge readily accessible and useful to all patrons irrespective of their learning styles or limitations. Multimedia materials with textual, visual, audio, and artifactual aspects could be selected whenever possible. Such materials could be of interest for quite diverse reasons to diverse groups of users. To further maximize access to special materials that patrons with diverse and out-of-the-mainstream needs, the library needs to run a strong interlibrary loan program—which is really temporary tactical collection development for an individual's sake. Special materials such as braille books and audio resources should be acquired for the visually or auditorially challenged patrons.

SERVICES

The classic mission and function of libraries to provide students, faculty, staff, and other user groups with information they need has not changed, but the scope and techniques to fulfill this function have broadened. A major component of providing adequate services is the recognition that the library must not only continue to perform traditional services but must at the same time adapt and develop new services to meet the changing needs of all patrons. The core of service is finding out what patrons need, providing for the need, and verifying that the need has been met. Some tips to enable the library to provide services to meet the needs of diverse patrons groups should include:

- Paying attention to segments of patron population that are often underserved—such as international patrons, minority patrons, patrons with disabilities, virtual patrons, and adult learners
- Identifying needed services—read professional literature
- Seeking patrons' view on the effectiveness of existing services
- Having patrons identify missing services
- Planning the identified services
- Evaluating and doing needed modifications

INSTRUCTION

Information literacy is proving to be a thread that is running through several of the services that libraries are currently providing. Instruction services are designed to teach library users how to use the library and locate information more effectively and efficiently. Instruction continues to grow in importance in the library for a couple of reasons. The twenty-first century is a century of data and information abundance. The complexity and expansiveness of information resources requires that user instruction be a high priority for library employees. Patrons are overwhelmed with the choices and number of potential sources that might be used. New technologies have penetrated and invaded and continue to transform every aspect of information storage, retrieval, and use. Consequently, patrons now go into "wandering land." They no longer stay within the controlled information environment of the library to search for information. Increasingly critical information sources are growing at an enormous rate and contain valuable information of a scholarly nature in almost every discipline. Often patrons prefer to go to cyberspace to retrieve needed information because of the relative ease of access and convenience, yet patrons have limited knowledge of the appropriateness of various information resources especially in interdisciplinary fields. It is important that patrons develop relevant information management skills to take full advantage of the resources available on both the Internet and the databases. Different user groups have varying levels of knowledge and competence in searching for information, especially electronic information. Often, patrons from low socioeconomic status and disadvantaged backgrounds are negatively impacted by the digital divide. Due to limited access or nonexisting access to adequate hardware and software, these patrons are gravely at a disadvantage in terms of taking full advantage of library resources to enhance their academic success. Developing and implementing an assertive instruction program could be useful in equipping library users to find needed information, and to navigate vast amounts of information quickly and easily. There are some specific questions which the library employees should answer while planning an adequate instruction program. These questions include:

- Whom do we teach?
- What do we teach?
- How do we teach it?
- How do we provide access to it?
- How do we market it?
- What do we need?
- Whom do we need?
- How do we assess our effectiveness?

Libraries offer course-related and assignment-related instruction sessions for patrons. These sessions provide information on the what, how, and when of databases, library catalogs, and services and give patrons the big picture. It is rarely possible to reach all patrons and ensure that they all understand the contents of the instruction session as a result of some variables which include: lack of adequate time to ensure that all patrons understood the contents of the session; varying levels of technological savoir-faire; varying learning styles of the patrons; varying levels of familiarity with the materials and skills presented; linguistic ability; and rate of absorption of new knowledge and skills. In order to provide for patrons who do not learn well in the instruction session setting, there are some other approaches to help them learn. These include:

- Web pages, which are a major gateway to resources and a major interface to services

- Tutorials—both online and in print formats
- Pathfinders and subject guides—both online and in print formats
- Quick Guides to e-resources, research strategies, and information literacy—both online and in print formats

These resources will allow patrons to learn how to navigate and use library resources independently and at the patron's pace and convenience. In addition to these benefits is the fact that patrons will have the information they need to retrieve and use information readily. When these helpful guides are electronically accessible, patrons can consult them irrespective of time and place. These resources should be designed in such a way that they are easy to access and not buried behind intermediate walls or pages, easily navigable, visually appealing, usable, and presented in a fashion that makes them instructive and understandable for a wide range of users. Furthermore, as much as possible the library should follow the following guidelines:

1. Consistent format
2. Manageable scope
3. Well constructed
4. Reliable and appropriate information
5. Readable and free of library jargons

The effectiveness of library instruction materials and approaches is further enhanced when methods of teaching modules, tutorials, Web pages, and pathfinders are accompanied with multimedia components that engage multiple senses and are not distracting, confusing, convoluted, and cluttered. Developing an aggressive liaison program is another strategy to bring the aggressive instruction program to library users. The liaison program should target all patron groups, especially those that are nonmainstream given the library environment. Whenever necessary, the liaison persons should set up research consultation services to provide individualized assistance.

REFERENCE SERVICES

Reference services are about assisting patrons by answering their questions, finding them information, directing them to sources, or connecting users and needed information, both print and nonprint. Patrons generally get reference assistance by:

1. Going to the physical reference desk
2. Using the Real Time Reference or virtual reference services
3. Emailing a reference question
4. Telephoning the reference desk
5. Scheduling a consultation session or research appointment

Patrons from most diverse groups have difficulty in accessing many services on campus, including the library. There are several means through which a library that is committed to diversity could meet the wide range of needs that diverse groups of patrons would have, and facilitate their academic success. The reference staff could plan activities that would be meaningful and useful in making it easy for all patrons, especially the underrepresented patrons, to know what the library has, what librarians can do for them, and how to take advantage of both the library human and material resources. Some of these activities include:

- Library orientation
- Library tour—traditional, virtual, and multilingual virtual tours
- Open house for all users—to advertise library presence, resources, and services
- Receptions for different patron groups, especially for underrepresented and underserved groups

There are also a variety of special activities which the reference librarians can do to make it easier for the diverse groups of users to feel welcome and to have a sense of belonging and acceptance. Some of these are:

- Special events programming such as essay or art contests or book reviews
- Contests with diversity themes
- Exhibits promoting different groups and topics
- Forums—a creative use of often-untapped resources

Most patrons feel uncomfortable and unsure of how to seek the information they need in the library. The climate of the library will greatly enhance the comfort level of patrons. Once they feel that they are safe they will come forward to request assistance. Patrons should be encouraged to make consultation appointments in advance or email in questions or needs, or use the virtual reference services so that each patron will have the opportunity to receive individualized reference services. Efforts should be made to answer the question as promptly as possible and the answers should refer patrons to appropriate sources and services. It would be useful to send useful and relevant brief factual information and relevant articles to the students to help them get started on their assignments. While working with them on the reference desk or one-on-one, frontline staff should:

1. Position the screen in such a way that there is co-browsing
2. Tell them what they are going to do
3. Audibly work their way through the search
4. Stop the reference interaction at various points and summarize the session thus far
5. Know when patrons need extra help and support

All these five steps would enhance the quality and effectiveness of reference transactions.

The hours the library is opened to users is a significant variable in meeting the needs of diverse user groups. The increasing number of nontraditional and returning adult students has made it crucial that the library consider when such patrons who juggle school, work, and family will want to use the library resources and services. The library should take advantage of new technologies that provide electronic access to resources and services so that patrons can use them as much as possible at any time and anywhere. Library evening and weekend hours should be carefully determined with the needs of special groups as the focus and not employee convenience.

FACILITIES

Facilities are very important in meeting the needs of diverse users. The different groups of users and the varying nature of their needs should constantly dictate decisions made in term of facilities acquisition, building, or designation. The floor plan should be designed to meet patrons' needs. Some facilities factors that are diversity sensitive include:

- Wheelchair-accessible stacks
- Individual and group use areas
- Lighting—bright and dim areas
- Pleasant, inviting, and stress-free environment
- Lockers
- Cubicles
- Computer labs

The library should also make available all the hardware and software necessary to access all information in all formats that are present in the collections. Some patrons absolutely depend on the library to provide electronic hardware and software they need because they do not own any. It would be very helpful to make available for patron use computer laboratories with work stations with Internet access and applications software such as word processing, spreadsheets, Excel, and PowerPoint. Reserve Reading Room facilities should be provided to enhance patrons' access to materials they cannot afford to buy or photocopy. The library should provide physically challenged patrons with useful adaptive technology such as closed caption devices, Kurzweil reading machines, visual enhancers, screen enlargement software, trackballs, and Versa Braille System equipment.

STAFFING

Employees could be the single most important resource and asset the library has because they represent the library, project the library image, market and sell the library, are the library's number one public relations officers, and plan and implement everything the library does. They will determine to a large extent how effective the library is in making its desire to serve diverse patrons adequately a reality.

The library should staff public services desks with competent and sufficient number of employees. This will ensure adequate desk coverage so that it will be possible for patrons to receive adequate attention and assistance. Having needed categories of employees on duty is another crucial strategy for meeting the needs of all patrons—for example, rovers or roamers, who roam the stacks to provide point-of-need assistance to confused, less library-savvy, and frustrated patrons; and systems employees, who assist the less technologically savvy patrons and serve as rescue guides such as when the systems crash, printers are not printing, or patrons lose documents and good searches.

Employee recruitment and retention are vital factors in enhancing the effectiveness of the library to promote diversity. Employees should reflect the reality of diversity because people like to see people who look like them and have similar qualities. To enrich the recruitment pool, the library should:

1. Post positions in national publications
2. Post positions in minority publications
3. Post positions in minority listservs

4. Mail positions to library and information sciences program deans
5. Contact specific minority organizations
6. Target mailing to potential applicants
7. Establish contacts at professional and scholarly conferences
8. Seek recommendations from prominent members of underrepresented and underserved populations
9. Use directories of ethnic professionals
10. Maintain a database of potential candidates (Winston and Haipeng 2000, 208)

Diverse library staff could be in a better position to design library facilities that are responsive to the needs of all patrons. Floor plan and access issues are significant issues in libraries. For example, employees with physical challenges will be very helpful in planning a library that is friendly to patrons with physical challenges. Such employees will be the voice of those who need special considerations in the design of library facilities. The more diversified the library employees are, the more representative will they be of the characteristics present among patrons. For instance, in the issue of study styles and preferences, the library will be attentive to the needs of patrons such as those who need less noise and distractions to concentrate, those who prefer to study alone, in a group, with little lighting, with bright lighting, with background noise, or without background noise.

Sometimes retaining diverse staff proves to be more difficult than recruiting them. There are some steps that the library can take to make it easier for them to stay. They include:

1. Forming a Library Diversity Committee
2. Organizing diversity sensitivity training activities
3. Providing information and activities to improve employees' people skills
4. Providing opportunity for open discussion for employees—too often fear, suspicion, and distrust prevent individuals, especially those with insufficient knowledge and experience with those different from them or those with diverse characteristics, from having honest discussions
5. Conducting Diversity Climate Surveys
6. Hiring outside consultants to advise when necessary

CLIMATE AND CULTURE

Kriza Jennings (Jennings 1996) affirms that the most pivotal questions in diversity discussions is "What do we have to do to create and foster a workplace climate where everyone feels welcomed, valued, and respected?" (Jennings 1996). The library needs to pay constant and conscious attention to ensure that the relationship and interactions between individuals in the library, be it among employees or between employees and patrons, is positive. This impacts the library climate and atmosphere. Research by CustomerSat and the Vanderbilt University Center for Services Marketing indicates that workplace climate attributes are among the strongest workplace-related drivers of customer satisfaction ("Workplace Climate Solutions"). The paramount significance of climate is further highlighted by this comment by a patron: "Last time we went to the library . . . to study . . . obviously, it's finals time . . . people are going to study. But when we walked in there looking for somewhere to sit down, it's like . . . they've never seen African American people before in their lives, or they've never seen African American people study before!" (Solorzano, Ceja, and Yosso 2000, 68). In order to make library experience positive for all patrons, the library should develop a mission that supports commitment to diversity and equitability and provide sensitivity training for employees.

COMMUNICATION

The area of communication, especially cross-cultural communication, is crucial to serving diverse patrons because:

1. Everything that occurs on the reference desk involves communication
2. Communication is a product of culture—it is culture bound
3. Communication issues affect human behavior

It would be suggested that library employees should develop interpersonal skill and a sensitivity to cultural differences. Employees' beliefs, values, assumptions, behaviors, and attitudes are mere manifestations of their culture. Since some of these components of culture could be learned, the library should give employees the opportunity to learn, unlearn, and exhibit the right ones while performing their duties. All patrons, irrespective of their uniqueness, stand to benefit from this because they avoid the negative impact of cultural myopia and of the inability to adjust which may include: (1) communication gap, (2) frustration—for both employees and patrons, and (3) portrayal of poor library image. The employees could promote a friendly, warm, nonthreatening, and supportive library climate if they:

- Pay more conscious attention to the communication process
- Develop relevant communication skills—such as active listening, paraphrasing, mirroring, and reflective questioning
- Become aware of communication blockers such as stereotyping
- Strive to provide equitable services
- Establish and maintain a supportive environment—know how to calm students down and help students to feel better about themselves and their information literacy skills
- Give specific feedback and send clear messages—it enhances understanding
- Check for patron understanding
- Give clear directions
- Become more aware of their choice of vocabulary, grammatical structures, and idiomatic expressions—to avoid confusion and misunderstanding
- Encourage responses and questions from diverse patrons
- Encourage responses and questions from diverse patrons
- Use calm, soothing, and pleasant tones

NONVERBAL COMMUNICATION

Employees need to realize the power of nonverbal communication. Though much of human nonverbal communication is culture bound and learned without conscious thought or effort, it has a huge effect on interpersonal relationship, perception, and climate. Body language such as gestures, postures, eye contact, facial expressions, tones of voice, spatial arrangements, patterns of touch, expressive movement, and conversational distance all play important roles in communication and they impact the comfort level of patrons. Sometimes these nonverbal channels seem to become even more powerful than what employees say. Employees should remember that though they are generally unconscious of nonverbal cues they should make an effort to controlling their body language. Different body language means different things in different cultures and cultural norms affect how people react to nonverbal communication cues or messages. Through enculturation people come to view the world in a particular way and accept certain interpretations for verbal and nonverbal messages. For example, raising eyebrows means:

1. Interest or surprise (North America)
2. Skepticism (Britain)
3. "Aren't you clever" (German)
4. "Hello" (Philippines)
5. "No!" (Arab)
6. Disagreement (Chinese) (Payne 2001)

Stress, tension, negative feelings, and misunderstanding destroy trust, a feeling of acceptance, and a positive climate. The importance of culture cannot be overemphasized. Different people do things and interpret things differently. Because of the rise in the number of patrons from different cultures, it would be desirable that library employees become knowledgeable of some common sources of miscommunication.

EYE CONTACT

Eye contact may seem to be insignificant, but it leads to some complications, misunderstanding, and ambiguity. Eye contact is a society behavior. In the United States of America, eye contact is almost a mandatory and expected part of communication and interaction. In some cultures making eye contact is considered rude and disrespectful, and in some it is even considered threatening and aggressive. But in some cultures it is a mark of respect, politeness, and interest. Some cultures even teach their young to focus on the neck of the person who is talking as a way to avoid eye contact. Therefore, library employees should learn to rightly decode the meaning of eye contact as they interact with patrons from different cultures.

CIRCLES THE INDEX FINGER AND THUMB

While working with a patron on the reference desk, a librarian may be excited that a patron understood, for instance, a search strategy and circles his or her index finger and thumb to indicate "Yes, OK, you got it!" In another culture circling one's index finger and thumb is vulgar. In some other cultures twisting an imaginary moustache means "OK."

HEAD NODDING

Humans sometimes regulate conversation with head nodding. In most cultures head nodding means "OK," "I'm following you," "Yes." "I agree with you." To others it simply means, "I am paying attention." But in India, the same gesture head nod indicates disagreement (Sharif, "Listening to Ourselves," 2003). Library employees need to understand that when a patron nods his or her head while a library employee is working with him or her, it does not necessarily mean the patron understands or agrees with the employee.

THE USE OF THE LEFT HAND

The use of the left hand could be a source of offense to a patron. A librarian on the reference desk may offer an object such as a book or an article he or she printed for a patron with his or her left hand. The librarian would expect the patron to be grateful for such kind gesture. But the patron may feel very offended by the librarian handing the patron the object with the left hand. Such a patron might completely avoid the library or avoid seeking assistance from that librarian. This is because the left hand signifies different things to different people. In the United States of America people do not pay attention to their use of their left hand because it doesn't mean anything to them. But "in most Arab and [African] countries, the left hand is considered "unclean" and is not put forward. . . . It is reserved only for certain 'hygienic functions' or blowing the nose. . . . Traditionally at meals the left hand is kept hidden in the folds of the robe" (Military Sealift Command 2004). Therefore, the frontline staff should be careful of how they use their left hand.

CONCLUSION

Today, diversity is a fact of life. To promote an awareness of diversity and an appreciation for it, it is imperative that the library resources, collections, services, facilities, staff, culture, and climate reflect a diverse representation and foci. They should be such to allow the different and many user groups to be happy and satisfied with the library. Though the diversity of the patron population can create practical challenges for the library, the library has no choice but to strive to meet the needs of all its patrons. The process and strategies necessary to make the library responsive to the needs of a diverse patron body demand effort, patience, and attention. Diversity awareness in all library activities is desirable because becoming more diversity-focused means becoming more relevant, more responsive, and more effective.

BIBLIOGRAPHY

Jennings, Kriza. Fostering a Workplace Climate for Diversity (1996). Available: http://64.233.161.104/search?q=cache:AWuj3RDkcacJ:www.arl.org/newsltr/185/foster.html+workplace+climate&hl=en.

Military Sealift Command. 2004. Taboos. Available: http://64.233.161.104/search?q=cache:U_JbJwtNmA0J:www.msc.navy.mil/msccent/taboos.htm+left+hand+culture+meaning&hl=en.

Osa, Justina O. 2003. "Collection Development: Curriculum Materials Center." *The Acquisitions Librarian* 30: 134.

Payne, Chuck. 2001. "I Think I Understand! Tips and Strategies for Successful Cross-cultural Communication." Available: http://64.233.161.104/search?q=cache:MWOB1dT3MPEJ:www2.mhc.ab.ca/users/cpayne/portfolio/cultcomm/understand.htm+raising+eyebrows+means+different+things+in+different+cultures&hl=en.

Sharif, Rebecca Z. 2003. "Listening to Ourselves." Available: http://64.233.161.104/search?q=cache:5J9GpYNfbSUJ:innerself.com/Relationships/listening.htm+head+nodding+culture+meaning&hl=en.

Solorzano, Daniel, Miguel Ceja, and Tara Yosso. 2000. "Critical Race Theory, Racial Microaggressions, and Campus Racial Climate: The Experiences of African American College Students." *Journal of Negro Education* 69, 1/2 (winter/spring): 68. In Whitmire, Ethelene. 2004. "The Campus Racial Climate and Undergraduates' Perceptions of the Academic Library." Portal: Libraries and the Academy 4, no. 3 (July). Available: http://muse.jhu.edu/journals/portal_libraries_and_the_academy/v004/4.3whitmire.html.

Winston, Mark D., and Li Haipeng. 2000. "Managing Diversity in Liberal Arts College Libraries." *College and Research Libraries* 61, no. 3 (May): 208.

"Workplace Climate Solutions." Available: http://64.233.161.104/search?q=cache:CMpYZcFlsTkJ:www.customersat.com/Solutions/HR/HR-climate.asp+workplace+climate&hl=en.

14 MAKING PEER RESEARCH ADVISORS A REALITY AT NCSU LIBRARIES

by Laura Blessing, Karen M. Brown Letarte, and Amy VanScoy

INTRODUCTION

In the spring of 2003, North Carolina State University (NCSU) Libraries began recruiting for its Peer Research Advisors program. The program has presented the libraries with both challenges and successes that we would like to share in this chapter.

Peer mentoring programs (often referred to as peer information counseling, or PIC programs) allow libraries to present a more diverse face to their public services by hiring students from underrepresented groups to assist with reference service and instruction and to participate in outreach activities. Since these programs emphasize peer-to-peer teaching, students of color feel more comfortable approaching other students for assistance at service points. Peer mentoring programs also provide an opportunity for students from diverse backgrounds to explore librarianship as a career option and to develop their information literacy skills. These kinds of programs have been in existence since the mid-1980s. Successful peer mentoring programs at other universities provided models upon which to base the design of a program at NCSU. Other universities that have implemented peer mentoring programs include the University of Michigan, the University of Arizona, Cleveland State University, Valdosta State University, and the University of Oregon (Winston and Downing 1998).

The planning stages for this program began in the fall of 2002, when the opportunity arose to apply for a campus grant providing up to $5,000 for new diversity initiatives. After considering several diversity programs answering various needs of the NCSU Libraries, the Libraries Diversity Committee decided that they wanted to pursue a peer program. The committee began writing a proposal for the peer grant. Unfortunately, when we contacted the head of the Office for Equal Opportunity with questions about the grant, we were told that we did not qualify for it because the libraries were not considered a college. There was not enough time left to apply for other grants that would begin in the spring. However, the libraries' Directors Council saw the proposal, and was so impressed with the idea, they decided to fund the program on a smaller scale through the student/temporary wages budget.

HISTORY OF THE PEER RESEARCH ADVISOR PROGRAM

In the fall of 2002, the NCSU Libraries Diversity Committee found itself confronting a number of challenges. The libraries were recruiting to fill the position for librarian for Professional Development and Diversity Initiatives. In light of this vacancy, the Libraries Diversity Committee's role in furthering the libraries' diversity goals was especially important. Having the position vacant had the advantage of guaranteeing that the Diversity Committee members develop diversity leadership skills. It has also enabled the library staff to see that advancing diversity is too important to be left to just one person. Despite this key leadership position being vacant, the Diversity Committee took the initiative to develop a vision and a plan for diversity in the NCSU Libraries.

DEVELOPING A VISION

At the beginning of the fiscal year, the Diversity Committee conducted a planning session to identify potential projects, initiatives, and priorities for the year. The committee laid some groundwork and identified some important campus groups with which to network. Thus when the campus diversity funding opportunity appeared on the horizon, the committee was prepared with several possible projects in mind.

Among the priorities that the committee wanted a potential project to address, three stood out. First, the committee was concerned about shortages in the profession and the need to recruit librarians of all backgrounds, but particularly those from diversity groups. Second, the committee also wanted an opportunity to work more closely with campus stakeholders, particularly the Office for Diversity and African American Affairs and the First Year College. Finally, the committee wanted to present a welcoming and more diverse public face, particularly in reference and instruction. This made the idea of a peer information counseling project rise to the top of the list.

PEER INFORMATION PROGRAMS

The main focus of a peer program is attracting students of color to librarianship. A peer program has the additional advantage of diversifying staff at main public service desks. NCSU's Peer Research Advisors program is not unique. Many have existed, including similar programs at the University of Minnesota, Cleveland State University, the University of Michigan, the University of Arizona, Valdosta State University, and the University or Oregon (Winston and Downing 1998, 4).

Winston and Downing define a peer information counseling program as "formally developed and managed efforts directed by a librarian (program coordinator) who recruits, hires, trains, and administers motivated students (peer information counselors) to work in public service areas and community outreach on behalf of the academic library" (Winston and Downing 1998, 1). A peer information counseling project would allow us to meet all three of our top priorities.

THE PROPOSAL

A subcommittee including several members of the Diversity Committee and the librarian for Instruction and Undergraduate Research was formed. The group was charged to write a proposal that identified the need for a peer information program and clearly explained how such a program was directly related to and supported the libraries' strategic goals as expressed in the Compact Plan. The proposal set forth the following objectives for the program:

- To strengthen support for university diversity efforts by the NCSU Libraries (as defined in the Compact Plan)
- To enhance the ability of undergraduates to use the library effectively
- To present a more welcoming and diverse face of library public services to students
- To provide role models for students from underrepresented groups
- To develop information literacy skills in the Peer Research Advisors students and enhance their academic success
- To enhance the educational experience of students from underrepresented groups
- To support the retention of students from underrepresented groups
- To recruit young, diverse people into science and technology librarianship

The subcommittee worked closely with the libraries' assistant director for Organizational Development, a member of the administrative council, in drafting the proposal. A question arose regarding the subcommittee's intent to require that applicants have minority status as defined by the U.S. Census. In seeking clarification to this question, we learned that we were ineligible to apply for the grant, which required that only colleges were eligible to receive this funding.

Although initially this seemed like an obstacle, ultimately, our ineligibility for the campus funding proved to be an advantage for the libraries.

About the same time, the vice provost for Diversity and African American Affairs was charged by the chancellor to create an advisory committee on diversity. The University Diversity Advisory Committee (UDAC) was formed in September of 2002. The committee includes broad representation from across campus, including the colleges, the graduate school, Multicultural Student Affairs, Facilities, and others. The libraries were invited to nominate a representative and the chair of the Libraries Diversity Committee was asked to serve in this capacity. This provided a wonderful opportunity for networking with others from across campus engaged in diversity work and especially for highlighting some of the libraries' initiatives. Through the University Committee, we were able to keep key members of the university community informed on the development of our Peer Researchers Advisors program.

Even though we were not able to apply for the campus grant funding, we did develop stronger relationships with other units on campus. We were able to educate the university administration about the libraries' mission and our ability to reach students in every college. What seemed at first to be an obstacle placed the libraries in the spotlight and gave us an opportunity to demonstrate to the campus community our unique strengths and commitment to diversity. The vice provost for Diversity and African American Affairs publicly praised the program and our commitment to diversity. This made it easy for us to gain the assistance of campus organizations that were essential to the success of the program, such as the Office of Multicultural Student Affairs, which assisted us with our targeted recruitment.

BUDGET AND RECRUITMENT PHILOSOPHY

Having learned that we did not qualify for the campus grant funding, we scrambled to see if there was any other funding available, but it was too late to apply for anything that would enable the program to start that fiscal year. The libraries' Directors Council heard about our efforts and offered to redirect $8,000 toward the Research and Information Services department budget for this program.

In working on the budget, the Diversity Committee found that we could hire three Peer Research Advisors to work approximately 10 hours per week for 32 weeks per year at an hourly salary of $9 for a total cost of $8,640 per year (10 hours per week $\times$ 32 weeks $\times$ $9 per hour = $2,880 $\times$ 3 Peer Research Advisors = $8,640). The Research and Information Services department was able to cover the amount over $8,000 through their wages budget.

With only three Peer Research Advisors, we were able to minimize equipment costs by sharing staff personal computers and office furniture and space already in place. We also minimized our recruiting costs by making contacts with key minority representatives on campus, asking them to email our announcement out to their members. Additionally, a small number of fliers were placed in key locations. This resulted in a near zero dollar cost for recruiting.

Although the cost of the program was relatively small in terms of dollars, it was a great cost in terms of supervision and management hours. We used existing professional staff to recruit, hire, and supervise the Peer Research Advisors. Primarily the assistant head of Research and Information Services and the librarian for Instruction and Undergraduate Research did this work. Both of these staff members also work with the Peer Research Advisors students on a weekly basis, taking approximately 10 hours of time.

You might ask why we would spend even this much money and staff resources on a program such as this when we were unable to obtain grant funding. In order to answer this, we must review why we wanted to invest resources in the program in the first place.

The goal of the Peer Research Advisors program is twofold: to provide a welcoming, diverse face to the public, and to recruit future librarians from minority populations. Both of these goals were seen as library-wide priorities. The second goal was seen as a need that the Research and Information Services department saw as relating directly to them. The facts that both the Research and Information Services department and the Diversity Committee were so committed to these initiatives helped in making this program a success.

We are beginning to see the seeds of the Peer Research Advisors' benefits in this area. When we recruited for student assistants for computer jobs in the fall of 2003, we had a high number of applicants who had previously applied for the Peer Research Advisors program. It appears that our Peer Research Advisors advertisements with underrepresented groups have inspired students of color to apply for other jobs within the libraries as well. Peer

Research Advisors students may decide not to pursue library careers after graduation; however, the NCSU Libraries administration believes that simply having diverse faces at public service points in libraries encourages underrepresented groups to consider librarianship as a career, while also helping to welcome users from diverse groups. When considering the need to recruit to the profession as well as the lack of diverse librarians, it is difficult to pass up the opportunity to become involved in a program like this.

IMPLEMENTATION

In general, implementing the Peer Research Advisors program required the same procedures as any student job in the library. However, due to its special goals, implementing the program did present some unique challenges. We were forewarned about some of the challenges after reading the *Leading Ideas* article on peer information counselor programs. The authors accurately depicted the challenges we were about to face and presented some useful solutions.

RECRUITMENT

Before beginning our recruiting, we developed a Web page (www.lib.ncsu.edu/pra/) explaining the program, including an online application form. Since the program was new and had special goals, we felt that we should explain these goals and clearly describe the responsibilities for the job. Staff members from other library departments, Distance Learning Services and Digital Library Initiatives, helped us to quickly publish a Web page and to create an application form that sent applicant information directly to the librarian for Instruction and Undergraduate Research, who had partial responsibility for hiring and implementation of the program. The online form not only made the recruiting process a little smoother, but aided in efforts to publicize the program. We were able to quickly and easily send email messages to campus partners that included the URL for the Web page. The partners then forwarded the message to students in our target groups. When it was time to recruit for the second semester, we updated the page with photographs of our current Peer Review Advisors (PRAs) and some enthusiastic quotes from them about the benefits of the program. We intended for the page to give the program credibility and to help potential applicants imagine themselves in the position.

We had high expectations for the Peer Research Advisors, requiring excellent customer service skills, dependability, teamwork skills, and interest in library research. In order to attract a large pool of applicants from a diverse group of students in the three-week time period that we had to fill the positions, we enlisted help from partners on campus who had shown support for the idea. For example, the Office of Multicultural Student Affairs was willing to send our job advertisement to all minority undergraduate students so that we could target our recruitment to that group. We also posted the job vacancy on a listserv for library supervisors. Some supervisors expressed enthusiasm for the program, explaining that they were happy to be able to reward high-performing students with a personal suggestion that they apply for this prestigious, high-paying job. As many library supervisors already know, word of mouth is often the best way to publicize jobs and attract good applicant pools.

Word of mouth definitely played a part in improving the candidate pool in our second round of interviews for the program. In fact, two of the candidates interviewed were friends of current Peer Research Advisors. Later, we were able to attract an excellent pool of candidates for another position in only two weeks that included friends of the Peer Research Advisors.

We decided to offer the job at a higher rate of pay than regular student jobs. We wanted to create a program with prestige that, as word about it began to spread on campus, would be attractive to other students not only for the pay rate, but also for the honor of securing the position. Libraries with concerns about creating a program that requires a higher pay rate could increase the prestige of the program in other ways. For example, the Peer Research Advisors were featured in an article about the program that appeared in a library publication. Professional photographs of the Peer Research Advisors accompanied the article. The students were excited about this honor and about the extra copies we gave them to send to the "folks back home." The vice provost and director of libraries also invited the women in the program to attend the Sisterhood Dinner on campus, along with members of the Libraries Diversity Committee. Small efforts such as these make the students feel honored and highlight the program on campus. Also, we believe that the higher pay rate is not necessary to attract a pool of qualified candidates. When we advertised a different position at a lower pay rate, we were still able to attract a diverse group of students; many were friends of the Peer Research Advisors.

PEER RESEARCH ADVISOR RESPONSIBILITIES

A major challenge of the program is to balance our commitment to provide the students with a challenging learning experience and our need to accomplish the work of our department. The Peer Research Advisors program has been successful in reference service, instruction, and outreach. Reference service has been the most successful responsibility for the students. In this capacity, they work at the main reference desk computer answering patron questions with the assistance, as needed, of a librarian. This service is beneficial to the students because they can clearly see that they are making a significant contribution and feel proud of their work. Their nightly service at the reference desk makes them visible to many other students and thus accomplishes one of the important goals of the program. Finally, by being able to rely on the Peer Research Advisors, we have been able to expand our service to include virtual reference in the evening without having to add additional permanent staff.

We had initially planned for the Peer Research Advisors to spend an equal amount of time in reference and in instruction-related activities. We envisioned the students assisting librarians in course-related instruction, especially in classes with a large number of freshmen or in large classes. We found this responsibility to be less productive because it was difficult for the students to fit the occasional instruction commitment into their busy schedules. One area of instruction where Peer Research Advisors are really able to contribute is with library tours. The Peer Research Advisors feel very knowledgeable about the content of the tour instruction, and we think that they have more credibility with undergraduates than the librarians.

The Peer Research Advisors also successfully participate in some of our outreach activities. They help staff the libraries' display at various information fairs. Having the Peer Research Advisors at our display helps to convey the message that the libraries value diversity in our staff and prospective students can't help but be attracted to the enthusiastic students at the display. In the third semester of the program, we are expanding the outreach responsibilities of the Peer Research Advisors by pairing them with a librarian to do presentations to campus groups. The reference librarian for Business and Management was very enthusiastic when we paired her with the Peer Research Advisor who is a graduating senior in the College of Management. After the presentation, the librarian complimented the student's performance and expressed regret that she hadn't asked the student to work with her earlier in the year.

ROLE CLARIFICATION

Winston and Downing emphasized the need to clarify the role of the Peer Research Advisors. This article stressed the importance of communicating with staff about what the students were supposed to be doing and how they were going to contribute to the work of the department and to also communicate with the students about the limits of their jobs. The Peer Research Advisors are highly motivated, intelligent students who, like many undergraduates, feel that they understand more about the complexities of research than they actually do. To address this issue, we prepared a handout for reference staff describing the goals of the program and suggesting ways to work productively with the students. Rather than simply talking to the students during training, we included a written clarification of their role in their initial expectations document. We provide expectations documents for all student employees in our department that clearly outline the expectations for their position, as well as how and where to take breaks, how to notify a supervisor of illness, etc. We adopted simple, concrete strategies, such as instructing the students to sit at the main computer alongside a librarian—thus making sure that they were never too far away from someone who had the experience to intervene and take over an advanced question. In the future, we would like to partner the Peer Research Advisors with one librarian with whom they can work on a regular basis. We think this would provide an opportunity for better teamwork between Peer Research Advisors and librarians, as well as an ideal opportunity for mentoring.

TRAINING

In addition to skill training, we scheduled a number of "show and tell" sessions to expose the Peer Research Advisors to the exciting work that librarians are doing outside the Research and Information Services department. Some examples of particularly successful sessions were a tour of the Digital Media Lab where patrons use scanning and usability equipment, a tour of Special Collections and University Archives, and a demo of the new electronic music course reserves service. The students were very enthusiastic about these sessions.

TIME COMMITMENT

The Peer Research Advisors program required a significant time commitment on the part of the librarians coordinating the program. The librarian for Instruction and Undergraduate

Research and the assistant head of Research and Information Services shared the responsibility. For hiring, training, and supervision of the program, the cost in staff time was about 10 hours per week for only three students. Introducing students to the library culture and making the job rewarding significantly increased the amount of time the coordinators spent on the program.

ASSESSMENT

Megan Oakleaf, librarian for Instruction and Undergraduate Research, and Amy VanScoy, Assistant Head of Resources, completed an assessment of the program in August 2003. Assessment of the Peer Research Advisors program really began with the initial proposal. We had several clearly articulated goals that we were then able to assess at the end of the first year. Knowing that assessment was critical, we collected statistics during recruiting. We also gave the Peer Research Advisors a pretest on their first day of work and a posttest at the end of their first semester that attempted to measure basic information literacy concepts. The posttest also included the questions that assessed their attitudes about librarianship and their willingness to consider a career in librarianship.

The following information is excerpted from the complete assessment. It summarizes the kind of assessment we did and what our conclusions were.

1. *To present a welcoming and diverse face of library public services to students.* We were able to recruit and hire a diverse group of students. The addition of the Peer Research Advisors increased the overall diversity of the reference staff, especially during the evening hours when many undergraduates use the library. The program also gives nonminority students an opportunity to see their minority peers in leadership positions.

2. *To develop the Peer Research Advisors' information literacy skills and contribute to their academic success.* Our posttest revealed growth in students' understanding of the research process, additional understanding of complex search strategies, and increased ability to evaluate information sources. Although we did not complete a formalized assessment to document increased academic success, anecdotal student comments show that we are meeting this outcome. For example, the Peer Research Advisors use reference services for their own research when not on duty. Two students reported that their grades improved during the semesters they worked as Peer Research Advisors. Two students also credited their experiences as Peer Research Advisors with inspiring them to do background research on companies to prepare for their interviews.

3. *To enhance the ability of undergraduates to use the library effectively.* While we did not complete formal assessment in this area, we did observe that undergraduates approach the Peer Research Advisors for help and return to them again and again. Future plans for the program include a formal evaluation of Peer Research Advisors' performance. From such a measure, we can infer that the transfer of skills to other undergraduates takes place.

4. *To recruit young diverse people into librarianship.* At the beginning of the program, all of the students were sophomores or juniors and said that they already had definite career plans and would not consider changing them. Still, we wanted to gauge whether or not a Peer Research Advisors program could influence an undecided student to consider librarianship and whether working as a Peer Research Advisor would help students to have a more accurate view of librarianship. To gauge their perceptions of librarianship as a career, Peer Research Advisors were asked two open-ended questions regarding (1) their impressions of librarians and (2) what might convince an undergraduate to pursue librarianship as a career.

In response to the question "Has your impression of the work that librarians do changed after working as a Peer Research Advisor," the qualitative data included the following comments:

> I really didn't understand how in depth the research process was. There are many aspects that a librarian, especially an NC State librarian, must know and understand in order to aid a patron in the research process.

> I definitely have gained respect and admiration for librarians, the amount of work they do, and [their] levels of education.

In response to the question "What might be most likely to convince an undergraduate student to pursue librarianship as a career," the qualitative data included the following comments:

> $ Texas! [Big money.] Other than that, I would probably enjoy being a librarian and wouldn't need much convincing.

> I believe that since the job allows you to help others, it would make them want to take on the job as a profession.

> First, the working environment was excellent. I thoroughly enjoyed my co-workers. Second, the technical aspect of the library is quite amazing.

These responses indicate that a program connecting Peer Research Advisors with recruiting opportunities could be very powerful.

What We Learned through the Process

1. It is important to get to know your campus community's diversity players. Although we were unable to apply for the campus money, the close relationship we forged with the University Diversity Advisory Committee and the Office for Diversity and African American Affairs helped the university's administration to see the libraries as partners in fostering diversity. The rules for eligibility for diversity funding were subsequently revised so that a unit no longer must be a college to submit a competitive project.
2. Although an individual or committee may be a diversity leader in your organization, diversity is everyone's responsibility. Decentralizing the responsibility for diversity helps to develop leadership skills across the library, in both the professional and support staff ranks. Although it was

a struggle to move forward without a diversity librarian, ultimately it was a very good thing for our organization because diversity could not be viewed as one person's responsibility.

3. Create a vision for diversity in your organization and understand your priorities. This will help you to be prepared when an unexpected opportunity comes your way.
4. Understand how diversity relates to your library's mission, goals, and strategic plan. You will be able to make a much stronger case for a project that you wish to undertake. Our ability to make a compelling case for the Peer Research Advisors program inspired the libraries' administration to provide the funding for the first year's program.
5. It is also becoming clear that one of the Diversity Committee's most important roles is to function as the research and development unit for diversity in the libraries, i.e., to serve as an incubator for diversity initiatives. The committee creates the conceptual framework for the initiative and develops the idea, laying the groundwork for implementation by identifying key stakeholders and garnering financial and administrative support. When the initiative is ready for implementation, it then becomes the responsibility of the implementing unit. This is the model we used to launch the Peer Research Advisors program and it has worked quite well. The Research and Information Services department now manages the program on its own.

CONCLUSION

Our experience launching the Peer Research Advisors program at North Carolina State University has been rich and exhilarating. Through commitment to our diversity goals and the creative use of available resources such as staff time, we have been able to make a measurable impact even with a relatively modest budget.

BIBLIOGRAPHY

Deese-Roberts, Susan, and Kathleen Keating. 2000. "Integrating a Library Strategies Peer Tutoring Program [at the University of New Mexico]." *Research Strategies* 17 (2/3): 223–229.

Holland, Maurita Peterson, and Christina Kelleher Powell. 1996. "Two Goals, One Course: Using Library School Students as Research Mentors [collaborative effort involving the School of Information, the College of Engineering, and the Engineering Library at the University of Michigan]." *Research Strategies* 14 (fall): 196–204.

Jones, Philip J., Vijith M. Varghese, and Janet H. Parsch. 2004. "Graduate Assistants at the University of Arkansas Libraries: Past, Future, and Significance, Part I." *Arkansas Libraries* 61 (4): 6–10.

Kathman, Jane McGurn, and Michael D. Kathman. 1998. "What Difference Does Diversity Make in Managing Student Employees?" *College and Research Libraries* 59 (4): 378–389.

Ronan, Jana, and Mimi Pappas. 2001. "Library Instruction Is a Two-Way Street: Students Receiving Course Credit for Peer Teaching [at the University of Florida]." *Education Libraries* 25 (1): 19–24.

Stelling, Prue. 1996. "Student to Student: Training Peer Advisors to Provide BI [at Binghamton University Library for a required course in the School of Education and Human Development]." *Research Strategies* 14 (winter): 50–55.

Winston, Mark, and Karen Downing. 1998. "Helping Students of Color Succeed: Implementing and Managing a Peer Information Counseling Program." *Leading Ideas* 3. Available: http://www.arl.org/diversity/leading/issue3/pic.html.

15 SPECIAL COLLECTIONS AS AN INTEGRAL PART OF A LIBRARY'S DIVERSITY INITIATIVE

by Tomaro I. Taylor and Lorel K. Reinstrom

INTRODUCTION

Library initiatives often reflect trends in administrative services to the patron community. Over the past twenty years or so, diversity and diversity-related issues have become primary focal points for libraries as collections, services, programming, and staffing are enhanced to provide support for the interests and needs of a rapidly changing user community. In the academic setting, libraries have witnessed not only diversification of student, staff, and faculty bodies but also changes in areas of study and scholarly research. As a result, academic libraries are utilizing varied means to guide and strengthen the diversity initiatives that they have established. One such way is in the recognition of special collections departments as elemental in supporting and cultivating library diversity initiatives.

Special collections departments can play a unique role in the advancement and reinforcement of library diversity initiatives by identifying institutional and community needs, developing collections that support those needs, and providing access to said collections. The department can be positioned at the forefront of its parent institution's diversity mission, goals, and activities through active collection development that emphasizes the acquisition of new diverse archival records and by selecting and utilizing resources available within the department to highlight diverse collections. The University of South Florida (USF) Tampa Library's Special Collections department has been able to foster the diversity-related efforts of the Tampa Library and its overarching institution (the University of South Florida) by providing access to collections that serve both historic and cultural research needs. Holdings, of which are comprised archival, book, and ephemeral collections of both regional and national prominence, not only provide insight into the lives of people, places, and organizations, but also provide ties to and for library, university, and community constituencies. In effect, the special collections department facilitates outreach, providing the resources needed to connect the library to its community and institutional affiliates. In this regard, special collections is a bridge that links a library's diversity initiatives with the resources needed for successful actuation and realization of diversity goals. By developing, building, processing, promoting, and maintaining diverse and diversity-related collections, special collections will lead the library's commitment to diversity in ways unparalleled by other departments and collections.

CULTIVATING COMMUNITY TIES THROUGH COLLECTION DEVELOPMENT

Collection development in special collections is not unlike collection development in other areas of a library: librarians must be knowledgeable about the subject area in which they collect and must know how to identify, select, and acquire pertinent resources. In established special collections departments, librarians and departmental heads may choose to acquire newly identified collections based on their ability to augment or "complete" particular collecting areas. Special collections' holdings also may consist of unsolicited donations that have been assessed for their potential value to the department. Whether collections and resources are acquired through purchase, active procurement, or gift, it is necessary for a special collections department to have a good collection development policy—one that clearly identifies the department's mission, goals, and target collecting areas—to aid in the process of selection. A collection development policy will guide the department in establishing parameters and developing means for expanded focal points and areas of interest. In the case of the Tampa Library's special collections, we refer to the library's mission statement and strategic plan to craft our collection development policy. The "Tampa Library Mission" imparts a significant amount of responsibility to Special Collections, as one of the primary goals of the Tampa Library is "to identify, acquire, preserve, and provide access to rare and unique research materials of cultural and historic significance." In accordance, "The University of South Florida Libraries Strategic Plan, 2002–2007" lists, as a major objective, the enhancement of "access to and use of special collections as resources of national distinction." By including these statements in the library's administrative documents, special collections is recognized as an important component for reaching the goals outlined by the Tampa Library and the USF Libraries System. As the library pursues new collections and increasingly processes materials of all types, there also will be continuous growth of diverse resources and, as a result, increased support to aid the library in this direction. Because the department has a pivotal role in the library's successfulness of accomplishing strategic goals, so too will special collections have a significant part in other areas of concern affecting patrons, university faculty and staff, and the community. This is critical in terms of diversity issues, as special collections departments establish institutional and community liaisons, identify hidden collections, and process and ensure the accessibility of resources. By upholding specific library initiatives, especially in regard to diversity, special collections departments will demonstrate their commitment to institutional endeavors and thereby garner support for their efforts.

The USF Tampa Library Special Collections "Collection Development Policy"* states as its mission to "focus its resources in areas where there is a reasonable expectation of being able to develop collections of excellence." In accordance, the department has a strong emphasis on Floridiana—manuscript collections, books, and ephemera with a primary focus on Florida. Of particular interest to the department are collections related to the historical development of Tampa's cultural past. Over time, the department has secured the organizational records of five prominent fraternal clubs founded at the turn of the twentieth century in Tampa's Ybor City—a multiethnic enclave that drew large numbers of immigrants to its folds with the lure of business prospects. The records of the Centro Asturiano (Spanish), Circulo Cubano (Cuban), L'Unione Italiana (Italian), Martí-Maceo (Afro-Cuban), and Centro

---

*A copy of the "University of South Florida Tampa Library Collection Development Policy: Special Collections Department—Tampa Campus Library" may be obtained from the library, 4202 E. Fowler Avenue, LIB122, Tampa, FL 33620-5400.

Español (Spanish) document the social and recreational activities of some of the more visible communities that established Ybor City. These collections provide insight into the cultural and ethnic history of Ybor City, illustrating the social, educational, and commercial needs of each population and the roles they had in the development of Tampa Bay society. To have overlooked collections of such importance would have been a great disservice to researchers, as the history of a people and their community may have been lost. But, by having an understanding of its community, and the roots that make up its present-day composition, the USF Special Collections is able to provide the resources needed for local research and analysis. The department also is able to connect to its community in a real, tangible way that helps build ties and create linkages with numerous people and organizations. Due to our efforts, we have sound contacts within the community who value and respect our endeavors.

Another important aspect of collection development, establishing community contacts, would be difficult if a special collections department did not have a solid history of collecting community records. Therefore, special collections departments must recognize the importance of collecting resources from within their local constituencies, as the USF Tampa Library has done. Ronald L. Becker makes an excellent point when he states: "Since archivists themselves are not a particularly diverse group, most repositories which try to document diversity within a region must therefore rely on special contacts within the communities" (Becker 1996, 41). In doing this, special collections can facilitate the development of relationships so necessary to attract potential donors in targeted areas. This is especially critical when working with diverse communities, as their archival records may not have been courted as much as other records for donation. With underdocumented groups, becoming a recognizable presence in the community boosts relationships, the potential for collaborative projects, and the assurance that donated materials will be in good hands.

There are many ways to build affiliations and encourage potential donations from targeted communities. One such way is to take an active role in the community by participating in or sponsoring events relative to the collecting goals of the department. In March 2004, the USF Tampa Library Special Collections erected an oversized display of photographs, membership ledgers, and other ephemera from the "Centro Asturiano Collection" as part of a reading and discussion of Nilo Cruz's *Anna in the Tropics*, which was held at the Centro Asturiano mutual aid society. The manned display highlighted the society's history and club activities, drawing numerous onlookers and giving us the opportunity to talk about our collections and the types of resources we have available. Even though most of our visitors wandered over to the display out of sheer curiosity, we were able to engage program attendees with an interesting and informative look into our special collections. Many visitors remarked that they didn't know that societal records had been preserved or that the documents and related materials could be used by the public; others either wanted to use the collection or donate more toward it. Publicizing our collection of Centro Asturiano materials not only generated interest in our archival holdings, it also acknowledged our investment in the historical records of diverse and underdocumented groups. Participating in this event demonstrated the department's pride in collecting, preserving, and maintaining the archival materials of one diverse community, thereby showing our commitment to all communities. With this project, we strengthened our ability to create community ties and reach out to historically underdocumented groups. Since our department makes it a priority to acquire and have available for use the community records of diverse groups, presenting some of these materials in an easily accessible format allowed us to spread the word of our endeavors to the greater community. As such, community liaisons and organizations, such as religious groups, fraternal societies, and local businesses, become cognizant of our efforts and are then able to provide us with leads and initial contacts to people and associations in targeted collecting areas. By making ourselves and our work known to diverse populations, we are able to "establish rapport and trust, two elements that are generally crucial to fostering good donor relations" (Neal 2002, 40).

There are many ways for special collections departments to cultivate relationships. Since it is especially important to identify and secure associates that are external to the organization—both departmentally and institutionally—units must find projects that support diversity missions and bring to the forefront collections identified as "diverse." Library outreach, whether through displays, brochures, presentations, or an easily locatable Web presence, demonstrates the department's commitment to building and maintaining diverse collections and reinforces the importance of special collections as a major player in library diversity initiatives. Just as we created a moveable display for a public event, so too have we designed exhibits for our own benefit and enjoyment. Musical scores performed by female artists were selected from the NationsBank African American Musical Heritage Collection and displayed in the library's main lobby during Women's History Month. A few months later, another lobby display featured photographs and ephemera from Ybor City mutual aid society collections. When special collections departments take action to promote and ensure access to diverse collections and archival materials, the community takes notice. Departmental support of the diversity-related goals promulgated by the library advance institutional missions and garner recognition for the contributions of special collections.

SUPPORTING LIBRARY DIVERSITY INITIATIVES THROUGH COLLECTIONS ACCESS

Processing, cataloguing, and creating finding aids for archival resources are important aspects of making collections access a priority and of providing tangible resources for outreach. Simply acquisitioning archival collections to increase the stature of an institution is not enough; collections must be acquired with the purpose of making them usable and useful. As part of the library, the special collections department must be active in maintaining collections that are of interest to researchers and that are viable for use. According to Becker, "Traditional collections should never sell themselves short as resources for developing and enhancing programs and services that recognize and respond to the diversity of their institutions. Nor should archivists allow institutional administrators or governing bodies to overlook the importance of archival collections as more and more universities issue diversity statements which elaborate affirmative action policies, advocate cultural and ethnic toleration among students, and propose plans for increasing diversity and fostering multiculturalism on campus but leave out references to the usefulness of special collections and archives in this effort" (Becker 1996, 46). The role of libraries, in the diversity initiatives of their overarching institutions, is critical as more and more support is needed to facilitate the research needs and interests of a diverse student, staff, and faculty body. And, as university communities nationwide are increasingly emphasizing the significance of diversity-related issues, it is time to recognize the important role that special collections can have in this realm.

To begin establishing the role of special collections departments relative to institutional diversity goals, there first must be an assessment of departmental holdings. By assessing special collections holdings, materials from typically underrepresented populations can be identified. Most important, librarians can cull backlogged collections for processing, evaluate the accessibility of previously processed collections, and make certain that all usable collections are highlighted so that communities are aware of their existence and research value potential. The USF Tampa Library Special Collections accomplished a similar endeavor by partnering with the Library's Diversity Committee to evaluate the department's diverse collections.

A small task force—members of the committee with significant representation from Special Collections (a librarian and a cataloguer)—devised a plan to "uncover" what were, in some cases, hidden collections. A graduate assistant compiled bibliographic research to determine what, when, and how similar projects had been undertaken. The librarian and cataloguer (the authors of this chapter) chose to assess collections related to their own personal interests—the papers of Tampa's Ybor City and West Tampa communities and African American people, businesses, and organizations. The project began with the identification of collections representative of the aforementioned research areas. We searched the library catalogue, perused Special Collections' shelves, and eventually enlisted the assistance of other librarians more knowledgeable than we. As our respective lists of collections grew, we were certain to discuss our progress with each other, as many collections overlapped the blanket categories we had created. For example, the "Papers of La Union Martí-Maceo" may be considered an "Ybor City" collection, because of the organization's establishment in the area, or an "African American" collection due to its ties to both the African American and Afro-Cuban communities. In this instance, we decided to include the collection as part of the "Ybor City" collections, which seemed a more relevant identifier than that of "African American."

Once we created comprehensive lists, we began sorting through the collections to determine the types of materials included therein. This was a significant part of the project, as many of the collections did not have abstracts or collection guides, nor had they been completely processed. We dove in, obviously interested in what the collections might yield, knowing how important our final product would be to the research community. For each of the identified collections, we drafted brief descriptions that included biographical or organizational information, provenance, and an overview of the types of items found in the collections (e.g., photographs, legal documents, correspondence, etc.). Brochures, which were created and made available to patrons visiting the Special Collections, later were converted into PDF format and made accessible through the Library's Diversity Committee Web pages. Emails were sent to the USF's departments of Africana Studies and Latin American and Caribbean Studies to inform faculty and staff of the availability of these collections. As more and more people become aware of our project, the department anticipates increased usage of these, and other, collections.

Looking beyond the department, even beyond the campus, we can conclude that our diverse collections assessment project has opened a gateway for researchers, ensuring availability and access to our collections and the overall recognition of their importance. By assuming a leadership role and our responsibility for making diverse collections a priority, this project enabled us to highlight diversity in the most effective and far-reaching methods possible. As Linda M. Matthews states, "We must find those things that make each of us distinctive—and promote those—and we must find the ties that bind us and weave those ever tighter" (Matthews 1996, 5).

CONCLUSION

Diversity initiatives play a significant role in the way many academic libraries operate in today's changing world. As patron needs change, and libraries adjust their services to reflect these changing needs, libraries must focus on those collections and resources that best serve the research interest of an ever-transforming population. Special collections materials often are comprised of resources that are both ethnically and culturally rich. Even though a wide range of diverse materials may be available in a special collections department, it does not mean that they are accessible, usable, or useful for the library community. Viable resources, whether new or established, often must be uncovered and identified to build and maintain a respected position in the diversity-related efforts of the institution. Therefore, it is necessary to ensure that diverse collections are targeted through both departmental and institutional objectives. How is this done? By making the acquisition of diverse collections a priority in the department's collection development policy and in the overarching library mission and strategic plan.

For a special collections department to become fully integrated into the administrative goals of its parent organization, it takes the perseverance and foresight of all involved; although a somewhat daunting challenge, it is an effort worthy of undertaking for departments, their libraries and institutions, and user communities. H. Thomas Hickerson states that "We should always be striving to document the under-documented. The spectrum of human experience and human interest is always expanding, and we have a responsibility to be inclusive within the range of our institutional mandates" (Hickerson 2001, 12). And, when our "institutional mandates" advance the inclusion of archival resources as significant to and necessary for meeting and surpassing established diversity initiatives, special collections are at the forefront to help lead the way.

BIBLIOGRAPHY

Becker, Ronald L. 1996. "Diversity and Traditional Collections at Rutgers University." *Provenance* 14: 37–47.

Hickerson, H. Thomas. 2001. "Ten Challenges for the Archival Community." *The American Archivist* 64, no. 6 (spring–summer): 6–16.

Matthews, Linda M. 1996. "Archives at the Millennium: Diversity, Community, and the World of Learning." *Provenance* 14, 1: 1–13.

Neal, Kathryn M. 2002. "Cultivating Diversity: The Donor Connection." *Collection Management* 27, no. 2: 33–42.

"Tampa Library Mission." 2002. Tampa: University of South Florida Libraries (January 2005). Available: www.lib.usf.edu/admin/mission/.

"University of South Florida Libraries Strategic Plan, 2002–2007." 2004. Tampa: University of South Florida Libraries (January 2005). Available: web.lib.usf.edu/usflibraries/admindocs/SP2002-07v4.pdf.

"University of South Florida Tampa Library Collection Development Policy: Special Collections Department—Tampa Campus Library." 2005. Tampa: University of South Florida Tampa Library Special Collections Department.

16 THE PAST IS NEVER DEAD. IT'S NOT EVEN PAST: THE ROLE OF THE DEPARTMENT OF ARCHIVES AND SPECIAL COLLECTIONS DURING THE "OPEN DOORS" COMMEMORATION OF THE FORTIETH ANNIVERSARY OF INTEGRATION AT THE UNIVERSITY OF MISSISSIPPI

by Jennifer Aronson and Jennifer Ford

INTRODUCTION

William Faulkner's memorable character Gavin Stevens in the novel *Requiem for a Nun* came to the conclusion that past events directly affect our present. Slavery, violence, and prejudice lay at the heart of Mississippi's difficult and troubled past. During the 2002–2003 academic year, the University of Mississippi directly confronted this legacy by commemorating the fortieth anniversary of its integration. University Chancellor Robert Khayat stated just prior to the anniversary, "We thought it was time to step forward about the realities of the past, and the realities of the future" (Haygood 2002, F01). The

University of Mississippi's Department of Archives and Special Collections involvement in this yearlong examination of its past and celebration of its progress had significant impact on the department including the growth of our civil rights collections, an increased interest and awareness in the department for the subject, a larger involvement with both the university and local communities, and the addition of new audiences for our research materials.

BACKGROUND

The segregation of Mississippi's system of higher education came to an end on the morning of October 1, 1962, when James Howard Meredith, a twenty-nine-year-old Air Force veteran and former student of Jackson State University, enrolled at the University of Mississippi. Meredith's enrollment ended over 100 years of segregation, but his triumph came only after years of preparation and a protracted court battle. The events surrounding the university's integration led to what *Time* magazine called "the gravest conflict between federal and state authority since the Civil War" (*Time* 1962, 15) and left the University of Mississippi with a legacy of violence and bigotry.

Resistance to change prompted a riot on the University of Mississippi campus the night of September 30, 1962, after Meredith arrived on campus. After several failed attempts to register Meredith, President John F. Kennedy ordered U.S. Marshals to escort Meredith to the University of Mississippi campus in preparation for his registration the next morning. Angry students, townspeople, and a large number of armed white supremacists from other

Figure 16-1. U.S. military troops surround the Lafayette County Court House, 1962. (Russell Barrett Collection, University of Mississippi Archives and Special Collections.)

states began to assemble at nightfall near the Lyceum, the oldest building on campus. President Kennedy called Federal Marshals, the federalized Mississippi National Guard, and other troops to restore order. The crowd attacked these troops surrounding the Lyceum with bricks, bottles, and lead pipes.

The night of violence ended with two men dead, 206 wounded marshals and soldiers, and over 200 arrested individuals. The morning brought scenes of burned cars, empty tear gas canisters, broken bricks, and the acrid smell of tear gas, but order had been restored and James Meredith began his first class at the University of Mississippi. The situation forced Meredith to bear such great loneliness and threats of physical violence that he wrote in *Look* magazine that "most of the time, I am perhaps the most segregated Negro in the world" (Meredith 1963, 70). After a year of unparalleled adversity, Meredith triumphed, receiving his BA degree from the university in August of 1963.

Since 1963, the University of Mississippi has become a stronger school due to the growth of a diverse student body. By the fortieth anniversary, nearly 13 percent of the university's students were African American (Joiner 2002). In 2002, when the University of Mississippi's School of Business Administration honored Meredith's son Joseph as its top graduate student, Dr. Meredith told television reporters that "It's the vindication of my life, my entire life" (Brumfield, July 24, 2002). The African American student and faculty population continues to grow at the University of Mississippi. The growth of all minority groups has fostered a vital university community.

In March 1997, James Meredith donated his collection to the Department of Archives and Special Collections. This collection contains over 250 linear feet of personal correspondence, speech and book manuscripts, and publications, collections of political brochures, and pamphlets that collectively document Dr. Meredith's unique perspective of this historically significant period. Scholars from all over the world regularly consult these important papers.

OPEN DOORS: BUILDING ON FORTY YEARS OF OPPORTUNITY IN HIGHER EDUCATION

The University of Mississippi observed its integration on several past anniversaries, but it was not until the fortieth anniversary that the university planned a large commemoration. In the spring of 2002, two members of the university community, Dr. Gloria Kellum, the vice chancellor for University Relations, and Dr. Susan Glisson, the head of the William Winter Institute for Racial Reconciliation, conceived an event honoring Dr. Meredith and those who protected him. A university-wide committee overseeing the event decided to dedicate the entire 2002–2003 academic year "to the courage of Dr. James H. Meredith '63, and to all the University of Mississippi students, faculty, alumni, and staff who stood up for open doors and opportunity for all on this campus" (Open Doors: Forty Years of Opportunity). The yearlong commemoration, named "Open Doors: Building on 40 Years of Opportunity in Higher Education," focused not only on the integration, but also on the strides the university made during the forty years that followed. The committee's goals for the year were to candidly and forthrightly acknowledge the University of Mississippi's past, to emphasize how far it had come, and to focus on how it could positively shape its future.

Figure 16-2. James H. Meredith and University of Mississippi students. (Robert Jordan, 2002.)

The Open Doors commemoration was centered on the dates of September 30th and October 1st, the anniversary of the riot and Meredith's enrollment. The university invited everyone who had a role during those tumultuous days in 1962 to observe the anniversary. Events included classroom talks by several key players such as Constance Baker Motley, Meredith's chief council in his year-and-a-half court battle, and Charles Moore, a Blackstar photographer who shot photographs of the riot for *Life* magazine, a commendation ceremony to honor National Guard, U.S. Army personnel, marshals, and other federal troops involved in the riot and aftermath, and a community dinner and a symbolic walk through the Lyceum. Mrs. Myrlie Evers-Williams, the wife of slain civil rights activist Medgar Evers, gave a speech in honor of James Meredith in front of a crowd of 2,000 people. Throughout the events, students and faculty recorded oral histories with many of the invited guests. James Meredith and his family were guests of honor during the two days.

The university continued to commemorate the anniversary throughout the year. The Open Doors Committee created brochures with self-guided tours of sites associated with the university's integration. The Department of Archives and Special Collections and the University Museums held several exhibitions focusing on civil rights and the integration. The History Department, Center for the Study of Southern Culture, and the William Winter Institute for Racial Reconciliation held several symposia including "Race and Sport: The Struggle for Equality On and Off the Field" and the first annual International Conference on Race, bringing national and international figures to campus.

The Department of Archives and Special Collections became involved early in the planning process. The university invited Special Collections Librarian Jennifer Ford to be a member of the organizational committee. The department was involved in several important aspects of the commemoration including helping extensively with the collection of donations, the creation and organization of the oral history collection, and producing several exhibitions.

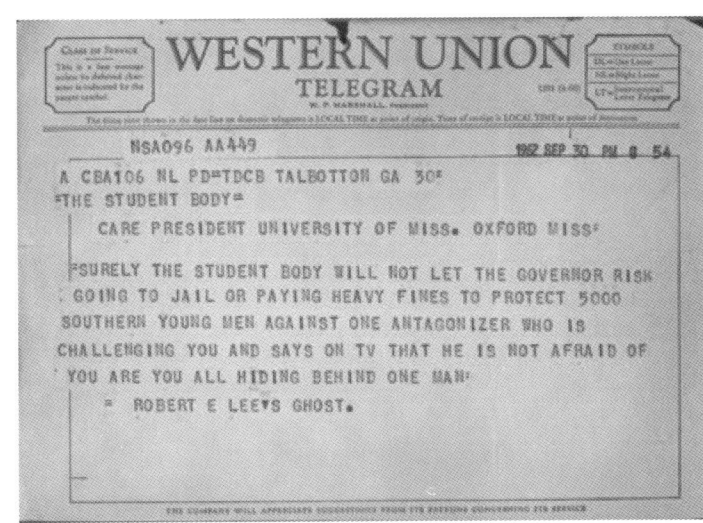

Figure 16-3. "Ghost of Robert E. Lee" telegram, 1962. (Thomas Cleveland Collection, University of Mississippi Archives and Special Collections.)

DONATIONS

The anniversary celebration provided the Department of Archives and Special Collections an excellent opportunity to seek donations of materials relating to the integration. Working with Special Collections, the Public Relations Department issued an appeal for donations in national and state newspapers, on radio programs, in printed publications, and on the Web site (http://www.olemiss.edu/opendoors):

> In commemoration of the 40th anniversary of the integration of the University of Mississippi, both Archives & Special Collections in the J. D. Williams Library and University Museums are calling all those who preserved historical materials relating to the 1962 integration to consider donating their materials to the University. Items such as letters, photographs, films, artifacts and oral histories relating to the integration and riot, will be valuable additions to the collections of the Museums and Special Collections. Please help us add to our lasting archive of this momentous event. Items will be considered for donation throughout this memorial year. Exhibitions are planned through the year to which these artifacts will be helpful.

During the events in September and October, several department members met directly with participants to accept donations. Many of those who returned for the commemoration had not seen the university campus in forty years. Understandably, some of these participants still perceived the university and Mississippi in a negative light. Through meeting directly with department staff, many changed their minds and were willing to donate their collections to the University of Mississippi. Other donors were unaware of the historical value of items they had saved. By talking directly with Special Collections staff members, participants were able to realize that their memorabilia would be an important resource for scholarship. Dr. Susan Glisson noted (April 21, 2004) this dynamic between the Special Collections staff and Open Doors participants: "The involvement of Special Collections was vital to the success of the Open Doors initiative. Its staff understood the significance of collection of the University's history and helped to make the donation process smooth, and I'm sure provided a level of comfort to potential donors that inspired some who would not have given items to them." The call for memorabilia resulted in a flood of donations to the archive including letters, photographs, film footage, broadsides, newspaper clippings, personal diaries, and even a tear gas canister.

In 1962, Second Lieutenant Henry Gallagher was a recent college graduate from Minnesota and a platoon leader with the U.S. Army 716th Military Police Battalion, then stationed at Fort Dix, New Jersey. In the early hours of Sunday, September 30th, his battalion flew to the U.S. Naval Air Station at Millington, Tennessee. Later that evening Gallagher rode in the lead vehicle escorting the battalion by convoy from Millington to Oxford, Mississippi, on the night of the riot. From October 1 through November, Gallagher served as the officer in charge of Meredith's security detail. He would return to Oxford for further duty on March 15th until May 8, 1963.

Gallagher's unit, nicknamed "the peanut patrol," had the difficult task of protecting James Meredith at all times. Due to his desire for a normal student life, Meredith asked these men to remain discrete. Gallagher developed a series of codes based on a numbered campus map he received on his first day. His unit used these codes when communicating by radio in an attempt to thwart anyone who might be listening and monitoring their movements. Gallagher donated his entire collection when he attended the anniversary events, including the codebooks, notes from the night of his arrival, photographs, and film footage. Gallagher's collection filled a void in Special Collections, as it provides the most in-depth glimpse into the day-to-day life of James Meredith on the university campus.

Figure 16-4. University of Mississippi Chancellor Robert Khayat, Jennifer Ford, Special Collections Librarian, and Henry Gallagher pose with items Gallagher donated to the University. (Robert Jordan, 2002.)

Dr. Thomas Cleveland, the president of the University of Mississippi's Associated Student Body during the 1963–1964 academic year, donated the correspondence he and his predecessor, Richard Wilson, received after Meredith enrolled at the university. The letters and their enclosures represent a wide variety of both positive and negative opinions from all over the nation. Of particular note are the numerous petitions sent to Ole Miss students by faculty and students from other universities.

Reverend Wofford K. Smith was the Episcopal chaplain of the University of Mississippi in 1962. Both Smith and Duncan M. Gray, Jr., the minister of St. Peter's Episcopal Church, attempted to pacify the violent crowd on the night of the riot. Their continued efforts supporting integration caused a backlash against Episcopalian events on campus and in Oxford. This collection contains many racially charged materials including angry letters and vandalized posters. The brutality of many of the pieces within the collection offer the scholar an extraordinary view into the Mississippi segregationist culture of the 1960s.

The publicity the archive received from the University Public Relations Department and the national media during the commemoration proved invaluable. Most donors gave materials to the department during the anniversary year, but people continue to contact the archive and present materials. During the summer of 2004, W. Wert Cooper, Jr., who was a senior majoring in commerce at the University of Mississippi when James Meredith enrolled at the University of Mississippi, donated a series of photographs of Oxford and the campus during the events surrounding Meredith's enrollment. Mr. Cooper donated his collection after he heard about the Open Doors Commemoration, and decided, rather than keeping the photographs, he would donate them so others could use them for research.

The gifts strengthened the archive and provided researchers with new materials for research. The result of reaching out to donors from different segments of the community was an influx of primary source materials coming into the department from former students, retired soldiers and marshals, African Americans from the community and state, Mississippians, and

Figure 16-5. Road blockade, 1962. (W. Wert Cooper, Jr. Collection, University of Mississippi Archives and Special Collections.)

reporters from all over the country. These new collections provide a variety of perspectives into the events that took place on campus. Until this point the civil rights–related collections focused on either university professors or James Meredith himself.

ORAL HISTORIES

Early in the planning stage, the Open Doors Committee decided that it was important to record oral histories with those involved in the riot and Meredith's integration. The yearlong commemoration provided access to many of those involved. It was important to record these histories because many of the participants were becoming older and the opportunity would not arise again.

A small group overseen by Dr. Glisson and Dr. Charles Wilson, director of the Center for the Study of Southern Culture, that included both Jennifer Aronson and Jennifer Ford, helped organize the oral history project. The group created a list of people it wanted to interview and sent out invitations. The group scheduled oral history recordings in several locations during the anniversary commemoration on campus. Working with the legal department, the subcommittee drew up an agreement that would allow the university to publish and use the oral histories for research and future projects.

Students and faculty members from the Department of History, the Center for the Study of Southern Culture, and the English Department volunteered to interview participants. The committee matched volunteers with the appropriate subjects. Each interviewer received biographies of the participants, a history of Meredith's admission to the University of Mississippi written by Dr. David Sansing, professor emeritus of history, and a list of suggested questions. The committee agreed to deposit the completed histories, recorded on MiniDV and audiocassette, in the Department of Archives and Special Collections.

The Open Doors Oral History Collection currently contains sixty-five interviews. Although the group recorded most of the interviews in September and October 2002, the William Winter Institute for Racial Reconciliation scheduled several other sessions and continues to record histories. The oral history participants include 1962 alumni who were active in student government, alumni who worked on the student newspaper *The Daily Mississippian*, Pan-Hellenic members, members of the student Hall of Fame, former National Guardsmen and military personnel, townspeople, attorneys, and government officials.

Like the other donations that Special Collections received, these oral histories provide a priceless resource to researchers. Although some of the histories record well-known figures in the Civil Rights Movement such as the U.S. Assistant District Attorney in 1962, Nicholas D. Katzenbach, and U.S. District Court Judge Constance Baker Motley, Meredith's chief council and a member of the NAACP's Legal Defense Fund, most of the collection captures the stories of everyday citizens who happened to be involved in an extraordinary event. The effect of the 1962 events on these varied groups of people had been previously ignored in history.

The committee also invited many of these unknown heroes to the university. Many had never returned to Oxford because of painful memories. Volunteers interviewed dozens of the more than 30,000 soldiers and marshals who risked their lives. These military personnel were finally honored and received a key to the city to acknowledge their role in the integration. Many of these personnel discuss in their oral histories the fact that they had not returned to Oxford until invited to attend these events. Some of them also talk about how they never or rarely talked about their involvement in such a critical moment in the movement. It is likely that some of these histories would have been lost if the project had not been organized.

Harold M. Antwine, Jr., who was a married Ole Miss student and a member of the Mississippi National Guard, remembers in his interview being awoken at 2:30 in the morning, as he was being federalized by the U.S. government. Antwine had mixed emotions about the event. Antwine soon changed his opinion when he realized "we were the invasion force. After I got hit by a few bricks, I started to take it personal and I changed my attitude and I was a federal soldier" (Grayson 2002).

The department has organized the oral histories and created a finding guide for the collection that is available on the Web. Researchers can view DVD copies made of each interview. The department hopes to put digital versions of some of the interviews on the Web and to transcribe many in the near future. The university, through a collaborative project between the William Winter Institute for Racial Reconciliation, Media Productions, and the Department of Archives and Special Collections, plans to create a film to distribute to elementary and high school students using the oral histories and materials from newly donated collections.

EXHIBITIONS

During the summer of 2002, the Department of Archives and Special Collections began planning a coordinated effort to document the anniversary with exhibitions in the library and around campus. The department decided to present three exhibits, each created by a different staff member, that highlighted the department's civil rights collections. Special Collections made the decision not to place its primary focus on materials from the James H. Meredith Collection because items from his collection were on permanent display in its exhibition space. The objective was to emphasize lesser-known collections that contained important civil rights materials unfamiliar to researchers. In addition to the physical exhibitions, the staff created Web sites to increase awareness and to allow greater access to these materials.

In the first exhibit of the series, "Civil Rights, Mississippi, and the Novelist's Craft," Library Specialist Leigh McWhite featured items found in the Special Collections' rare book and manuscript collections. The display showcased authors who used real life or fictional events surrounding the Mississippi Civil Rights Movement. Several of the authors' novels used the infamous murders of Emmett Till, Medgar Evers, and Freedom Summer workers Michael Schwerner, James Chaney, and Andrew Goodman as the subject matter. The exhibition highlighted both well-known authors such as Eudora Welty and John Grisham and some lesser-known authors through the use of first-edition novels, manuscripts, and uncorrected galleys.

The second exhibition focused on the department's photography collections. Jennifer Aronson, curator of Visual Collections, assembled a series of photographs from three different collections offering viewers a glimpse of the Mississippi school system before integration. The exhibit "Segregation Through the Lens: African American Schools in Mississippi" included several different collections, such as the images of historically African American Mississippi institutions Piney Woods Country Life School and the Mississippi Industrial College, but the John E. Phay Collection served as the primary focus.

John E. Phay shot the exhibited photographs as part of studies and surveys conducted by the Bureau of Educational Research at the University of Mississippi. These photographs, taken of every African American school in thirteen counties in Mississippi, provide a stark view of what the state of Mississippi considered a "separate but equal" school system. The images of impressive buildings and well-dressed students found in the Piney Woods Country Life School and the Mississippi Industrial College collections, both private institutions, sharply contrast the Phay images. The great interest expressed by visitors and researchers

Figure 16-6. Jackson's Chapel School, Grenada County, Mississippi, April, 1955. (John E. Phay Collection, University of Mississippi Archives and Special Collections.)

who viewed the exhibit led to the completion of the processing of the Phay collection as well as additional exhibitions and presentations. The online exhibition brought and continues to bring many inquiries from researchers.

The final exhibition, "We Can Not Walk Alone," devoted to the experiences and family histories of Lafayette County's African American community, proved to be the most challenging exhibit up to that point due to the many individuals involved, but it served as an invaluable experience into community outreach. In 1993, Mrs. Susie Marshall, a longtime resident of Oxford, Mississippi, received a Mississippi Humanities Council grant for her coordinated project "Changes in the African American Family in Oxford/Lafayette County and Mississippi." Sponsored by a local club, the Senior Sewing and Savings Club, the Oxford Development Association, and the Mississippi Humanities Council, the project consisted of three public presentations held in the spring of 1996.

From the success of these three presentations focusing on African American history, Mrs. Marshall and other members of the working group conceived the idea of chronicling the history of the African American community in Lafayette County. Several families wrote short family narratives and donated or loaned photographs. These narratives, written in the words of family members along with other community memories, form the nucleus of the materials. The collection also includes information about local African American businesses, clubs, churches, and events.

In 2002, the Department of Archives and Special Collections heard about this resource from Dr. Glisson, who had worked with Mrs. Marshall on several community projects. Ford thought an exhibit of the materials would work well as one of the three Open Doors exhibitions. Ford and Aronson met with Mrs. Marshall and Mrs. Niler Franklin to discuss working on a collaborative project. The group made an agreement allowing Special Collections to use pieces in an exhibit. In exchange for the loan, Special Collections organized and transcribed the written histories and created a finding aid for the collection. The organized collection will become the first collection housed at the African American Community Center in the historic Burns Methodist Church in Oxford, Mississippi. Special Collections, working

Figure 16-7. Class from the Del Mont Seminary, Oxford, Mississippi. Photographer Unknown, 1927. (Lafayette County African American Collection, University of Mississippi Archives and Special Collections.)

in partnership with the William Winter Institute, plans to publish a book of the exhibition to raise funds for the restoration of the building.

In addition to the exhibition and Web site, Ford and Aronson presented two talks about the collection during African History Month in February 2003. The first presentation, a brown bag lunch in Special Collections, attracted over seventy members of the university and the local African American community. After hearing about the presentation, several other local groups extended invitations to speak.

A departure from the standard permanent gift practice, Special Collections felt it was important to exhibit the loaned collection. These events allowed us to build our relationship with the local African American community, which in the past has been distrustful of the University of Mississippi because of its ugly history. It was also important to us to organize the collection, so that no matter where it was stored it would be preserved and accessible. The hope is that through the exhibition more local African American community members will donate either to our archive or to the community center.

OUTCOME

The University of Mississippi built a strong foundation within several communities during the Open Doors celebration. The events surrounding the commemoration were so successful that the University of Alabama used the events as a blueprint for its anniversary celebration "Opening Doors, Opening Minds."

The national publicity of the events surrounding the anniversary brought Special Collections free and welcome publicity. We used this notoriety to gather new donations and to publicize collections already in our possession. The positive publicity surrounding Open Doors undoubtedly contributed to many new additions. The events also allowed the University of Mississippi to create an excellent oral history collection that contains interviews with those who have been previously silent.

Another outcome of all these events was the strengthening of ties between Special Collections and other campus departments. We continued to work with the William Winter Institute on several projects, including the creation of a film about the Freedom Riders for elementary and high school students. Under the institute's direction, the staff also volunteered and gave presentations during a youth weekend held for students from Rome and Batesville, Mississippi, as part of the institute's community outreach. We have also worked extensively with University Relations on several other projects including helping with the celebration of the restoration and opening of the Oxford Depot. Dr. Gloria Kellum, vice-chancellor for University Relations, told the department in April 2004 that our "participation as a member of the planning committee was invaluable to the overall success of this historic occasion. The Open Doors celebration will be remembered as one of the landmark events in the life of our University, and you played a major role in its success" (Kellum 2004).

Special Collections realized its own importance as an educational tool for the university and state. During the Open Doors celebration it became clear that many of the students on campus did not know what had happened. Several professors attended the presentation the department had throughout the year or visited our exhibitions and expressed interest in having us present talks to students. After returning from the National Diversity in Libraries conference, Ford and Aronson presented several talks about their involvement in the Open Doors initiative to several graduate and undergraduate classes.

Besides focusing on university students and faculty, we have continued additional outreach projects. During the summers of 2003 and 2004, Special Collections worked with groups of students from the Sunflower County Freedom Project. Founded in 1998, the Freedom Project is a nonprofit organization dedicated to developing educational excellence among young children living in one of the poorest areas of the country. Students spend the summer at an intensive six-week program held at the University of Mississippi. In 2003, Special Collections gave a presentation to the group about Mississippi and the Civil Rights Movement. Due to the success of this presentation, Chris Meyers, director of the Freedom Project, approached us and asked if we could create a program to correspond with the group's documentary history class. Ford, with help from Aronson, created weekly lesson plans using primary source materials from the collections. Each week the group focused on the different periods surrounding the Civil War.

The Freedom Summer project was very labor intensive, but extremely rewarding for the department. It is unusual for a university archive to work with elementary school students, but our positive experiences during the Open Doors commemoration led us to believe in the importance of community outreach.

BIBLIOGRAPHY

Aronson, Jennifer. November 2002. "Segregation through the Lens: African American Schools before Integration." University: University of Mississippi, Department of Archives and Special Collections. Available: http://www.olemiss.edu/depts/general_library/files/archives/exhibits/civilrights/segregation/index.html.

Brumfield, Patsy R. July 24, 2002. "Events Set to Mark Integration Anniversary." University: University of Mississippi. Available: http://www.olemiss.edu/cgi-bin/news2000/display.pl?id=2653&mode=full.

Brumfield, Patsy R. September 27, 2002. "Integration Anniversary Draws Many to Campus." University: University of Mississippi. Available: http://www.olemiss.edu/cgi-bin/news2000/display.pl?id=2768&mode=full.

Doyle, William. 2001. *An American Insurrection: The Battle of Oxford, Mississippi*. New York: Doubleday.

Doyle, William. 2002. "Forgotten Soldiers of the Integration Fight." *The New York Times* (September 28): A17.

Ford, Jennifer, and Jennifer Aronson. 2003. "We Cannot Walk Alone: Images and History of the African American Community. Lafayette County, Mississippi." University: University of Mississippi, Department of Archives and Special Collections. Available: http://www.olemiss.edu/depts/general_library/files/archives/exhibits/civilrights/aa/index.htm.

Glisson, Susan. 2004. Email to Jennifer Aronson, April 22.

Grayson, April. 2002. Open Doors Oral History. Interview with Harold Antwine, Jr., September 30.

Halbfinger, David M. 2002. "40 Years after Infamy, Ole Miss Looks to Reflect and Heal." *The New York Times* (September 23): A1.

Haygood, Wil. 2002. "A Mississippi Odyssey: In 1962, James Meredith Gave Ole Miss a Crash Course in Civil Rights. Forty Years Later, the Lessons Continue." *The Washington Post* (September 29): F01.

Joiner, Lottie. 2002. "Ole Miss Reflects on Deadly Integration." *Crisis (The New)* 109, no. 6 (November/December): 10–11.

Kellum, Gloria. 2004. Email to Jennifer Ford, April.

McWhite, Leigh. 2002. "Civil Rights, Mississippi, and the Novelist's Craft." University: University of Mississippi, Department of Archives and Special Collections. Available: http://www.olemiss.edu/depts/general_library/files/archives/exhibits/civilrights/novelist/index.htm.

Meredith, James H. 1963. "I Can't Fight Alone." *Look* 19 (April): 70–78.

Moore, Angela. October 1, 2002. "Thousands Commemorate Anniversary of Integration." University: University of Mississippi. Available: http://www.olemiss.edu/cgi-bin/news2000/display.pl?id=2770&mode=full.

"Open Doors: Forty Years of Opportunity." 2002. University: University of Mississippi. Available: http://www.olemiss.edu/opendoors/.

Time. 1962. "The Edge of Violence." 80, no. 14 (October 5): 15–17.

17 THE HBCU LIBRARY ALLIANCE AND SOLINET: PARTNERS IN INCLUSION

by Loretta Parham, Janice R. Franklin, and Kate Nevins

INTRODUCTION

Historically black colleges and universities (HBCUs) evolved from a segregated South with a mission to educate newly freed slaves emancipated after the Civil War with the promise of equal opportunity under the law as Americans. In spite of struggles to survive, HBCUs have flourished, educating thousands of professionals who have made outstanding contributions to the growth and prosperity of their country. Today, HBCUs and the libraries that reside within their historic walls are considered American treasures. By executive order, the White House Initiative on HBCUs bestows special national recognition to these 103 institutions for their value in American society. The libraries of HBCUs have supported the mission and preserved the legacy of black achievement in a wealth of priceless collections. Realizing this rich heritage and the need to work together to strengthen and integrate libraries into teaching and learning activities on their campuses, 96 librarians representing 103 HBCUs met in Atlanta, Georgia, on October 28 and 29, 2002, to answer a call for cooperation at a historic HBCU Library Initiative conference. The conference sought to explore opportunities for collaboration and strategize about ways to increase advocacy for HBCU libraries.

THE CRY FOR UNITY

The idea for the initiative grew out of a meeting in 2001 of the board of directors of the Southeastern Library Network (SOLINET). SOLINET, a membership organization of more than 2,600 libraries, strengthens libraries and the communities they support through cooperation, leadership, and services. Serving on the SOLINET board at that time were directors of two HBCU libraries, Loretta O'Brien Parham (then at Hampton University, now at the Atlanta University Center) and Janice R. Franklin (at Alabama State University). Parham and Franklin were able to observe the work of SOLINET member libraries belonging to the Association of Southeastern Research Libraries (ASERL), and spoke about the need to develop a similar collaborative model to address issues pertinent to HBCU libraries. Further exploration revealed that the HBCU library directors and deans had never met as a body, had never convened to share ideas, talk, and network or laugh together, and were without a platform for advocacy. No existing organization or committee offered an agenda or venue on behalf of all of the libraries on the designated White House HBCU Initiative; not in the American Library Association (ALA), not in the Black Caucus of the ALA (BCALA), not in the National Association for Equal Opportunity in Higher Education (NAFEO), and not in the United Negro College Fund (UNCF). The "Association of 1890 Library Deans and Directors" represents eighteen land-grant HBCU institutions, but not the other eighty-five HBCU libraries. Upon closer examination, it was noted that 72 percent of the HBCUs are within the geographic region served by SOLINET (ten southeastern states and the Caribbean); many of the remaining HBCUs are in states contiguous to the Southeast. This reality was discussed during a retreat of the SOLINET board. What started out as an airing of mutual concerns took on a different focus, leading to the development of a strategic goal for the SOLINET board, to foster cooperation among libraries with diverse populations in HBCUs and the Caribbean. The SOLINET board and Kate Nevins, executive director, embraced the idea with enthusiasm.

As an initial step, SOLINET assigned staff to work on the HBCU initiative and established an electronic discussion forum for the HBCU library deans and directors. This dialogue, begun in November 2001, served to engage the HBCU library deans and directors along with the executive director of the Council on Libraries and Information Resources (CLIR). CLIR, along with SOLINET, provided financial support to plan and host the first meeting of HBCU library deans and directors. Eleven months later, the HBCU Library Initiative was formally born on Monday morning, October 28, 2002.

ANSWERING THE CALL

The goal to develop an action plan for collaboration led to the establishment of a steering committee that included HBCU librarians and SOLINET staff under the visionary leadership of the executive director, Kate Nevins. In addition to Nevins, Parham, and Franklin, other steering members included Elsie Stephens Weatherington (Virginia State University), Emma Bradford Perry (Southern University and A&M College), Tommy Holton (Dillard University), and Jennifer Bliss (HBCU project director at SOLINET). The decision was made to convene a meeting of library deans and directors from HBCUs in order to determine common opportunities and challenges that could be addressed jointly. The committee enlisted the aid of Merryll Penson, executive director for library services at the Board of Regents of the University System of Georgia, to facilitate the meeting activities. SOLINET staff assisted in arrangements and logistics with additional assistance provided by Dean Gunn of the Clark Atlanta Library School, Brenda Banks of the Georgia Department of Archives and History, and Althea Jenkins of Florida State University. Letters of announcement were sent to college and university presidents informing them of the meeting opportunity for their library directors and deans.

A position paper set the stage for conference discussions and outcomes. Submitted by Franklin, *A Call for Cooperation Among HBCU Libraries: Opportunities for Consideration* provided the foundation for gathering input and consensus at the meeting after approximately eighteen months of dialogue among the HBCU librarians over the electronic list and during SOLINET Annual Membership meetings. Four potential areas for cooperation were identified in the paper: (1) preservation and digitization of cultural materials, (2) information and advocacy, (3) human resources for shared expertise, recruitment, and staff development, and (4) strategies for better access to collections and facilities.

Appropriately, Atlanta was selected for the meeting location. The efforts of the Steering Committee and the individual passion of its members resulted in 101 libraries sending representatives to the meeting, a resounding cry in support of collaboration.

MEETING OUTCOMES

The meeting began with a statement of vision and charge presented by the chair of the Steering Committee, Loretta Parham:

> I hope that we can work toward a vision for an entity that can represent and present the HBCU library with reliable authority, an entity that can promote our interests, position us for collaborative development of virtual and print collections, and place the HBCU library in a position to reinvent for the most strategic disbursements and benefits.

A stirring and emotional roll call followed with each library institution called out in order of founding date (beginning in 1837), to the rhythmic and pulsating cadence of the Atlanta-based Giwaya Mata African Dance and Drum Ensemble. For one and a half days, breakout sessions and discussions about the HBCU libraries were conducted. Participants were vocal and eager to share, mentor on the spot, and offer ideas about a possible future. Deana B. Marcum, then executive director of CLIR, and Susan Perry, senior advisor for the Andrew W. Mellon Foundation, provided luncheon remarks. An arousing and thought-provoking dinner keynote was delivered by Dianne Boardley Suber, president of Saint Augustine's College in Raleigh, North Carolina. Dr. Suber's comments challenged the attendees to think and act "outside the box" in planning for the future of libraries for African American students.

By the closing day of the meeting, a spirit of cooperation and a strong breeze of commitment were felt by all as they united to determine ways of strengthening library programs and services at HBCUs. Participants sensed a new and historic undertaking of extreme importance at a time of scarce resources and heightened expectations.

SINCE THE MEETING

The Steering Committee is now continuing its work at the request of the conference attendees who empowered this group to plan for the new consortium. The initiative now has a name, the HBCU Library Alliance; the organizational bylaws are in place; the Web site is active (www.hbculibraries.org); committees are working; a statistical study is underway; and a planning grant funded by the Andrew W. Mellon Foundation has been successfully completed.

Members of the HBCU Library Alliance elected their first board of directors in 2004. Those board members were:

- Loretta O'Brien Parham (chair), Director/Chief Executive Officer of the Robert W. Woodruff Library, Atlanta University Center
- Yildiz Binkley, Director of Libraries and Media Centers, Tennessee State University
- Zenobia Blackmon, Head Librarian, Trenholm State Technical College
- Janice R. Franklin, Director of the University Library and Learning Resource Center, Alabama State University

- Tommy S. Holton, Dean of Library/Learning Resources, Dillard University
- Karen McDaniel, Director of Libraries, Kentucky State University
- Anita Moore, Head Librarian, Rust College
- Emma Bradford Perry, Dean of Libraries, Southern University and A&M College
- Elsie Stephens Weatherington, Dean of Library and Media Services, Virginia State University

Holton chairs a statistics committee, which is preparing an assessment of the HBCU libraries to identify needs and priorities and enable institutions to effectively allocate resources for improving library services and strengthening educational programs. The study, funded by SOLINET, the Library Statistics Program of the National Commission on Libraries and Information Science, and the Andrew W. Mellon Foundation, will be forthcoming.

Through SOLINET, the Andrew W. Mellon Foundation provided a planning grant to develop leadership programming for HBCU libraries. The grant, which was completed in 2004, supported a collaborative process for assessing the roles of HBCU librarians on their campuses and identifying obstacles to the full integration of libraries into campus programs for teaching and learning. The planning effort included librarians and presidents from HBCUs. It was led by Consuella Askew, chief librarian and chair of Library and Information Services at Medgar Evers College in New York. The full report, "Strengthening Libraries at Historically Black Colleges and Universities," was completed in August 2004 and is available on the HBCU Library Alliance Web site (www.hbculibraries.org/NewsEvents/htm).

As a result of the planning effort, SOLINET and the HBCU Library Alliance have recently received additional funding from the Andrew W. Mellon Foundation to support a two-year leadership development program for HBCU libraries. The grant also provides funds for an HBCU Library Alliance Program Officer. The Leadership Development program will take place in 2005 and 2006. It will seek to develop stronger library leadership within the HBCU community, leadership that can overcome obstacles and transform HBCU libraries into effective partners in the teaching and learning process.

FROM HERE

> We have to elevate our role, challenge our staffs, and promote always our existence. We must have the consensus that we do not all bring the same thing to the table . . . but we can certainly dine. We need to develop and deliver a plan of action. And then we must be willing . . . to step up to the line and be baptized, so to speak, to get full-body wet in the work of the HBCU library and information center.
>
> —Loretta O'Brien Parham, chair of the HBCU Library Alliance

It has been no small feat to garner the unanimous commitment of the HBCU libraries. However, the decision was made on October 29, 2002, to move forward and do the work that is needed for the success of an organization whose purpose is to collaborate for greater strength and productivity of its members and their constituencies. The population of libraries that comprises the membership is not homogeneous. It includes institutions that are racially diverse; public, private, and church-affiliated; small and large; federal- and state-assisted; two-year, four-year, graduate, and doctoral degree-granting educational centers. For this reason, the need for a more accurate picture of the membership has prompted efforts to build portals of information and compile data that have never before been made available. Such information has value not only to HBCUs but also to majority institutions and agencies that may be unaware of the impact of HBCUs and their library collections. The possibilities appear limitless as the work of the initiative now takes shape.

In the year 2000, the same year that Franklin and Parham began their tenure on the SOLINET board, President Clinton proclaimed September 17 through September 23, 2000, as National Historically Black Colleges and Universities Week. In a press release issued by the White House Office of the Press Secretary on September 14, 2000, President Clinton made the following statements:

> Rooted in the segregated South of more than a century ago, Historically Black Colleges and Universities (HBCUs) for decades were the sole source of higher education for African Americans. Generations of African American educators, physicians, lawyers, scientists, and other professionals found at HBCUs the knowledge, experience, and encouragement they needed to reach their full potential. . . . The faculty and staff of HBCUs have created a nurturing environment for their students, set high academic standards and expectations, and served as inspiring role models for the young people around them. . . . In addition to educating many of our Nation's most distinguished African American professionals, HBCUs reach out to improve the quality of life in surrounding communities. . . . For well over a century, HBCUs have made their mark as vital institutions of higher learning. They have educated millions of young people, and today they maintain their lead role in preparing African Americans and students of all races for the challenge and opportunities of this new century.

These words ring hollow without the work of the many African American librarians who have labored tirelessly to ensure high-quality resources and services in the libraries of these great institutions. It is a personal privilege and a significant responsibility to work at an HBCU on behalf of its constituency. The libraries of HBCU institutions have been symbols of democracy in providing access to information for the descendents of slaves who believed that education would lift them up from slavery into a promised land of equality. As culture keepers for this great people, librarians of HBCUs continue their quest to serve well their institutions with the conviction and faith that they must preserve this glorious legacy. It is with this purpose in mind that the call for cooperation was answered among libraries of HBCUs, uniting to form a consortium that will represent the diverse, multitype, HBCU libraries, libraries with a common history and a common purpose that are rich in contribution to the American story and the education and experiences of the African American.

18 THE DIVERSITY LIBRARIANS' NETWORK

by Kawanna Bright, Jayati Chaudhuri, and Maud Mundava

INTRODUCTION

The Diversity Librarians' Network (DLN), located online at http://www.lib.utk.edu/residents/dln/, was developed by the University of Tennessee (UT) Minority Resident Librarians in order to bring together diverse librarians from diversity training programs (primarily defined here as residency, fellowship, and internship programs), as well as interested faculty, students, and human resources professionals, into a forum for sharing ideas and networking. The term *Diversity Librarians'* used on the Web site refers to both current and future librarians from culturally diverse backgrounds. Though the primary focus is placed on those diverse librarians who have completed, are completing, or will complete a diversity training program, all diverse librarians are invited to share their experiences and expertise as a part of the network.

WHO IS DEVELOPING THE NETWORK?

The network's developers are three recent MLS (Master of Library Science) graduates who are in their second year as Minority Librarian Residents at the UT Libraries. The residents serve on the libraries' Diversity Committee. They are fully committed to the committee's goals which include the following:

- Promoting diversity in the libraries' collections and its workforce
- Making the library a more welcoming environment for an increasingly diverse staff and student body
- Taking a leadership role in enhancing diversity on campus and in the library profession

Diversity Librarians' Network

About the Network
Network Home
Overview
How to Get Involved
LAMA Diversity Grant Proposal
2004 ALA Diversity Fair Poster Session
FAQ

Diversity Training Programs
Program Profiles
 Programs Currently Accepting Applications
How to Include Your Program's Information

News & Announcements
Diversity Events & Activities Calendar
• Submit a calendar event
News & Announcements

Resource Lists
Employment
• Post a job
Scholarships and Awards

The **Diversity Librarians' Network (DLN)** is being developed by the University of Tennessee Libraries' Minority Resident Librarians in order to bring together diversity librarians from library residency, fellowship, and internship programs (as well as interested faculty, students, and human resources professionals) into a forum for sharing ideas and networking. "The terms "Diversity Librarians" and "Diverse Librarians" primarily refer to both current and future librarians from culturally diverse backgrounds (including those from historically underrepresented racial and ethnic populations). However, the Network is also open to those representing other aspects of diversity, including but not limited to sexual orientation, religion, and disabilities. Though the primary focus is placed on those diverse librarians who have completed, are completing or will complete residency, internship, and fellowship programs, all diverse librarians are invited to share their experiences and expertise as a part of this network.

In addition to fostering a forum for sharing and networking, our mission is to create a resource that will serve as a single point of reference for all library professionals interested in diversity. The website and discussion list will offer up-to-date listings of current programs preparing diverse librarians for careers in librarianship, current open position announcements, diversity development opportunities, and relevant discussions in the library profession that promote diversity in libraries.

The network may appeal to the following groups of people:

• Current diversity training program leaders and mentors in search of information to help them evaluate and update their own programs.

• Libraries interested in beginning a diversity training program at their own institutions.

• Diverse students currently enrolled in library and information science programs in search of information on current training programs and considering applying for positions.

• Administrators and other program coordinators of diversity training programs interested in sharing information about their programs with others in similar positions.

• Diversity training programs interested in finding well qualified candidates.

• Current diversity training program participants in search of networking connections with previous participants who have similar experiences.

• Previous diversity training program participants looking to mentor and share their experiences with current and future program participants.

For more information about the DLN, its background, and its activities please use the links located in the About the Network section of the left navigation pane or view the Lama Cultural Diversity Grant Application.

 The **Diversity Librarians' Network** is the recipient of the 2004 LAMA Cultural Diversity Grant.

Connecting (Requires Registration)
Electronic Discussion Board

Diversity Residents, Interns & Fellows (Current & past)

• Submit your information

Sharing
Mentoring Opportunities

• Sign up to be a mentor
• Sign up to be a mentee

Blogs (Current program participants)

Succeeding
What Others are Saying...

• How are we doing? Let us know! Submit comments, suggestions, or questions

Contact Us!
dln@lib.utk.edu
Page Last Updated:
June 21, 2005
Page Visits Since 05/09/05:
00003020

Figure 18-1. Diversity Librarians' Network Web Page

WHY IS IT BEING DEVELOPED?

The need for a service such as the DLN was initially based on a failure to retrieve more up-to-date and accurate information on diversity librarian training programs when searching the Internet. The Google search that we performed provided an immediate insight into why a more comprehensive and updated information resource on these programs was needed. For instance, most results were out-of-date open position announcements for individual programs dating as far back as 1998. In addition, found hidden in the Google search results for minority librarian residency programs was the ARL Residency and Internship Programs Database, a resource that would preferably appear if not first, at least on the first page of results. A search of the database for programs with the word *minority* in the description only located seven listings, three of which were for the same program in three different years. Subsequent searches for *diversity* and *underrepresented* resulted in similar problems, with overlap being the most noticeable.

As a result, the development of a Web site and electronic discussion board (EDB) that offered up-to-date listings of current programs, and a structured bibliography on residency programs was inevitable. Creating a Web site such as this was therefore envisioned as a way to alleviate the frustration and time related to the current methods for gathering this information.

FEATURES OF THE DLN

PURPOSE

Our mission is to create a resource that will serve as a single point of reference for all library professionals interested in diversity. The Web site and EDB will offer up-to-date listings of current programs that prepare diverse librarians for careers in librarianship, diversity development opportunities, current open position announcements, and relevant discussions in the library profession.

INTENDED AUDIENCE

The DLN offers a number of resources that will appeal to a wide audience. The network is specifically targeted toward the following:

- Current diversity training program leaders and mentors in search of information to help them evaluate and update their own programs
- Libraries interested in beginning a diversity training program at their own institutions
- Diverse students currently enrolled in library and information science programs in search of information on current training programs and considering applying for positions
- Administrators and other program coordinators of diversity training programs interested in sharing information about their programs with others in similar positions
- Diversity training programs interested in finding well-qualified candidates
- Current diversity training program participants in search of networking connections with previous participants who have similar experiences
- Previous diversity training program participants looking to mentor and share their experiences with current and future program participants

GOALS AND OBJECTIVES

One of the primary goals of the DLN is to promote information sharing and communication among current, past, and future participants in programs that train diverse librarians. The network will also enable future participants and emerging programs to obtain more up-to-date and comprehensive information. The network's goals include mentoring and networking opportunities for program participants and other diverse librarians, as well as connecting program administrators and future program participants.

The prime objective of the DLN within the first year of operation is to create an engaged community of participants. This could be achieved by identifying and contacting potential participants for the EDB and initiating professional and social events to facilitate the sharing of work experiences, accomplishments, and challenges. A brochure will be created and distributed in order to market the EDB and Web site to the Library and Information Science schools and future residents.

Another fundamental objective of the network is to make the EDB and the Web site lively and responsive with current awareness tools. In order to achieve this objective the network will post timely notices of diversity awareness and skill development opportunities to a targeted audience. The network will also scan the library literature for discussions of relevant issues that can be posted on the Web site.

Another key objective of our network is to facilitate networking between new program participants and faculty advisors (particularly past participants) across the country by providing a readily available forum for participants and interested library faculty to connect. Other objectives for the network include planning for its future and longevity by pursuing other means of support and possibly transfer of hosting responsibilities to a national organization.

With the demonstrated need defined, the audience identified, and a sense that this resource would be well received and well used, the developers of the network moved on to the next step of the DLN's creation: locating funding. As members of the UT Libraries' Diversity Committee, the residents were aware of the fact that the committee had been awarded a cultural diversity grant from the Library Administration and Management Association (LAMA) in 2002. Following the recommendation of the Diversity Committee, the residents applied for the grant.

IMPLEMENTATION: FROM DEVELOPMENT TO LAUNCH

FUNDING AND USE OF FUNDS

The DLN received initial funding from the LAMA *Cultural Diversity* grant. The $1,000 grant, awarded in June 2004, was slated to provide a means for initial development of the network's components and to facilitate the network's launch. Much of the funding was requested expressly for the purpose of advertising and recruiting users to the network.

The importance of making potential users aware of the network was reflected in the detailed budget breakdown included in the LAMA grant application. One hundred dollars in funding was requested to cover the cost of mailing informative letters and brochures designed to introduce the project to potential users. This contact funding would also cover the cost of telephone calls used to facilitate information gathering, make networking arrangements, and promote the project.

The largest part of the grant money received was designated for the development of a brochure and the production of other advertisement materials for the network. The brochures will be the key means of informing others in the field of this important resource, thus the decision to expend 40 percent of the total funding toward the development of an impressive handout. Remaining funds will be used to develop other methods of project advertisement, including posters and bookmarks.

Recognizing the need to utilize face-to-face contact for networking and information sharing, part of the requested funds were designated for the planning and support of a networking reception at the 2005 ALA Annual Meeting in Chicago. Funds will be used for the advertisement of this event, as well as for the provision of refreshments for attendees.

The remaining funds were initially requested for use in locating a Web hosting service with the ability to support both a Web site and an electronic discussion board (EDB). During the beta-testing of these two resources on the UT Libraries' Web server, it was determined that both the network's Web site and the EDB should remain on the UT Libraries' Server. This Web space was extended by the libraries to the project in-kind. The funds initially earmarked for the support of these resources will be rerouted to the support of other areas of the network, including future networking events and advertising efforts.

How to Get Involved

Joining the Network is easy!

Many of the Network's components are open to anyone who visits the site. Those interested in learning more about the details of programs included in the Network, locating information on programs with openings, getting help with job searching, or locating information on diversity related events and activities can browse the site without registration or log-in.

http://www.lib.utk.edu/residents/dln

Networking

Those interested in participating in the Electronic Discussion Board (EDB) and networking with other members will need to register via the EDB to select a user name and password.

http://www.lib.utk.edu/residents/dln/edb/

Mentoring

Those interested in serving as mentors or mentees should visit our Mentoring Opportunities section:

http://www.lib.utk.edu/residents/dln/mentoring.html

The Network's Developers:

The DLN is being developed by the 2003-2005 Minority Resident Librarians at the University of Tennessee Libraries.

Kawanna Bright is a 2003 graduate of the University of Washington Information School.

Jayati Chaudhuri is a 2002 graduate of the University of Rhode Island Graduate School of Library and Information Studies.

Maud Mundava is a 2003 graduate of The State University of New York at Buffalo, School of Informatics.

Contact us at:

dln@lib.utk.edu

The Diversity Librarians' Network

http://www.lib.utk.edu/residents/dln

Figure 18-2. Diversity Librarians' Network Brochure

What is the Diversity Librarians' Network (DLN)?

The DLN is About Connecting:

The DLN is designed to bring together diverse librarians who have completed, are completing or will complete a recruitment program (primarily defined here as residency, fellowship, and internship programs) in order to share their experiences and expertise. Although the site is designed primarily for this population, all diverse librarians are invited to share their experiences and expertise as a part of the Network. We also encourage the participation of library faculty, students and human resources professionals interested in diversity issues in librarianship.

The terms "Diversity Librarians" and "Diverse Librarians" primarily refer to both current and future librarians from culturally diverse backgrounds (including those from historically underrepresented racial and ethnic populations). However, the Network is also open to those representing other aspects of diversity, including but not limited to sexual orientation, religion, and disabilities.

Prospects for making connections include mentoring opportunities, an Electronic Discussion Board (EDB), and a list of former and current program participants.

The DLN is About Sharing:

Sharing experiences, news, and other information is an important part of the DLN. The information sharing focus of the DLN is highlighted by the recruitment program profiles featured on the site. These profiles offer pertinent information on the programs currently in existence including contact information and how to apply.

Other opportunities for sharing are also available through the Network including the EDB; diversity resource lists that feature scholarships, awards, and employment information; a residents' blog; and an area for diversity events and news.

The DLN is About Succeeding!

The DLN recognizes the importance of networking in the successful recruitment, development, and future careers of diverse librarians. The benefits of membership in the DLN include:

- Mentoring, networking opportunities, and information sharing.
- Access to current and up-to-date information resources on diversity recruitment programs and any other information that promotes diversity in libraries.
- Access to links to the existing programs, development opportunities, and relevant discussions in the library profession.
- An opportunity to contribute your ideas and expertise.
- Access to timely notices of diversity events and activities.

Visit us at:
http://www.lib.utk.edu/residents/dln

Figure 18-2. Diversity Librarians' Network Brochure (*Continued*)

WEB SITE COMPONENTS

The components of the DLN Web site represent aspects of the network that we felt were most important to emphasize to potential users. The majority of the components chosen for inclusion were selected in response to a need for an information resource for diverse librarians or on diversity in librarianship that either did not exist or was not up to date. The selected components also had to fit within the initial purpose of the network. These selected components were placed into these general categories: Diversity Training Programs, News and Announcements, Resource Lists, Connecting, Sharing, and Succeeding.

DIVERSITY TRAINING PROGRAMS

The section on Diversity Training Programs includes two of the most important components of the network and the Web site: Program Profiles and Programs Currently Accepting Applications. The Program Profiles area includes individual listings of library residency, fellowship, and internship programs that currently exist. These informative profiles offer information on the programs that is most sought after by others. This includes: how the program is funded, the number of participants accepted, why the program initially began, the purpose of the program, and other details concerning the operation of the program. The information included in the profiles is of interest to those who want to develop similar programs at their institutions, as well as to those interested in participating in a program. Any program that wishes to have a profile included on the site can submit the online "How to Include Your Programs Information" form (http://www.lib.utk.edu/residents/dln/how.html) to request the inclusion of their program.

The Programs Currently Accepting Applications section lists the programs that are currently recruiting for participants. These listings include general program information and more detailed information on the application procedures, candidate qualifications, and short position descriptions. Each listing includes information on where to locate more details about the program and information on application deadlines.

NEWS AND ANNOUNCEMENTS

The News and Announcements section includes a Diversity Events and Activities calendar. This calendar is compiled through a combination of our efforts and the efforts of other members of the network. We collect events for the calendar via Web searches, from listserv announcements, and by word of mouth. Other members of the network are encouraged to submit events through an online form to help keep us informed about other events in a timely manner. Those events that focus on diversity in librarianship, diversity training opportunities, and diversity conferences and meetings are the most sought after for the calendar.

RESOURCE LISTS

The Resource Lists section of the Web site includes individual pages that offer detailed links and information on topics of particular interest to diverse librarians. Currently this section consists of a list of employment resources and a list of scholarships and awards resources. The employment resources list includes a Jobs of Interest section where jobs that refer directly to an aspect of diversity are posted. Members of the network are also invited to post positions on the Jobs of Interest list for the purpose of making larger groups of minority candidates aware of the position. The scholarships and awards list includes links and information on funding opportunities for diverse librarians, including special conference scholarships, fellowships, and educational awards. Other resource lists will be added as the network continues to develop.

CONNECTING

The Connecting, Sharing, and Succeeding sections of the Web site are titled by descriptive terms used to emphasize three of the network's major goals. The Connecting area of the

Web site includes components that require registration and login to use. The two components included in this area are the electronic discussion board (EDB) and the Diversity Residents, Interns, and Fellows list.

The purpose of the EDB is to offer a forum for members of the network to discuss issues related to the network and to diversity in librarianship. The EDB requires a login to post or respond to messages, but can be browsed without a login. The board is separated by different topics to improve the ease of use and to help users locate the forums they wish to participate in most. Topics expected to be covered on the board include questions about particular programs, requests for information and help with program development, questions and discussions concerning hot diversity topics in librarianship, and job postings.

The Diversity Residents, Interns, and Fellows list (DRIF list) also requires a login to view and cannot be perused without a login. Members of the network will use the same login and password for both the EDB and the DRIF list. The DRIF list will consist of a roster of names of former and present participants in diversity training programs. Information included on the list will range from a name and program title entry only to a full profile. Full profiles include information on current position, title, location, areas of work, research interests, and contact information. Participants who choose to include full profiles will also have the option of volunteering to be contacts to discuss the program that they completed or to discuss possible research collaborations with other members of the network. Members of the network interested in being included in the list can apply through an online information form included in the connecting section.

SHARING

The Sharing section of the Web site features a mentoring component and an informal Web log (blog) component. The Mentoring Opportunities section allows interested users to self-identify as possible mentors or mentees. The major focus of the mentoring component of the network is to connect two members of the network with a mutual interest in forming a successful and supportive mentoring relationship. With this in mind, both mentees and mentors can utilize the links to their respective online information forms in the Mentoring Opportunities section to include their names in the lists of potential mentees and mentors.

The Blogs section of the Web site is an attempt to allow interested users to get a more informal glimpse into a residency, fellowship, or internship program. Current participants in different programs will be encouraged to begin their own blogs as a means of chronicling their program experiences. These blogs will allow others to read a firsthand and fresh account of the activities and projects undertaken by the program participants. Currently the UT Libraries have the only blog listed on the site. Participants in other programs will be contacted with the suggestion that they consider establishing their own program blog that can be included on the network's site.

SUCCEEDING

The Succeeding section of the Web site will consist of the collected comments from users of the Web site. "What Others Are Saying" will allow us to share comments and suggestions from visitors to the site with others interested in the progress of the project. This section also includes a form that can be used to contribute to the "What Others Are Saying" compilation as well as contact us with other questions about the network.

WEB SITE DESIGN

The initial design of the network's Web site branched out of the design of the logo for the DLN. The DLN logo was in place and emphasized the issues of connecting, sharing, and succeeding. We wanted to continue the emphasis on these three concepts and chose to place them as major categories on the site. The remaining categories were based on the components that had already been selected for inclusion in the network.

Any component that fit into the concept of connecting, sharing, or succeeding was placed into that general category. Components that dealt with the network in general were placed in a category called "About the Network." We placed a lot of emphasis on maintaining an updated list of diversity training programs and considered it one of the stronger components of the site. With this in mind, information on training programs was placed into a category of its own. This was followed by a category for news and announcements and a category for resource lists. The original design of the Web site placed all of the categories and components into a navigation scheme that dominated the left side of the Web page. However, further conversations between us led to a two-column navigation scheme with page content placed in the middle of each page. This two-column design allowed us to place components that dealt more with the static provision of information on one side of the page and components that dealt more with dynamic sharing of information on the other.

Other aspects of Web site design, including color schemes, font selection, and page layout, have currently been based on our preferences. All of these site aspects will be continuously reviewed and open to modification based on the feedback that we receive from the users of the network.

GATHERING FEEDBACK

Once the beta-version of the Web site, including the information collection forms, was available online, we needed to gather initial feedback from others in the field on the direction of the network. We wanted to use any opportunity that we could to have others comment on the network's components, as well as the general layout of the site.

ALA ANNUAL CONFERENCE, JUNE 2004

Our first large-scale opportunity to share information about the network came at the 2004 ALA Annual Conference in Orlando. We participated in two activities that allowed us to present the network to different audiences. The first and largest opportunity was the Diversity Fair Poster Session. We developed a large poster that included information on the network's Web site and its components, and also the projected timeline for the formal launch of the project. Hundreds of attendees visited the Diversity Fair and a large number stopped by our table to discuss the project. We handed out materials that garnered future feedback on

The Diversity Librarians' Network

The DLN is designed to bring together diverse librarians who have completed, are completing or will complete a recruitment program (primarily defined here as residency, fellowship, and internship programs) in order to share their experiences and expertise.

Although the site is designed primarily for this population, all diverse librarians are invited to share their experiences and expertise as part of the Network. We also encourage the participation of library faculty, students and human resources professionals interested in diversity issues in librarianship.

"The terms "Diversity Librarians" and "Diverse Librarians" primarily refer to both current and future librarians from culturally diverse backgrounds (including those from historically underrepresented racial and ethnic populations). However, the Network is also open to those representing other aspects of diversity, including but not limited to sexual orientation, religion, and disabilities.

* Mentoring Opportunities

* Electronic Discussion Board

* List of former and current program participants

* Recruitment Program Profiles

* Diversity Resource Lists that feature scholarships, awards, and employment information

* Residents' Blog

* Diversity Calendar of Events and News

The benefits of membership in the DLN include:

* Mentoring, networking, and information sharing opportunities.

* Access to current and up-to-date information resources on diversity recruitment programs and any other information that promotes diversity in libraries.

* Access to links to the existing programs, development opportunities, and relevant discussions in the library profession.

* An opportunity to contribute your ideas and expertise.

* Access to timely notices of diversity events and activities.

Figure 18-3. Diversity Librarians' Network Poster

the Web site and made note of suggestions and comments offered by fair attendees. One of the most popular methods of gathering feedback was the distribution of buttons that featured the DLN logo and included the link to the Web site.

Our second opportunity to share information about the network during ALA was at the LAMA Diversity Officers Discussion Group meeting. This group provides a forum to LAMA members "whose job assignments and interests include responsibilities for developing or implementing diversity training and/or diversity awareness programs" (LAMA 2005). With this group's interest in sharing information and discussing strategies for program development, Jill Keally, a member of the group and major sounding board for the DLN project, thought they would be a good resource for gathering more structured feedback and invited us to attend the meeting. The meeting in Orlando also included non-LAMA members with an interest in diversity programs, producing a good turnout for announcing the network. Initial feedback was promising and included an invitation to return at the midwinter meeting in Boston to update the group on the status of the network.

PERSONAL REQUESTS FOR REVIEW AND FEEDBACK

Another method of gathering feedback on the beta-Web site involved personal requests for review and help sent out to colleagues and acquaintances from the field. Each of us sent out a number of emails describing the project and asking our colleagues and friends to give us their opinions of the Web site's design and usability. No set number of people was selected for these personal requests and not everyone replied, but we did receive a number of responses that included suggestions for the layout of the site, selection of questions used on the online forms, and practice responses to the online forms. All of these responses allowed us to gauge our level of success in terms of development of the site and to evaluate areas of the site that needed continued work.

UNIVERSITY OF MINNESOTA LIBRARIES TRAINING INSTITUTE FOR EARLY CAREER LIBRARIANS FROM TRADITIONALLY UNDERREPRESENTED GROUPS

Two of the residents had the opportunity to attend the University of Minnesota Libraries Training Institute for Early Career Librarians from Traditionally Underrepresented Groups in October 2004. This institute offers leadership training and other professional development skills for a select number of new librarians from underrepresented populations. Attending this week-long institute offered an opportunity to share the impending launch of the DLN with over thirty potential users. The attendees and presenters of this institute represented different sections of our project's intended audiences, including current and former program participants, potential mentors and mentees, and members of the field interested in diversity issues. The residents were able to use this opportunity to share the purpose and goals of the project with others and to encourage these potential users to investigate the site in the future.

STEPS TO LAUNCH

The steps to the launch of the DLN took effect after the final beta-testing of the site was completed. The first step toward launch was to apply for human subjects' approval from the UT Library Human Subjects Departmental Review Committee (DRC). The DRC reviewed the project and gave it approval to enter into the next step: approval from the UT Institutional Review Board (IRB). During the IRB review, the feedback received in the previous months was utilized to make final changes and updates to the site. This included finalizing the design of the Web site, improving the appearance, functionality of the pages, and the online forms.

TECHNICAL CHALLENGES

During the development of the network's Web site, the residents faced a number of technical challenges related to functionality of online forms, software selection for the EDB, software selection for the residents' blog, and privacy and protection of particular Web pages within the site. In an effort to keep costs low, free software was chosen for both the EDB and the residents' blog. In addition, Paul Cummins, a member of the UT Libraries' Systems Department, provided technical assistance for the installation and setup of the network since protecting the libraries' online security was of the utmost importance to us.

The final technical problem encountered involved placing password protections on the Diversity Residents, Fellows, and Interns List pages. Once again, Paul Cummins worked diligently to find a solution. After a week Paul managed to get the software which was to be used for the EDB. This software utilizes user names and passwords that are compatible with the software used to build the Web site. With this in place, we were able to protect the pages without requiring members to memorize different user names and passwords for different areas of our site.

With all of the technical challenges conquered, we only had to await word from the IRB. In December of 2004 we finally received notice that our project had passed final review and had the approval of the IRB. We were ready to launch.

LAUNCH STRATEGY

The launch strategy of the DLN was separated into stages to allow us to make contact with members of our intended audiences in a focused manner. The first stage of contact involved sending letters introducing the network and inviting participation in the network to the coordinators of identified residency, fellowship, and internship programs. These letters included a link to our online information form and also included print copies of the same form and self-addressed and stamped envelopes for easy replies. We are currently awaiting the responses to this stage of contact.

The second stage consisted of using the 2005 Midwinter Meeting in Boston as an opportunity to announce the launch of the DLN to a large number of librarians in the field. Over 200 brochures that described the project were handed out by us and our colleagues from the UT Libraries, including the dean and the head of Access and Delivery Services at various meetings during the conference. Announcements concerning the launch of the network were made during an all-day recruitment forum; a Diversity Interest, Networking, and Exchange meeting; a meeting of the LAMA Diversity Officers Discussion Group; and at other meetings and events.

Stage three of launching the DLN will consist of sending introductory emails to diversity-related listservs in the field of librarianship. These emails will serve to make parties interested in diversity aware of the new resource and will act as an invitation to investigate and participate in the network.

Stage four of the launch of the DLN will consist of contacting ALA-accredited graduate schools and asking them to share copies of the DLN brochure with interested students in their programs, as well as interested faculty and staff members. This stage of the launch is especially focused on catching potential participants in diversity training programs who will be able to utilize the network to learn about the programs that they may be qualified to apply for in the future.

The final DLN launch stage will consist of making personal contact with former and current diversity training program participants. These participants will be identified through Web searches and from records made available on program Web sites. These potential members of the network will be contacted via a personal letter that will describe the network to them and invite them to participate in any capacity.

MARKETING STRATEGY

Marketing the DLN has proven to be both the easiest and most difficult aspects of the project. We have discovered that the opportunities to discuss the project abound, but our goal is not just to tell others about it. We want to make the DLN as important to others within the field of librarianship as it is to us. With this in mind, we worked on a number of components of the project with the idea of making them "memorable."

The name of the project itself was carefully discussed throughout the project's development. Our original title proved to be inadequate, only conveying one small part of the project's intention. We felt that the Diversity Librarians' Network not only better conveyed who and what the project was for, but also proved to be a more inclusive title to describe our intended audiences. This title decision also rested on wanting a name that would be seen as familiar to users without already being in use by another resource.

Along with the project's name came the design of the project's logo. We wanted to create a logo that conveyed diversity and was also easily recognized and remembered by anyone who saw it. The logo was intentionally given a simple but colorful design, so as not to overwhelm any advertising objects that it is placed on while still being eye-catching. The logo appears on every page within the Web site and is always a link back to the network's home page. The circular shape of the logo also lends itself well to buttons, a method of marketing that was used during the testing phase of the project and will be used again in the future. Our logo is designed to be portable and can easily be utilized on other Web sites and printed resources.

Further marketing of the DLN will include links to the Web site and descriptions of the project placed prominently on other Web sites and resources in the field of librarianship. National organizations and groups like the Ethnic Caucuses of ALA and the ALA Office of Diversity will be approached as possible avenues for marketing the network, whether online or in brochures or other printed information resources that they create. ALA-accredited schools will be encouraged to list the DLN as a resource of interests for their students.

VISION OF THE FUTURE: WHERE DO WE GO FROM HERE?

In the future the network will hold formal and informal meetings at ALA annual and midwinter conferences, National Diversity in Libraries conferences, or any other major conference that can strengthen our networking capability. The gatherings will enable us to generate novel and innovative ideas and to build new relationships to sustain this service. The network will also continue to gather and add information to the Web site, monitor the EDB, and promote both resources. As the site grows, we will begin the process of completing research on the network and applying for future funding support.

EVALUATION

We will use comments, suggestions, and other feedback from the Web site to update, upgrade, and improve the service. An evaluation form for both the Web site and the brochure is currently being developed to get feedback from our audience. Responses to queries for information from other academic institutions will also reflect the success of our service, as will be the number of programs that request inclusion on the site and the number of people who sign up to participate on the EDB.

THE FUTURE

The Diversity Librarian Network has nearly limitless potential for future growth and advancement. As more people become involved in the project, it will become more successful. In the future the DLN hopes to gain recognition as a diversity information resource with national professional organizations. The network also hopes to present preconference workshops that can bring together those who have created residency programs and those who want to create a program. Eventually, the network anticipates furthering its publicity and involvement to the international community such as the International Federation of Library Association and Institutions.

LESSONS LEARNED

The development of the DLN has been an immense undertaking and achievement. Throughout the process we have learned many things about research, making connections, and the amount of work that it takes to get such a large-scale project off the ground. We have learned the importance of making connections with others who have an interest in the project's development and are willing to share their experiences and knowledge. We have also learned the importance of "knowing the ropes" when attempting to develop a project at a large academic university. Most of all, we have learned that something that starts out as an idea can grow into something much more substantial and important than we ever imagined.

WHAT'S LEFT TO BE DONE

Many aspects of the network are already in place. The majority of the work that remains to be done involves bringing in the participants who will make it a success. Marketing strategies are already in place and will be used to further the goals of the network. We will also begin the process of writing about and performing research based on the network. Finally, formal evaluations of the project will need to be completed. This will allow us to garner a sense of how far we have come from the initial planning to the actual implementation. We will also use the evaluation process to help with the continued improvement and development of the network.

The productive partnerships formed by those involved in this networking service will help librarians foster and sustain diversity in their institutions while building an overall commitment to diversity at their institutions and within the library profession. The support network created for diverse librarians will increase their representation and advancement in the field of librarianship, including administration and management. This will contribute to the creation of a more welcoming environment for all in the libraries. The contacts made through this service will lead to future partnerships between administrators in the library field and national organizations with interests in diversity issues and affairs. The main goal of facilitating and fostering ongoing participation in diversity awareness and initiatives can easily be achieved through the hard work of a dedicated few.

19 FINAL THOUGHTS ON DIVERSITY IN LIBRARIES

by Loretta Parham

The final thought is, enough with the thinking on this topic and onward with the plan of action. Throughout the chapters of *Achieving Diversity: A How-To-Do-It Manual for Librarians* library staff from a wide variety of libraries have offered evidence of their action that is meant to enrich the workplace by incorporating principles of diversity that ultimately contribute to the success and satisfaction of both library information seekers and information providers. It is our hope that readers of the book will incorporate, add to, and improve on specific actions, collections, programs, activities, and efforts infusing diversity into the life of their library.

In the library the issues of differences are largely unchanged from the days of the first ALA Diversity Office in 1997 (Balderrama 2000, 194–214). Then the issues were about the recruitment of students of color into library schools, the recruitment, hiring, retention, and promotion of a diverse workforce, communications, outreach, and leadership that with purpose surrounds organizational goals and objectives with diversity deliverables. It is much the same these days, although we do include people that are different due to physical challenges and people that expand the parameters of the phrase a "person of color."

My husband, a retired U.S. military officer, is fond of reminding me that "you never go back the same way you came." The application of this military strategy when we are on a journey is that by traveling a different road we see something that was not seen on the journey out, we hear different things, we take in different sites and scenery and experience different people. I've come to appreciate this sage advice and as a result I have discovered places, paths, and people that might otherwise have gone totally unknown to me.

The same can be said of diversity in the workplace, in our social groups, and in our play. That is, doing things differently, including different people, planning differently, can beautify the landscape of our organizations and make difference of opinion and viewpoint an important and valuable outcome. It is an assignment for everyone in the organization, from trustee to volunteer. "Strategic choices and courageous decisions bring the value of diversity to life—no matter where we are within the library organization. Supportive directors help. Supportive staff helps. Strong and vocal trustees help. Strategic plans with goals and objectives help. Ultimately, however, our own personal decisions, choices, and actions impact how diversity is hindered or facilitated" (Balderrama 2000, 194–214).

Indeed, through thoughtful application of the practical examples presented in this book, we can see things differently in all our libraries, and enrich our lives, by taking a different path.

BIBLIOGRAPHY

Balderrama, Sandra Rios. 2000. "This Trend Called Diversity." *Library Trends* 49(1): 194–214.

20 CELEBRATING DIVERSITY IN LIBRARIES: A SELECTED BIBLIOGRAPHY

by Molly Royse

GENERAL WORKS ON DIVERSITY

Cox, Taylor. 2001. *Creating the Multicultural Organization: A Strategy for Capturing the Power of Diversity*. San Francisco: Jossey-Bass.
Cross, Elsie Y. 2000. *Managing Diversity—the Courage to Lead*. Westport, CT: Quorum Books.
The Drama of Diversity and Democracy: Higher Education and American Commitments. 1995. Washington, DC: Association of American Colleges and Universities.
Gardenswartz, Lee, and Anita Rowe. 1998. *Managing Diversity: A Complete Desk Reference and Planning Guide*. 2nd ed. New York: McGraw-Hill.
Gentile, Mary C. 2000. *Differences That Work: Organizational Excellence Through Diversity*. Prospect Heights, IL: Waveland Press.
Gore, Albert. 2000. *Best Practices in Achieving Workforce Diversity: U.S. Department of Commerce and Vice President Al Gore's National Partnership for Reinventing Government Benchmarking Study*. Washington, DC: U.S. Department of Commerce.
Miller, Frederick A., and Judith H. Katz. 2002. *The Inclusion Breakthrough: Unleashing the Real Power of Diversity*. San Francisco: Berrett-Koehler.
Musil, Caryn McTighe. 1995. *Diversity in Higher Education: A Work in Progress*. Washington, DC: Association of American Colleges and Universities.
Thomas, R. Roosevelt, Jr. 1996. *Redefining Diversity*. New York: American Management Association.
Thomas, R. Roosevelt, Jr. 1999. *Building a House for Diversity: How a Fable about a Giraffe and an Elephant Offers New Strategies for Today's Workforce*. New York: American Management Association.

DIVERSITY AND LIBRARIES

Alire, Camila A., and Frederick J. Stielow. 1995. "Minorities and the Symbolic Potential of the Academic Library: Reinventing Tradition." *College and Research Libraries* 56 (November): 509–517.

Balderrama, Sandra Rios. 2000. "This Trend Called Diversity." *Library Trends* 49.1 (summer): 194–214.

Buttlar, Lois. 1994. "Facilitating Cultural Diversity in College and University Libraries." *Journal of Academic Librarianship* 20 (March): 10–14.

Chadley, Otis A. 1992. "Addressing Cultural Diversity in Academic and Research Libraries." *College and Research Libraries* 53 (May): 206–214.

Cultural Diversity Programming in ARL Libraries, SPEC Kit 165. 1990. Washington, DC: Office of Management Services, Association of Research Libraries.

Curry, Deborah A., Susan Griswold Blandy, and Lynne M. Martin, eds. 1994. *Racial and Ethnic Diversity in Academic Libraries: Multicultural Issues*. New York: Haworth Press.

DuMont, Rosemary Ruhig, Lois Buttlar, and William Caynon. 1994. *Multiculturalism in Libraries*. Westport, CT: Greenwood Press.

East, Dennis, and Errol Lam. 1995. "In Search of Multiculturalism in the Library Science Curriculum." *Journal of Education for Library and Information Science* 36 (summer): 199–216.

Hill, Katherine Hoover, ed. 1994. *Diversity and Multiculturalism in Libraries*. Greenwich, CT: JAI Press.

Hoxeng, Holly. 2000. "Addressing Diversity in the Public Library Community with Diversity on the Library Staff." *Colorado Libraries* 26 (summer): 14–15.

Jennings, Kriza. 1995. "Seven Components of a Successful Library-Wide Diversity Program." *ARL: A Bimonthly Newsletter of Research Library Issues and Actions* 180 (May): 12–13.

Jones, DeEtta. 1999. "The Definition of Diversity: Two Views, a More Inclusive Definition." *Journal of Library Administration* 27: 5–15.

Josey, E. J. 1999. "Diversity: Political and Societal Barriers." *Journal of Library Administration* 27: 191–202.

Jones, Emily J., Corinne O. Nelson, and John Berry. 1999. "Culturally Competent Librarianship." *Library Journal* 124 (September 1): 148–150.

LaGuardia, Cheryl, Christine K. Oka, and Adan Griego. 1994. "Living Diversity: Making It Work." In *Diversity and Multiculturalism in Libraries*, edited by Katherine Hoover Hill. Greenwich, CT: JAI Press. 215–226.

Lenox, Mary F. 1993. "Enhancing Ethnic and Racial Diversity: The New Challenge for Libraries." *Illinois Libraries* 75.5 (fall): 292–295.

Martin, Rebecca. 1994. *Libraries and the Changing Face of Academia: Responses to Growing Multicultural Populations*. Metuchen, NJ: Scarecrow Press.

McCook, Kathleen de la Pena. 2000. *Ethnic Diversity in Library and Information Science*. Champaign: University of Illinois, Graduate School of Library and Information Science.

Miller, Rush G. 1994. "Leading the Way to Diversity: The Academic Library's Role in Promoting Multiculturalism." In *Diversity and Multiculturalism in Libraries*, edited by Katherine Hoover Hill. Greenwich, CT: JAI Press. 1–18.

Neely, Teresa Y. 1999. "Diversity Initiatives and Programs: The National Approach." *Journal of Library Administration* 27: 123–144.

Neely, Teresa Y., and Kuang-Hwei Lee-Smeltzer, eds. 2002. *Diversity Now: People, Collections, and Services in Academic Libraries*. New York: Haworth Press.

Paris, Lee Anne H. 1997. "Response to Diversity: A Comparison of the Libraries at Stanford and UCLA." *Journal of Academic Librarianship* 23 (March): 91–99.

Riggs, Donald E., and Patricia A. Tarin, eds. 1994. *Cultural Diversity in Libraries*. New York: Neal-Schuman.

Stoffle, Carla J., and Patricia A. Tarin. 1994. "No Place for Neutrality: The Case for Multiculturalism." *Library Journal* 119 (July): 46–49.

Sykes, Vivian. 1994. "Perspectives on Cultural Diversity." In *Cultural Diversity in Libraries*, edited by Donald E. Riggs and Patricia A. Tarin. New York: Neal-Schuman. 1–10.

Trujillo, Roberto G., and David C. Weber. 1991. "Academic Library Responses to Cultural Diversity: A Position Paper for the 1990s." *Journal of Academic Librarianship* 17 (July): 157–161.

Welburn, William C. 1999. "Multicultural Curriculum in Higher Education." *Journal of Library Administration* 27: 157–169.

Yates, Carol J., Rafaela Castro, and Lillian Castillo-Speed. 1994. "Voices of Diversity in University of California Libraries: Impact, Initiatives and Impediments for Cultural and Racial Equity." In *Diversity and Multiculturalism in Libraries*, edited by Katherine Hoover Hill. Greenwich, CT: JAI Press. 19–28.

ORGANIZATION AND MANAGEMENT

Butler, Meredith A., and Gloria R. DeSole. 1993. "Creating the Multicultural Organization—A Call to Action." *Journal of Library Administration* 19: 155–174.

Dow, Gail M. 1995. "When a Plan Comes Together: The Denver Public Library's Diversity Plan." *Colorado Libraries* 21 (summer): 34–38.

Dyson, Allan J. 1989. "Reaching Out for Outreach: A University Library Develops a New Position to Serve the School's Multicultural Students." *American Libraries* 20 (November): 952–954.

Gerhard, Kristin H., and Jeanne M. K. Boydston. 1993. "A Library Committee on Diversity and Its Role in a Library Diversity Program." *College and Research Libraries* 54 (July): 335–343.

Jordan, Elaine. 1994. "The University of Michigan Library's Diversity Committee." In *Cultural Diversity in Libraries*, edited by Donald E. Riggs and Patricia A. Tarin. New York: Neal-Schuman. 95–107.

Li, Haipeng. 1999. "Diversity in the Library: What Could Happen at the Institutional Level." *Journal of Library Administration* 27: 145–156.

Nance-Mitchell, Veronica E. 1996. "A Multicultural Library: Strategies for the Twenty-First Century." *College and Research Libraries* 57 (September): 405–413.

Owens, Irene. 2000. "A Managerial/Leadership Approach to Maintaining Diversity in Libraries." *Texas Library Journal* 76 (spring): 20–27.

Ranson, Charles. 1994. "The Diversity Librarian." In *Cultural Diversity in Libraries*, edited by Donald E. Riggs and Patricia A. Tarin. New York: Neal-Schuman. 165–171.

Riggs, Donald E. 1994. "Top Management's Commitment and Role." In *Cultural Diversity in Libraries*, edited by Donald E. Riggs and Patricia A. Tarin. New York: Neal-Schuman. 23–35.

Sannwald, W. 1999. "Managing Diversity: The City of San Diego Experience." *Library Administration and Management* 13.1: 18–22.

Simmons-Welburn, Janice. 1999. "Using Culture as a Construct for Achieving Diversity in Human Resources Management." *Library Administration and Management* 13 (fall): 205–209.

Stoffle, Carla J. 1994. "Moving to Diversity: Institutional Philosophy and Role." In *Cultural Diversity in Libraries*, edited by Donald E. Riggs and Patricia A. Tarin. New York: Neal-Schuman. 11–22.

Welburn, William C. 1994. "Rethinking Theoretical Assumptions about Diversity: Challenges for College and University Library Planning." In *Diversity and Multiculturalism in Libraries*, edited by Katherine Hoover Hill. Greenwich, CT: JAI Press. 75–84.

Welch, Janet E., and R. Errol Lam. 1991. "The Library and the Pluralistic Campus in the Year 2000: Implications for Administrators." *Library Administration and Management* 5 (fall): 212–216.

Williams, James F. 1999. "Managing Diversity: Library Management in Light of the Dismantling of Affirmative Action." *Journal of Library Administration* 27: 27–48.

Winston, Mark, ed. 1999. *Managing Multiculturalism and Diversity in the Library: Principles and Issues for Administrators*. New York: Haworth.

SERVICES AND ACCESS

Alire, Camila, and Orlando Archibeque. 1998. *Serving Latino Communities: A How-to-Do-It Manual for Librarians*. New York: Neal-Schuman.

Berry, John N. 1999. "Culturally Competent Service: A New Mandate to Serve a New Majority." *Library Journal* 124 (September 1): 112.

Dame, Melvina Azar. 1993. *Serving Linguistically and Culturally Diverse Students*. New York: Neal-Schuman.

Downing, Karen E., Barbara MacAdam, and Darlene P. Nichols, eds. 1993. *Reaching a Multicultural Student Community: A Handbook for Academic Librarians*. Westport, CT: Greenwood Press.

Graves, Gail, and Barbara Kay Adams. 1993. "Library Instruction and Cultural Diversity: Programming in an Academic Library." *Mississippi Libraries* 57 (winter): 89–101.

Jacobson, Trudi E., and Helene C. Williams, eds. 2000. *Teaching the New Library to Today's Users: Reaching International, Minority, Senior Citizens, Gay/Lesbian, First-Generation, At-Risk, Graduate and Returning Students, and Distance Learners*. New York: Neal-Schuman.

Kuharets, Irina, Brigid Cahalan, and Fed Gitner, eds. 2001. *Bridging Cultures: Ethnic Services in the Libraries of New York State*. Albany, NY: New York Library Association, Ethnic Services Round Table.

Lin, Poping. 1994. "Library Instruction for Culturally Diverse Populations: A Comparative Approach." *Research Strategies* 12.3: 168–173.

Liu, Mengxiong. 1995. "Ethnicity and Information Seeking." *Reference Librarian* 5: 49/50, 123–134.

Liu, Mengxiong, and Bernice Redfern. 1997. "Information-Seeking Behavior of Multicultural Students: A Case Study at San Jose State University." *College and Research Libraries* 58: 348–354.

MacAdam, Barbara, and Darlene Nichols. 1989. "Peer Information Counseling: An Academic Library Program for Minority Students." *Journal of Academic Librarianship* 15.4 (September): 204–209.

Martin, Rebecca R. 1994. "Changing the University Climate: Three Libraries Respond to Multicultural Students." *Journal of Academic Librarianship* 20 (March): 2–9.

Metoyer, Cheryl A. 2000. "Missing Links in Reaching Culturally Diverse Students in Academic Libraries." *Journal of Academic Librarianship* 26.3 (May): 157–158.

Osborne, Nancy Seale, and Cecilia Poon. 1995. "Serving Diverse Library Populations

through the Specialized Instructional Services Concept." *Reference Librarian* 51–52: 285–294.
Pontau, Donna Z. 1994. "Transforming Academic Libraries for Employees and Students with Disabilities." In *Diversity and Multiculturalism in Libraries*, edited by Katherine Hoover Hill. Greenwich, CT: JAI Press. 157–173.
Rios, Francisco A., ed. 1996. *Teacher Thinking in Cultural Contexts*. Albany: State University of New York Press.
Rubin, Rhea Joyce. 2001. *Planning for Library Services to People with Disabilities*. Chicago: American Library Association.
Sarkodie-Mensah, Kwasi. 1992. "Dealing with International Students in a Multicultural Era." *Journal of Academic Librarianship* 18 (September): 214–216.
Whitmire, Ethelene. 1999. "Racial Differences in the Academic Library Experiences of Undergraduates." *Journal of Academic Librarianship* 25 (January): 33–37.
Winston, Mark, and Karen Downing. 1998. "Helping Students of Color Succeed: Implementing and Managing a Peer Information Counseling Program." *Leading Ideas* 3 (July): 2–5. Available: www.arl.org/diversity/leading/issue3/pic.html.

STAFF DEVELOPMENT AND TRAINING

Gomez, Cheryl. 1994. "Cultural Diversity Staff Training: The Challenge." In *Diversity and Multiculturalism in Libraries*, edited by Katherine Hoover Hill. Greenwich, CT: JAI Press. 29–42.
Janes, Phoebe, and Ellen Meltzer. 1990. "Origins and Attitudes: Training Reference Librarians for a Pluralistic World." *Reference Librarian* 30: 145–155.
Kendall, Frances E. 1994. "Creating a Multicultural Environment in the Library." In *Cultural Diversity in Libraries*, edited by Donald E. Riggs and Patricia A. Tarin. New York: Neal-Schuman. 75–94.
Leonard, G. 1991. "The Ways We Serve." *Library Administration and Management* 5.4: 204–211.
Simmons-Welburn, Janice. 1999. "Diversity Dialogue Groups: A Model for Enhancing Work Place Diversity." *Journal of Library Administration* 27: 111–121.
Simmons-Welburn, Janice. 2001. "Addressing Diversity in Library Staff Training." In *Staff Development: A Practical Guide*, 3rd ed., edited by Elizabeth F. Avery, Terry Dahlin, and Deborah A. Carvery. Chicago: American Library Association. 74–77.
Wheeler, Maurice B. 1994. "Cultural Diversity Staff Development Activities: What's in It for Me?" In *Cultural Diversity in Libraries*, edited by Donald E. Riggs and Patricia A. Tarin. New York: Neal-Schuman. 109–129.

RECRUITMENT, HIRING, AND RETENTION

Buttlar, Lois, and William Caynon. 1992. "Recruitment of Librarians into the Profession: The Minority Perspective." *Library and Information Science Research* 14 (September): 259–280.

Cohen, Lucy R. 1994. "Recruitment and Retention." In *Cultural Diversity in Libraries*, edited by Donald E. Riggs and Patricia A. Tarin. New York: Neal-Schuman. 65–74.

Echavarria, Tami. 1990. "Minority Recruitment: A Success Story." *College and Research Libraries News* 51 (November): 962–964.

Edwards, Ronald G. 1999. "Recruiting More Minorities to the Library Profession: Responding to the Need for Diversity." In *Racing Toward Tomorrow: Proceedings of the Ninth National Conference of the Association of College and Research Libraries, April 8–11, 1999*, edited by Hugh A. Thompson. Chicago: American Library Association. 178–185.

Glaviano, Cliff, and R. Errol Lam. 1990. "Academic Libraries and Affirmative Action: Approaching Cultural Diversity in the 1990s." *College and Research Libraries* 51 (November): 513–523.

Howland, Joan. 1999. "Beyond Recruitment: Retention and Promotion Strategies to Ensure Diversity and Success." *Library Administration and Management* 13 (winter): 4–14.

Josey, E. J. 1993. "The Challenges of Cultural Diversity in the Recruitment of Faculty and Students from Diverse Backgrounds." *Journal of Education for Library and Information Science* 34 (fall): 302–311.

Knowles, Em Claire, and Linda Jolivet. 1991. "Recruiting the Underrepresented: Collaborative Efforts between Library Educators and Library Practitioners." *Library Administration and Management* 5 (fall): 189–193.

McCook, Kathleen de la Pena, and Paula Geist. 1993. "Diversity Deferred: Where Are the Minority Librarians?" *Library Journal* 118 (November 1): 35–38.

Reese, Gregory L. 1999. *Stop Talking, Start Doing: Attracting People of Color to the Library Profession*. Chicago: American Library Association.

Verny, Carol. 2002. "Ohio Goes Recruiting for Minority Librarians." *American Libraries* (August): 52–55.

Winston, Mark. 1998. "The Role of Recruitment in Achieving Goals Related to Diversity." *College and Research Libraries* 59 (May): 240–247.

Wright, Joyce C. 1990. "Recruitment and Retention of Minorities in Academic Libraries: A Plan of Action for the 1990s." *Illinois Libraries* 72 (November): 621–625.

INTERN AND RESIDENCY PROGRAMS

Brewer, Julie. 1997. "Post-Master's Residency Programs: Enhancing the Development of New Professionals and Minority Recruitment in Academic and Research Libraries." *College and Research Libraries* 58 (November): 528–537.

Cawthorne, Jon E., and Teri B. Wiel. 1986. "Internships/Residencies: Exploring the Possibilities for the Future." In *In Our Own Voices: The Changing Face of Librarianship*, edited by Teresa Y. Neely and Khafre K. Abif. Lanham, MD: Scarecrow Press. 121–124.

Cogell, Raquel V., and Cindy A. Gruwell, eds. 2001. *Diversity in Libraries: Academic Residency Programs*. Westport, CT: Greenwood Press.

DeBeau-Melting, Linda, and Karen M. Beavers. 1994. "Positioning for Change: The Diversity Internship as a Good Beginning." In *Diversity and Multiculturalism in Libraries*, edited by Katherine Hoover Hill. Greenwich, CT: JAI Press. 227–242.

Diaz, Jose O., and Kristina Starkhus. 1994. "Increasing Minority Representation in Academic Libraries: The Minority Librarian Intern Program at the Ohio State University." *College and Research Libraries* 55 (January): 41–46.

Internship, Residency, and Fellowship Programs in ARL Libraries, SPEC Kit 188. 1992. Washington, DC: Association for Research Libraries.

Quarton, B. 2002. "Five Steps to an Effective Internship Program." *College and Research Libraries* 63: 109–111.

Wrighten, Mary G. "The Significance of a Minority Reference Internship Program." In *Racial and Ethnic Diversity in Academic Libraries: Multicultural Issues*, edited by Deborah A. Curry, Susan Griswold Blandy, and Lynne M. Martin. New York: Haworth Press. 57–66.

COLLECTION DEVELOPMENT AND MANAGEMENT

"Accommodating Diversity: Searching Across Collections." 1999. *Information Retrieval and Library Automation* 35.4 (September): 9.

Buttlar, Lois, and L. R. Wynar. 1992. "Cultural Pluralism and Ethnic Diversity: Authors as Information Users in the Field of Ethnic Studies." *Collection Management* 16.3: 13–33.

Diaz, Joseph Robert. 1994. "Collection Development in Multicultural Studies." In *Cultural Diversity in Libraries*, edited by Donald E. Riggs and Patricia A. Tarin. New York: Neal-Schuman. 185–198.

Figueredo, Danilo H. 1994. "The Many We Are: Guidelines for Multicultural Collections Based on the Bloomfield College Project." In *Diversity and Multiculturalism in Libraries*, edited by Katherine Hoover Hill. Greenwich, CT: JAI Press. 63–74.

Johnson-Cooper, Glendora. 1994. "Building Racially Diverse Collections: An Afrocentric Approach." In *Racial and Ethnic Diversity in Academic Libraries: Multicultural Issues*, edited by Deborah A. Curry, Susan Griswold Blandy, and Lynne M. Martin. New York: Haworth Press. 153–170.

LaFond, Deborah M., Mary K. Van Ullen, and Richard D. Irving. 2000. "Diversity in Collection Development: Comparing Access Strategies to Alternative Press Periodicals." *College and Research Libraries* 61 (March): 136–144.

Nuckolls, Karen A. 1995. "Subject Access to Diversity Materials: The Library of Congress Subject Heading Shortfall." In *Racial and Ethnic Diversity in Academic Libraries: Multicultural Issues*, edited by Deborah A. Curry, Susan Griswold Blandy, and Lynne M. Martin. New York: Haworth Press. 241–251.

Pettingill, Ann, and Pamela Morgan. 1996. "Building a Retrospective Multicultural Collection: A Practical Approach." *Collection Building* 15: 10–16.

Serebnick, Judith, and Frank Quinn. 1995. "Measuring Diversity of Opinion in Public Library Collections." *Library Quarterly* 65.1 (January): 1–38.

Totten, Herman L., and Risa W. Brown. 1994. *Culturally Diverse Library Collections for Children*. New York: Neal-Schuman.

Totten, Herman L., Risa W. Brown, and Carolyn Garner. 1996. *Culturally Diverse Library Collections for Youth*. New York: Neal-Schuman.

IV SAMPLES OF SUCCESSFUL DIVERSITY DOCUMENTS

American Library Association Staff Diversity and Inclusion Action Plan

ALA Mission
To provide leadership for the development, promotion, and improvement of library and information services and the profession of librarianship in order to enhance learning and ensure access to information for all.

ALA's Commitment to Diversity
Diversity is one of the five key action areas adopted by the membership of the American Library Association to fulfill its mission of providing the highest quality library and information services for all people. The Association actively promotes equal access to information for all people through libraries; encourages development of library services for diverse populations; advocates for the recruitment of underrepresented groups and individuals with disabilities to the profession; and deeply commits to fostering a diverse and inclusive work environment for its staff.

The Diversity Vision
The American Library Association recognizes that in addition to race, creed, color, religion, gender, disability and national origin, there are a multitude of differences (language origin, regional and geographic background, economic class, education, learning and communication styles, sexual orientation and personal lifestyle) that individuals bring to the workplace. It is this diversity that contributes a deeper level of understanding and competence to our daily work. The American Library Association envisions a richly, diverse workforce providing a high level of service to the membership in an environment where respect, appreciation, equity and inclusion are core values.

Summary of Goals
The Diversity and Inclusion goals of the American Library Association and the strategies that have been outlined to meet them are dynamic in that we expect them to grow and change over time. Specifically we aim to:

1. Ensure that ALA maintains a welcoming and safe environment for all staff.
2. Encourage diversity efforts at the highest level of leadership.
3. Recruit and retain an excellent and diverse workforce at all levels of the organization.
4. Provide models for the profession in the development and implementation of diversity initiatives, training and programs.
5. Make available continued learning, personal and professional leadership opportunities and development training to staff at every level.
6. Incorporate diverse views and voices in every aspect or our work.
7. Promote and sustain a harassment free, barrier free, open communication work environment.

American Library Association

C. Internal Environment Issues

DIVERSITY

ISSUE 4: *How do we create a climate that values diversity?*

We believe that diversity provides multiple perspectives and broadens views of issues and problems and leads to more effective solutions. Our efforts to promote and develop library collections, services, and staff that are representative of our diverse community will have a major impact on our success as a research library. These efforts include the recruitment and retention of library staff at all levels from a variety of backgrounds, particularly from those groups underrepresented in our workforce. We should also seek to develop a culture that values diversity and ensure that diversity is incorporated into our collections and services. The issue is not should we have diversity, but how to make it play a central role in our thinking and planning for the Libraries' future.

Strategy 1: *Improve minority recruitment and retention efforts for librarian, professional staff, and support staff.*
Strategic Initiatives:
   A. Create a position in the Libraries for a recent minority library school graduate that makes good on our investment in ARL's "Initiative to Create a Diverse Workforce."
   B. Obtain funding through the Minority Faculty Fellowship Program to create a position for a minority librarian.
   C. Work with University Human Resources to attract more minority applicants to professional and support staff positions.
   D. Develop a program to mentor minority staff.
Operational Goals:
   A. Investigate additional options for advertising to potential minority applicants.
   B. Educate search and screen committee members on their role in recruiting minority applicants.
   C. Provide diversity training to all staff.

Strategy 2: *Demonstrate through our decisions about collections and services that the Libraries value diversity.*
Strategic Initiative:
   A. Create and fill a multicultural librarian position to provide outreach to diversity programs at IU.
Operational Goals:
   A. Ensure that our facilities, exhibits, publications, and staffing at public service desks reflect the diversity of the community we serve.
   B. Take advantage of opportunities to build collections of interest to underrepresented groups.

Strategy 3: *Develop processes to incorporate thinking about diversity in our day-to-day activities.*
Strategic Initiatives:
   A. Appoint and charge a diversity committee to work with the Libraries Human Resources on diversity initiatives.
   B. Monitor our progress in increasing the diversity of staff at all levels.
   C. Conduct periodic assessment of the needs of minority faculty, students, and staff for library collections and services.
Operational Goals:
   A. Encourage staff to participate in diversity programs on campus and at national conferences.
   B. Work with the Office of Multicultural Affairs to expose staff to additional diversity programming.

Return to Contents

Indiana University Libraries' Diversity Plan

University of Louisville Libraries' Diversity Plan
September 28, 2005

Employee Diversity

Goal 1: Increase minority employment in the profession.

Strategies:
- Participate in career days at local high schools.
- Increase endowment for minority internship program.
- Establish contact with local volunteer, community outreach, and pre-professional minority organizations.
- Work with minority student groups and organizations on the UofL campuses.

Goal 2: Review and revise hiring practices.

Strategies:
- Review ARL resources and related institutions' best practices on hiring procedures.
- Investigate use of specialized recruitment tools.
- Identify MLS programs that have African Americans enrolled.
- Compile list of all professional library and information science list-servs targeting minority groups.
- Compile a list of other news organizations geared towards local and national minority groups.
- Advertise open positions through all appropriate lists and to all appropriate groups and organizations.

Goal 3: Retain minority hires.

Strategies:
- Develop a mentorship program.

Diversity Education for Libraries' Administrators, Faculty, Staff and Students

Goal 4: Determine the current diversity climate within the libraries.

Strategies:
- Conduct a diversity climate survey.
- Monitor Deyta Inc surveys for indications of service issues.

Goal 5: Expand diversity training opportunities in the libraries.

University of Louisville Libraries' Diversity Plan

Curricular and Programmatic Diversity

Goal 6: Create a welcoming, inclusive environment for study and research.

Strategies:
- Sponsor at least one event a year that features a minority author.
- Sponsor at least two exhibits a year that feature African American history or authors.
- Ensure library collections reflect campus diversity.
- Identify ways to communicate diversity efforts to the campus community.
- Create links to diversity resources from the libraries' Web pages.

(*Continued*)

SAMPLES OF SUCCESSFUL DIVERSITY DOCUMENTS 219

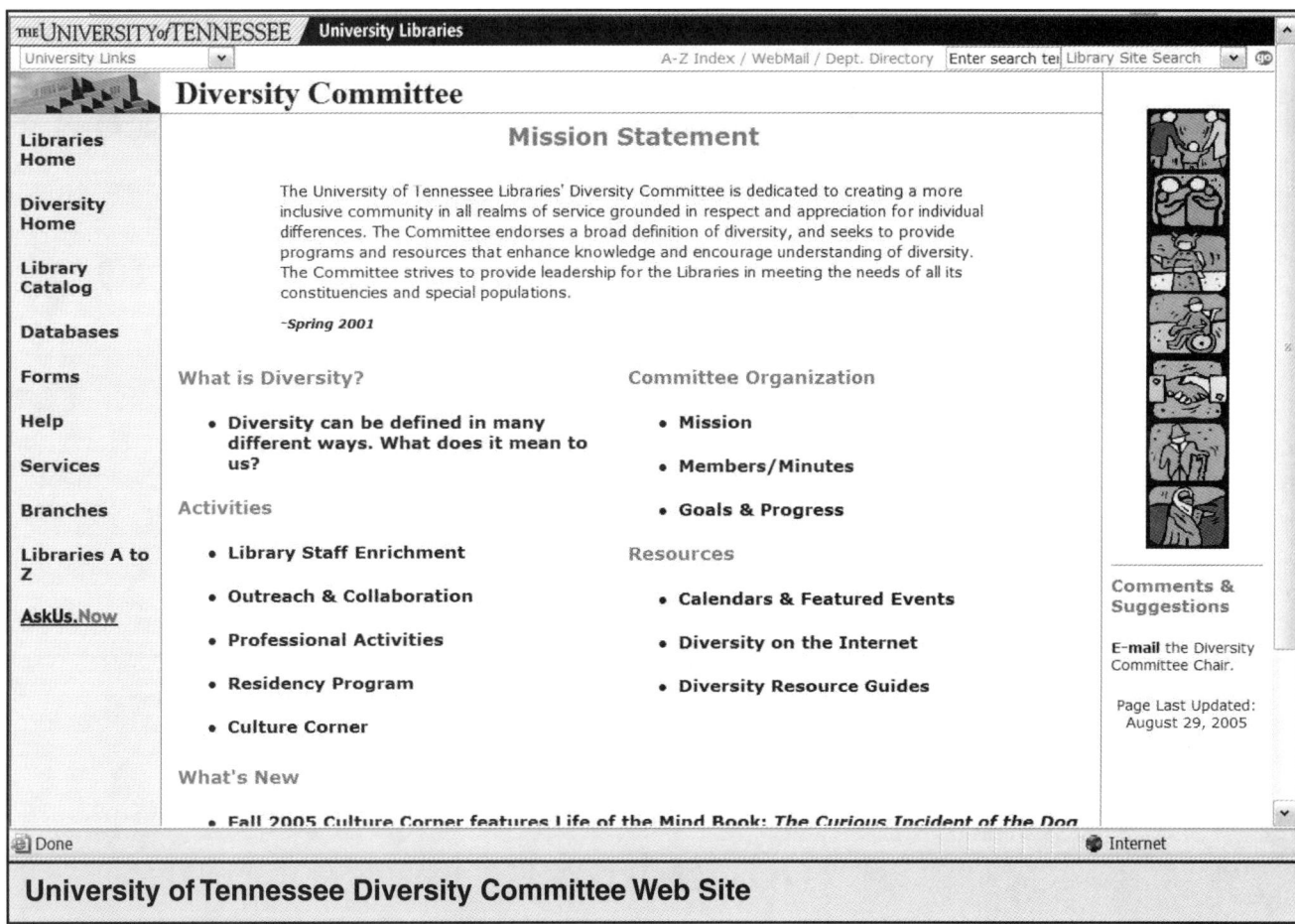

University of Tennessee Diversity Committee Web Site

Diversity is a commitment to recognizing and appreciating the variety of characteristics that make individuals unique in an atmosphere that promotes and celebrates individual and collective achievement.

Examples of these characteristics are: age; cognitive style; culture; disability (mental, learning, physical); economic background; education; ethnicity; gender; geographic background; language(s) spoken; marital/partnered status; physical appearance; political affiliation; race; religious beliefs; sexual orientation.

THE UNIVERSITY OF TENNESSEE LIBRARIES DIVERSITY COMMITTEE
SPRING 2001; REVISED JANUARY 200

University of Tennessee Libraries' Diversity Definition Plan

Diversity Committee

Mission

The University of Tennessee Libraries' Diversity Committee is dedicated to creating a more inclusive community in all realms of service grounded in respect and appreciation for individual differences. The Committee endorses a **broad definition of diversity**, and seeks to provide programs and resources that enhance knowledge and encourage understanding of diversity. The Committee strives to provide leadership for the Libraries in meeting the needs of all its constituencies and special populations.

Excerpts from University of Tennessee Libraries' Planning Documents that relate to diversity:

From *Library Plan 2002-2006*:
"Commit to the value of a broad approach to diversity that includes ethnic, cultural, religious, gender and experiential differences.
- Mount a long-term diversity program through the work of the Diversity Committee
- Initiate a dialogue within the Libraries to define and examine diversity issues
- Undertake a program of outreach to international students
- Set priorities and take action to ensure a diverse library staff, collection, and environment"

Also from *Library Plan 2002-2006* - under *Organizational Values*:
"The University Libraries value diversity in staff, users, and collections and work to provide a climate of openness, acceptance, and respect for individuals and points of view."

From *Priority Action Items for 2002* - A priority under the *Personnel* heading:
"Create a diverse and welcoming library environment guided by the results of the Diversity Climate survey."

From *Strategic Priorities for 2001* - Under the *Personnel* heading:
"Develop a plan to address diversity and a welcoming library environment."

University of Tennessee Libraries' Diversity Committee Mission Statement

University of Tennessee
University Libraries (UL) Climate Survey
Fall 2001

The University of Tennessee Libraries' Diversity Committee is asking library employees for input on diversity issues. This survey will assess your perceptions of the general work climate in the University Libraries (UL), as well as your reactions regarding the more specific climate for diversity. Your responses will provide the Diversity Committee with guidance about the types of programs that will be beneficial to the staff.

Your responses are anonymous and confidential. Questionnaires should be returned by **October 31, 2001** to the **UT Office of Equity and Diversity** in the envelope provided. No one will ever see the information in such a way that personal identities could be ascertained.

Your participation is completely voluntary. Although it will be helpful to have as many completed questionnaires returned as possible, you may decline to participate. **Please do not complete a questionnaire if you are not yet 18 years old.** Regulations intended to protect human subjects do not allow us to survey staff under the age of 18. If you have any questions, please contact Thura Mack, Chair of the University Libraries' Diversity Committee.

Thank you for your help.

Instructions
The questions in this survey cover several areas of work climate, as well as individual perceptions and attitudes. Please be honest in your responses and try not to leave any questions blank. The entire questionnaire should take about 30 minutes to complete.

Demographic Information

A. **Race/Ethnicity (check one):**
- African
- African American
- American Indian or Alaskan Native
- Asian or Pacific Islander
- Causasian
- Hispanic
- Other (Please describe)

B. **Position (check one):**
- Student Library Assistant
- Graduate Assistant
- Non-exempt Staff
- Exempt Staff
- Faculty

C. What is your country of origin? _____
D. What is your gender? ___ M ___ F
E. What is your age? _____ years
F. How long have you worked at UL? _____ years
G. Do you have supervisory responsibilities? ___ Yes ___ No
H. Were you aware, before this survey, that UL has a Diversity Committee? ___ Yes ___ No
I. Are you familiar with the UL Diversity Committee's definition of diversity? ___ Yes ___ No
J. Are you familiar with the diversity components of the Libraries' current planning documents? ___ Yes ___ No
K. Do you consider yourself to be a member of an under-represented group? ___ Yes ___ No
   If yes, please briefly explain why:

University of Tennessee Climate Survey

Ekstrom Library—Public Services—Reference—Intern/Lecturer, Latisha Reynolds

Teaches information literacy classes and provides reference assistance. Serves on various committees and teams to support the work of the libraries and the University. Serves as the Chair of the Diversity Task Force and as a representative on the university-wide diversity group. Provides outreach to students through volunteer activities and events.

Kornhauser Health Sciences Library—Intern/Lecturer, John Chenault

Provides reference services for patrons of the Health Science Library, including assistance with using and searching electronic resources, and locating print journals, serials, and monographs in the stacks. Responsible for designing and teaching citation management software courses for library patrons.

University of Louisville Libraries' Intern Job Description

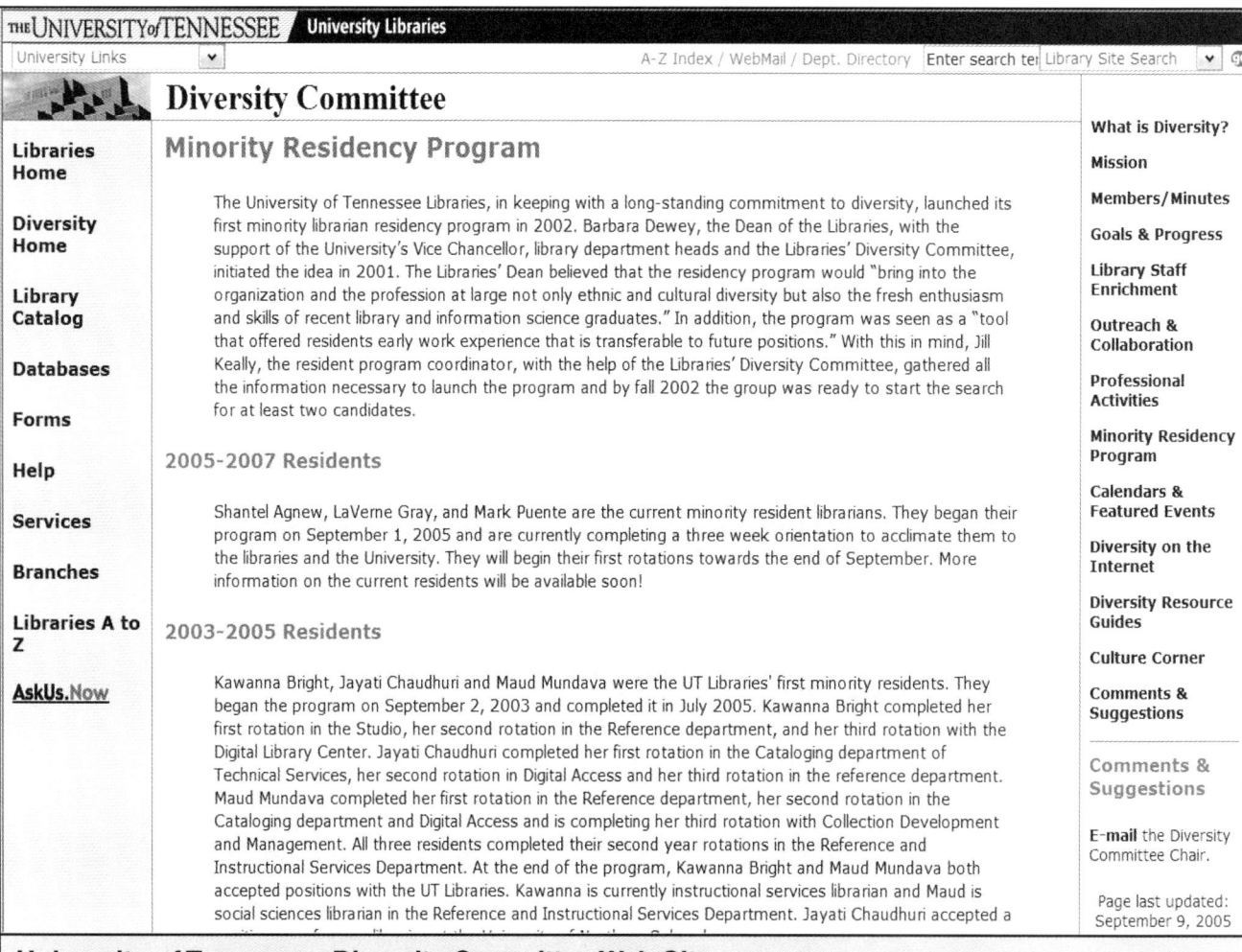

University of Tennessee Diversity Committee Web Site

INDEX

A
Abdul-Jabbar, Kareem, 36
academic libraries
    diverse library staff for, 61–67, 73
    outreach services in, 132–135
access
    to special collections, 166–167, 168
    works on, 208–209
accountability, 25
ACRL
    See Association of College and Research Libraries
"Adaptor" library, 21, 25
advisory groups, 85
affirmative action, 34
African Americans
    HBCU Library Alliance, 182–186
    library climate and, 147–148
    number of librarians, 69
    Open Doors exhibition and, 178–179
    University of Louisville Libraries and, 62, 67
    University of Maryland Eastern Shore and, 117–124
    University of Mississippi integration and, 170–171
ALA
    See American Library Association
Aleph 500 automated library system
    of Frederick Douglass Library, 119, 120–121
    impact in library, 117–118
ALISE
    See Association of Library and Information Science Education
Alsup, City of St. Petersburg v., 17
American Council on Education, 46
American Libraries, 72, 132
American Library Association (ALA)
    diversity in recruitment and, 79, 80
    diversity issues, 203
    Diversity Librarians' Network and, 195–197
    recruitment resources, 90
    Spectrum Initiative of, 71
    Staff Diversity and Inclusion Action Plan, 215
American Library Association (ALA) Office for Research and Statistics
    diversity of librarians, 33
    on minority librarians, 102
Andrew W. Mellon Foundation, 184, 185
Anna in the Tropics (Cruz), 165
Antwine, Harold M., Jr., 177
archival collections, 166
    See also special collections departments
Aristotle, 93
ARL
    See Association of Research Libraries
Aronson, Jennifer, 169–180
ASERL (Association of South East Research Libraries), 65
Askew, Consuella, 185
assessment
    of diversity initiatives, 66
    library needs assessment, 138–141
    of library's climate for diversity, 47–48
    of multicultural programs, 128
    of Peer Research Advisors program, 159–161
    See also diversity assessment
Association for Assessment in Counseling, 4

225

"Association of 1890 Library Deans and Directors", 183
Association of College and Research Libraries (ACRL)
  Institute for Information Literacy Immersion Program, 78
  recruiting demographics, 93
  Task Force on Recruitment, 63–65, 81–83
Association of Library and Information Science Education (ALISE)
  admission procedures, 65
  Library and Information Science Education Statistical Report, 33
  on minority librarians, 102
Association of Research Libraries (ARL)
  CIRLA Fellows Program and, 95
  diversity workshop, 5–6
  online diversity assessment course, 14
  Program Officer for Training and Diversity, 90
  recruiting demographics, 93
  Residency and Internship Programs Database, 189
  Task Force on Recruitment, 63–65
  University of Arizona library, 70
Association of South East Research Libraries (ASERL), 65
awareness-based training, 18

B

Balderrama, Sandra Rios, 203
Ballard-Thrower, Rhea, 16–31
Bangs, Patricia, 5
Banks, Brenda, 183
Becker, Ronald L., 165, 166
Beckwith, Harry, 37, 40–41
Bennis, James, 96
Berry, John, 84
best practices
  See diversity in library, best practices
Beyond Race and Gender: Unleashing the Power of Your Total Workforce by Managing Diversity (Thomas), 17
bibliographic database, of Frederick Douglass Library, 121
bibliography, works on diversity, 205–211
Binkley, Yildiz, 184
Blackmon, Zenobia, 184
Blessing, Laura, 152–161
Bliss, Jennifer, 183

Blogs section, Diversity Librarians' Network, 194
Board of Education, Brown v.
  diversity in workplace and, 17
  multicultural outreach librarian and, 126, 127
Boardley Suber, Dianne, 184
body language, 149
Bonnette, Ashley, 72, 74
Bothmer, James A., 74
brand, 38–40
Bright, Kawanna, 187–202
Brooks, Sharon D., 117–124
Brown Letarte, Karen M., 152–161
Brown v. Board of Education
  diversity in workplace and, 17
  multicultural outreach librarian and, 126, 127
Brown v. State of Louisiana, 17
Brumfield, Patsy R., 171
budget, 155
Building a House for Diversity: How a Fable about a Giraffe and an Elephant Offers New Strategies for Today's Workforce (Thomas), 4
Burton, Jametoria, 76–89

C

California Librarians Recruitment Project, 83
A Call for Cooperation Among HBCU Libraries: Opportunities for Consideration (Franklin), 183
Canada, diversity in libraries, 51–55
career development, 96–97
Carnevale, Anthony Patrick, 16, 17
Ceja, Miguel, 147–148
Census Canada, 51–52
"Changes in the African American Family in Oxford/Lafayette County and Mississippi" project, 178
Charter of Rights and Freedoms, 52
Chaudhuri, Jayati, 187–202
Chesapeake Information and Research Library Alliance (CIRLA) Fellows program
  brochure, 98–101
  conclusion about, 97
  demographics background, 93–94
  highlights, 94–97
Chicago Multi-type Library System, 103
City of St. Petersburg v. Alsup, 17
civic organizations, 85
Civil Rights Act of 1964, 17

"Civil Rights, Mississippi, and the Novelist's Craft" exhibition, 177
Cleveland, Thomas, 175
climate, library, 147–148
Clinton, Bill, 55, 186
coach figures, 35
Coats, Reed, 5
collection development policy
    for diversity, 142
    for special collections department, 164
collections
    diversity tips, 141–142
    needs assessment, 139
    special collections departments, 163–168
    works on, 211
Collins, Jim, 42
Columbus Metropolitan Library system, 5
commitment, 70
communication
    about library diversity program, 48–49
    for diverse library user services, 148–150
    of diverse strategy, 73
community records, 165
community ties, 164–166
competencies, 96
computers
    of Frederick Douglass Library, 118
    laptops of University of Maryland Eastern Shore, 121–122
    of library facilities, 146
Conference Board of Canada, 52
conferences, 87
Confucius, 97
Connecting area, Diversity Librarian's Network Web site, 193–194
connectors, 38
Cooper, W. Wert, Jr., 175
Coordinator of Personnel Programs, UMD Libraries, 10
Copley, Frank Barkley, 19
"Core Competencies and Learning Outcomes Statement" (CIRLA Fellows Program), 96
Cornell University Library Junior Fellows Program
    conclusion about, 111–112
    description of, 103–106
Courtney, Hugh
    posture types, 20–21
    strategic planning uncertainty, 19–20
    team-based strategic planning, 24, 25
Covey, Steven, 36
Cox, Taylor, Jr., 13
cross-cultural communication, 148–150
Cruz, Nilo, 165
Cultural Diversity grant, 106, 190–191
culture, library, 147–148
culture, organizational, 69
Cummins, Paul, 198
CustomerSat, 147

D

Dakshinamurti, Ganga B., 51–55
Delaware Conference Academy, 117
delegation, 25
delivery systems, 129
Department of Archives and Special Collections
    See University of Mississippi's Department of Archives and Special Collections
design, Diversity Librarians' Network Web site, 195
Dewey, John, 96
digital divide
    definition of, 118
    distance education, 119–120
    impact of technology in library, 117–118
    integrated library system, 120–121
    laptops, wireless environment, 121–122
    library instruction services for, 143–144
    online resources, 122–123
    technology history, 118–119
    training, instruction, 123–124
Digital Divide Network, 118
Dinkins, Joia, 77
displays
    for multicultural outreach, 126
    of special collections department, 165, 166
distance education, 119–120
diversity
    in Canadian libraries, 51–55
    CIRLA Fellows Program, 93–101
    communication and, 148–150
    definition of, 3–4
    Diversity Librarian's Network, 187–202

HBCU Library Alliance and SOLINET, 182–186
issues in library, 138
libraries and, 203
library diversity program, strategies for, 46–49
library needs assessment for, 138–141
library staff, 61–67
library user services, 141–148
multicultural outreach librarian, 126–135
people and, 51
in recruitment, 71–73, 76
in recruitment, evolution of, 79–83
recruitment stories, 76–79
recruitment strategies, 84–87
recruitment/retention today, 84
in retention, 73–74, 87–89
serving, 137–138
special collections departments, 163–168
in staffing, 69–70
strategic plan sample, 26–31
strategic planning and, 18–19
team-based strategic planning and, 22–26
today, 16–17
University of Maryland Eastern Shore and, 117–124
value of, 46
in workplace, 17–18
works on, 205–211
Diversity, Five Laws of, 36–37
diversity assessment
diversity definition, 3–4
rationale for, 4–5
research, adaptability of, 13–14
research/efforts in libraries, 5–6
University of Maryland Libraries' assessments, 6–13
diversity documents
American Library Association Staff Diversity and Inclusion Action Plan, 215
Indiana University Libraries' Diversity Plan, 216
University of Louisville Libraries' Diversity Plan, 217–218
University of Louisville Libraries' Intern Job Description, 223
University of Tennessee Diversity Committee Web site, 219
University of Tennessee Libraries' Diversity Committee Mission Statement, 221
University of Tennessee Libraries' Diversity Definition Plan, 220
University of Tennessee University Libraries Climate Survey, 222
University of Tennessee University Libraries Minority Residency Program, 224
diversity in library, best practices
be standout player, 35–36
brand for, 38–40
get in game, 34–35
marketing, 40–41
overview of, 33–34
rules, play by, 36–37
scenario planning exercise, 44
specialist role, 37–38
triple threat position, 42–43
versatility, 41–42
Diversity Librarian's Network (DLN)
ALA Annual Conference and, 195, 197
developers of, 187
development reasons, 188–189
evaluation of, 200
features of, 189
feedback, 195, 197
future growth/work, 201–202
goals, objectives of, 190
implementation of, 190–192
launch strategy, 199
marketing strategy, 199–200
poster, 196
purpose of, 187
steps to launch, 198
technical challenges, 198
University of Minnesota Libraries training Institute for Early Career Librarians, 197–198
vision of future, 200
Web page, 188
Web site components, 192–194
Web site design, 195
Diversity Necklace (Olsen), 53
Diversity Now (Neely and Lee-Smeltzer), 5
Diversity Residents, Interns, and Fellows list (DRIF list), 194
diversity training, 17–18
Diversity Training Programs section, 193
DLN
  See Diversity Librarian's Network

documents
   See diversity documents
Domingue, Alexandria L., 7–9
donations, 173–176
Downing, Karen
   on peer information counseling program, 153–154, 156
   peer mentoring programs, 152
   on role of Peer Research Advisors, 158
DRIF list (Diversity Residents, Interns, and Fellows list), 194

E
education, 48
Edwards, Ronald, 72
electronic discussion board (EDB)
   of Diversity Librarians' Network, 189
   funds for, 191
   goals and, 190
   purpose of, 194
Ely, Robin J., 3
Employment Equity Act, 52
environment
   See library environment
equity, 53
evaluation
   of Diversity Librarians' Network, 200
   of library's climate for diversity, 47–48
   See also assessment
Evers, Medgar, 172
Evers-Williams, Myrlie, 172
exhibitions, 177–179
ExLibris, 117, 119
eye contact, 149
eyebrow raising, 149

F
"Faces of a Profession" (video), 64–65
facilitator, 22–23
facilities
   diversity tips, 146
   needs assessment, 140
Fairfax County Public Library (FCPL) system, 5
Faulkner, William, 169
feedback, 195, 197
Festival Latino, 127
financial assistance, 85–86
First Joint Librarians of Color Conference, 90–91
Five Laws of Diversity, 36–37
floor plan, of library facilities, 146, 147
Fogg, C. Davis, 22–26
Ford, Barbara, 82
Ford, Jennifer, 169–180
Fortas, Abe, 17
Franklin, Janice R., 182–186
Franklin, Niler, 178
Frederick Douglass Library
   digital divide, 118
   distance education, 119–120
   impact of technology in library, 117–118
   integrated library system, 120–121
   laptops, wireless environment, 121–122
   online resources, 122–123
   technology history, 118–119
   training, instruction, 123–124

G
Gallagher, Henry, 174
Gandhi, Mahatma, 39
Garvin, David, 35–36
Georgetown University, 94
GLISA (Graduate Library Institute for Spanish-Speaking Americans), 83
Glisson, Susan
   Department of Archives and Special Collections and, 178
   Open Doors commemoration and, 171, 174
   Open Doors Oral History Collection and, 176
goals, 47
Goldstein, Leonard, 16
Good to Great! (Collins), 42
Goodwin, Jane, 5
Graduate Library Institute for Spanish-Speaking Americans (GLISA), 83
graduate programs
   See library and information science (LIS) graduate programs
Grady, Jennifer, 69, 102–103
grant
   for CIRLA Fellows Program, 94
   Cultural Diversity Grant, 106
   for Diversity Librarians' Network, 190–191
   for HBCU Library Alliance, 184, 185
   Peer Research Advisors program and, 152, 154, 155

for University of Notre Dame Libraries' Summer Program, 111
Granville A. Bunton Pan African Collection, 67
Gray, Duncan M., Jr., 175
Grayson, April, 177
Grow Your Own campaign, 84
Gunn, Dean, 183

H

Haipeng, Li, 146–147
Hall, Stuart, 55
Hall, Tracie D.
  ALA Office for Diversity director, 90
  Grow Your Own campaign, 84
  librarian demographics, 69
  library diversity practices, 33–44
  on recruitment of high school students, 102–103
hand, left, 150
Hanes v. Shuttlesworth, 17
Hanges, Paul J., 12
Havener, W. Michael, 76–89
Hawkins, Ernestine
  on diversity action, 70
  minorities in library, 33
  on recruitment, 76
Haygood, Wil, 169
HBCU Library Alliance, 182–186
HBCUs (historically black colleges and universities), 182–186
head nodding, 150
Hickerson, H. Thomas, 168
High Impact Tools and Activities for Strategic Planning: Creative Techniques for Facilitating Your Organization's Planning Process (Napier et al.), 19
high school students
  Cornell University Library Junior Fellows Program, 103–106
  librarianship recruitment, 102–103
  recruitment initiatives, 111–112
  University of Notre Dame Libraries' Summer Program, 106–111
higher education, diversity in, 46
hiring
  See recruitment
historically black colleges and universities (HBCUs), 182–186
Hoffman, Irene M., 93–101
Holiday, Deloice G., 126–135

Holton, Tommy S., 183, 185
Howard University Law Library, 28–31

I

ILL (Inter Library Loan), 122
IMLS
  See Institute of Museum and Library Services
immigration, to Canada, 52
Indiana University Libraries, 126–135, 216
Institute for Early Career Librarians, 78
Institute for Information Literacy Immersion Program, 78
Institute of Museum and Library Services (IMLS)
  CIRLA Fellows Program and, 93, 94
  grants from, 103
instruction
  diversity tips, 143–144
  at Frederick Douglass Library, 122–123
integrated library system, 120–121
integration
  of University of Mississippi, 170–171
  University of Mississippi's commemoration of, 169–170, 171–180
Inter Library Loan (ILL), 122
Interactive Video Network (IVN) system, 119–120
internships, 66, 210–211
Issues in Advancing Diversity through Assessment (Sedlacek), 4

J

Jacoby, Tamar, 17
Jenkins, Althea, 183
Jennings, Kriza, 147
Job Shadow day, 103
job shadowing, 106
John E. Phay Collection, 177–178
Johnson, Earvin "Magic", 42
Johnson v. Virginia, 17
Joiner, Lottie, 171
Jones, DeEtta, 3–4
Jordan, Michael, 33
Josey, E. J., 80–81

K

Kansas State University diversity program, 46, 130

Kayongo, Jessica, 102–112
Keally, Jill, 197
Keller, Kirsten, 12
Kellum, Gloria, 171, 180
Kennedy, John F., 170, 171
Kentucky, 66–67
Kerzner, Harold, 18, 19
Khayat, Robert, 169, 174
knowledge, 38
knowledge management, 63
Knowledge River Program, 84
Knowles, Em Clair, 81–82
Kochan, Thomas, 18, 19

L

LaCroix, Michael, 74
Lafayette County Court House (Oxford, Mississippi), 170
LaFleur, LeRoy, 102–112
LAMA
   See Library Administration and Management Association
laptops, 119, 121–122
Lasch-Quinn, Elisabeth, 17–18
leadership, 47
Leading Ideas, 156
Learning Curriculum, 10
left hand, 150
Leslie, Lisa M., 12
"Let Recruitment Begin with Me" (Perry), 72
liaison program, 144
librarians
   CIRLA Fellows Program, 93–101
   demographics of, 69
   diverse library environment and, 61–62
   Diversity Librarian's Network, 187–202
   recruitment, Jamie's story of, 76–78
   recruitment of diverse library workforce, 63–65, 71–73, 130–132
   retention of, 65, 73–74
   staff diversity, 69–70
   technology and, 119
   work of, 62–63
   See also multicultural outreach librarian
librarianship, high school student programs, 102–112

library
   climate/culture, 147–148
   diversity and, 203
   diversity in Canadian libraries, 51–55
   diversity in libraries, works on, 205–211
   diversity of, 21–22
   Five Laws of Diversity, 36–37
   HBCU Library Alliance, 182–186
   retention strategies, 88
   role of, 129
   special collections departments, 163–168
   strategic plan, sample, 26–31
   strategic planning postures, 20–21
   team-based strategic planning, 22–26
   See also diversity in library, best practices
library, diversity assessment
   diversity definition, 3–4
   rationale for, 4–5
   research, adaptability of, 13–14
   research/efforts in libraries, 5–6
   University of Maryland Libraries' assessments, 6–13
Library Administration and Management Association (LAMA)
   Cultural Diversity grant, 106, 190–191
   Diversity Officers Discussion Group meeting, 197
library and information science (LIS) graduate programs
   evolution of recruitment, 79–83
   recruiting practices, 76
   recruiting stories, 76–79
   recruitment/retention suggestions, 84–89
   recruitment/retention today, 84
library diversity program
   assessment/evaluation, 47–48
   communication/publicity, 48–49
   education/programming, 48
   organization/planning, 46–47
   special collections departments and, 163–168
   value of diversity, 46
library environment
   diverse, 61–62
   facilities, diversity and, 146
   library staff and, 147
   needs assessment, 140–141

Library Journal, 84
library services, 140
    See also library user services
library staff
    academic librarians' work, 62–63
    assessment of diversity initiatives, 66
    case study, 66–67
    CIRLA Fellows Program, 93–101
    communication for user services, 148–150
    diverse academic library environment, 61–62
    diversity tips, 146–147
    high school students, reaching, 102–112
    minority students, success of, 66
    needs assessment, 140
    Peer Research Advisors program, 152–161
    recruiting practices, 76
    recruitment, evolution of, 79–83
    recruitment of, 63–65, 71–73
    recruitment resources, 90–92
    recruitment stories, 76–79
    recruitment strategies, 84–87
    recruitment/retention of, 84, 130–132
    retention of, 65, 73–74, 87–89
    staffing, 69–70
    UMD Libraries' diversity assessment, 7–13
    of University of Louisville Libraries, 67
    works on, 209–211
library user services
    communication and, 148–150
    diversity, serving, 137–138
    diversity issues, 138
    needs assessment, 138–141
    tips/practices for, 141–148
LIS
    See library and information science (LIS) graduate programs
"Listening to Ourselves" (Sharif), 150
logo
    brand for diversity programs, 38–39
    of Diversity Librarians' Network, 200
Look magazine, 171
"Looking for Leaders in the Information Age" (video by Ohio Library Council), 103
Love, Johannieque B.
    assessment of diversity initiatives, 66
    on diversity assessment, 3, 5, 14

M

Madden, Amy, 55
management
    of diversity, 17
    works on, 207–208
Manitoba, Canada, 52
Marcum, Deana B., 184
marketing
    for diversity initiatives, 40–41
    of Diversity Librarians' Network, 199–200
    library outreach services, 129, 130
Marshall, Suse, 178
master's programs
    See library and information science (LIS) graduate programs
Matthews, Linda M., 167
maven, 38
McDaniel, Karen, 185
McWhite, Leigh, 177
"Me? A Librarian?" (video by Ohio Library Council), 103
Mead, Margaret, 46
mentoring
    in CIRLA Fellows Program, 95
    Diversity Librarian's Network and, 190
    importance of, 9
    of Jametoria Burton, 77, 78
    of LIS students, 85
    new librarians, 87
    recruitment of librarians, 72
    REFORMA/UCLA Mentor Program, 82
    for staff retention, 73–74
    See also Peer Research Advisors program, NCSU Libraries
Mentoring Opportunities section, Diversity Librarians' Web site, 194
Meredith, James Howard
    Henry Gallagher and, 174
    Open Doors commemoration and, 175
    Open Doors Oral History Collection and, 176–177
    University of Mississippi's integration and, 170–171, 172
Meredith, Joseph, 171
MetaLib, 122
Meyers, Chris, 180

Military Sealift Command, 150
Mills, Grace M., 16–31
minorities
    in Canada, 52
    librarian demographics, 69
    in library, limitations for, 33
    library staff, 67
    in LIS programs, 80
    minority librarians, 102
    minority residency program, 48
    recruitment of diverse library workforce, 71–73
    recruitment of high school students, 103–112
    UMD Libraries' diversity assessment and, 8
    See also diversity
Minority Internship/Scholarship in MLIS program, 83
"Minority Representation in Library and Information Science Programs" (Josey), 80–81
minority students
    Peer Research Advisors program, 152–161
    success of, 66
Mintzberg, Henry, 18, 19
mission statement
    for diversity program, 47
    of Tampa Library, 164
    in team-based strategic planning, 24
    University of Tennessee Libraries' Diversity Committee Mission Statement, 221
Mississippi, 170–171
    See also University of Mississippi's Department of Archives and Special Collections
Moore, Anita, 185
Moore, Charles, 172
Mossison, Ann M., 18
Motley, Constance Baker, 172
Multicultural Orientation festival, 127
multicultural outreach librarian
    assessment of multicultural programs, 128
    diverse workforce and, 130–132
    diversity challenges, 126–127
    job of, 127–128
    outreach services, 132–135
    promotion of outreach services, 129
multicultural programs, 128
Multiculturalism Act of 1988, 52
multilingual services, 54

multimedia materials, 142
Mundava, Maud, 187–202

N

Napier, Rod, 19
National Center for Education Statistics, 33
National Diversity in Libraries (NDIL) Conference, 87
National Historically Black Colleges and Universities Week, 186
National Library of Canada, 53
Native Americans, 69
NCSU (North Carolina State University) Libraries, 152–161
NDIL (National Diversity in Libraries) Conference, 87
Neal, Kathryn M., 165
needs assessment, 138–141
Neely, Teresa, 33–34
network
    See Diversity Librarians' Network
networking, 96
Nevins, Kate, 182–186
News and Announcements section, Diversity Librarian's Network Web site, 193
Nishii, Lisa N., 7–9
nonverbal communication, 149
Norlin, Elaina, 132
North Carolina State University (NCSU) Libraries, 152–161

O

objectives, 24
OCLC (Online Computer Library Center) system, 118
Offord, Jerome, Jr., 90
Ohio Library Council, 103
Olsen, T., 53
Online Computer Library Center (OCLC) system, 118
online resources, 122–123
"Open Doors: Building on 40 Years of Opportunity in Higher Education" commemoration
    background, 170–171
    creation of, 169–170
    description of, 171–173
    donations for, 173–176
    exhibitions, 177–179
    Oral History Collection, 176–177
    outcome of, 179–180

oral histories, 172, 176–177
organization
    of library diversity program, 46–47
    works on, 207–208
organizational climate
    library climate/culture, 147–148
    UMD Libraries' diversity assessment and, 7–9
    See also diversity assessment
organizational culture, 69
Osa, Justina O., 137–150
outreach programs, 165–166
outreach services
    in academic libraries, 132–135
    assessment of, 128
    diversity promotion through, 132
    promotion of, 129

P

Pan African Studies Program, 67
Parham, Loretta
    on diversity and libraries, 203
    HBCU Library Alliance and, 182–186
Payne, Chuck, 149
peer information programs, 153–154
Peer Research Advisors program, NCSU Libraries
    assessment of, 159–161
    budget, recruitment, 155–156
    focus of peer information programs, 153–154
    history of, 153
    idea of, 152
    implementation, 156
    peer research advisor responsibilities, 157–158
    proposal, 154–155
    recruitment, 156–157
    role clarification, 158
    time commitment, 158–159
    training, 158
    vision of, 153
Penson, Merryll, 183
Perry, Emma Bradford
    diversity in recruitment, staffing, retention, 69–74
    HBCU Library Alliance and, 183, 185
Perry, Susan, 184
Phay, John E., 177–178
Philadelphia Free Library, 103
planning, 46–47
    See also strategic planning

priority issues, 24
Prism Fellowship Program, University of Rhode Island Graduate School of Library and Information Studies, 77–78, 86
professional development, 96
professional organizations, 88–89
program development, 25
programming, 48
promotion
    of Diversity Librarians' Network, 199
    of diversity programs, 39, 40–41
    of librarianship, 64
publicity, 39, 49

Q

quotations, diversity, 55

R

Race Experts: How Racial Etiquette, Sensitivity Training, and New Age Therapy Hijacked the Civil Rights Revolution (Lasch-Quinn), 18
race/ethnicity, 69
racial segregation, 17
Rader, Hannelore B., 61–67
Ranganathan, Shiyali Ramamrita, 36
Raschke, Gregory, 73
Raver, Jana L., 7–9
Rea, Peter, 18, 19
recruiting practices
    evolution of recruitment, 79–83
    Jametoria Burton's story, 76–78
    overview of, 76
    practical suggestions, 84–87
    recruitment/retention today, 84
    resources for, 90–92
    retention strategies, 87–89
    W. Michael Havener's story, 78–79
"Recruiting the Underrepresented to Academic Libraries" (Association of College and Research Libraries), 81–83
recruitment
    CIRLA Fellows Program, 93–101
    of diverse library staff, 63–65, 71–73, 146–147
    evolution of, 79–83
    of high school students, 102–112
    Peer Research Advisors program and, 153, 155–157, 160

today, 84
works on, 209–210
Reese, Gregory L.
　on diversity action, 70
　minorities in library, 33
　on recruitment, 76
reference services, 144–145
REFORMA/UCLA Mentor Program, 82
Reinstrom, Lorel K., 163–168
Requiem for a Nun (Faulkner), 169
research
　adaptability of, 13
　peer research advisors, 152–161
research libraries, CIRLA Fellows program
　brochure, 98–101
　conclusion about, 97
　demographics background, 93–94
　highlights, 94–97
Research Port, 122
"Reserving the Right to Play" library, 21, 25
residency programs
　for minorities, 48
　University of Tennessee University Libraries Minority Residency Program, 224
　works on, 210–211
Resource Lists section, Diversity Librarians' Network Web site, 193
resources
　diversity in libraries bibliography, 205–211
　online, 122–123
　for recruitment, 90–92
retention
　of diverse library staff, 65, 73–74, 146–147
　recommendations for, 81
　strategies, 87
　today, 84
　works on, 209–210
retirements
　recruitment of high school students and, 102
　of research librarians, 93
Revels, Ira, 102–112
review, 25–26
riot, 170–171
"The Role of Assessment in Advancing Diversity for Libraries" (Association of Research Libraries workshop), 6, 14

Rounds, Marvella, 117–124
Royse, Molly
　"Celebrating Diversity in Libraries: A Selected Bibliography", 205–211
　"Practical Strategies for Building a Library Diversity Program", 46–49
rules, play by, 36–37

S

salary, 65
salesmen, 38
sample, 26–31
　See also diversity documents
Sansing, David, 176
scenario planning exercise, 44
scheduling, 86
scholarship
　for LIS students, 85–86
　from Teenage Library Association of Texas, 83
Sedlacek, William E., 4
segregation
　integration at University of Mississippi, 170–171
　racial, court cases on, 17
"Segregation Through the Lens: African American Schools in Mississippi" exhibition, 177
Seidenberg, Ivan, 55
Sensitivity Training Model, 18
services
　of library, diversity tips, 142
　needs assessment, 139
　works on, 208–209
　See also library user services
SFX tool, 122
"Shaper" library, 20–21, 24
Sharif, Rebecca Z., 150
Sharing section, Diversity Librarians' Web site, 194
Shields, Theodosia F., 117–124
Shuttlesworth, Hanes v., 17
Simmons-Welburn, Janice, 78
situation analysis, 23–24
skill-based training, 18
Smith, Wofford K., 175
SOLINET (Southeastern Library Network), 182–186
Solorzano, Daniel, 147–148
Sophocles, 94
Southeastern Library Network (SOLINET), 182–186

SPEC kits, 65
special collections departments
   access to, 166–167
   conclusion, 167–168
   development, community ties and, 164–166
   role in diversity, 163
   University of Mississippi's Department of Archives and Special Collections, 169–180
Special Libraries Associations' Affirmative Action Subcommittees, 83
specialist effect, 37–38
Spectrum Initiative
   contributions of, 84
   diversity strides with, 79
   purpose of, 71
   recruitment of minority librarians, 102
staff
   See library staff
staffing
   diversity in, 69–70
   diversity tips, 146–147
   library, needs assessment, 140
State of Louisiana, Brown v., 17
State University of New York (SUNY) library system, 83
Stoffle, Carla, 70
Stone, Susan Carol, 16, 17
Stop Talking, Start Doing! (Reese and Hawkins), 70, 76
strategic planning
   conclusion, 31
   definition of, 16
   diversity in workplace, 17–18
   diversity today, 16–17
   history of, 18–19
   library posture, analysis of, 20–21
   look of libraries, 21–22
   sample library strategic plan, 26–31
   team-based strategic planning, 22–26
   uncertainty of, 19–20
strategies, team-based strategic planning, 24–25
strategy building exercise, 44
Strategy Under Uncertainty (Courtney et al.), 19–21
"Strengthening Libraries at Historically Black Colleges and Universities" (HBCU Library Alliance), 185
students
   diversity of library student assistant workers, 67
   multicultural outreach librarian and, 126–128
   outreach services and, 132–135
   Peer Research Advisors program for, 152–161
   See also minority students
Succeeding section, Diversity Librarian's Web site, 194
Summer Program of the University of Notre Dame Libraries, 106–112
Sunflower County Freedom Project, 180
SUNY (State University of New York) library system, 83

T
TALA (Teenage Library Association of Texas), 83
"Tampa Library Mission" (University of South Florida Libraries), 164
Task Force on Recruitment of Underrepresented Minorities, 63–65, 81–83
Taylor, Frederick W., 18–19
Taylor, Tomaro I., 163–168
Teaching Tolerance Magazine, 55
team-based strategic planning
   description of, 22–23
   steps of, 23–26
Team-Based Strategic Planning: A Complete Guide to Structuring, Facilitating, and Implementing the Process (Fogg), 22–26
technology
   digital divide at University of Maryland Eastern Shore, 117–124
   for diverse library environment, 61, 63
   Diversity Librarian's Network Web site and, 198
   information literacy instruction, 143–144
   library staff services and, 146
   reference services and, 145
Teenage Library Association of Texas (TALA), 83
Thomas, David A., 3
Thomas, R. Roosevelt, Jr.
   managing diversity, 4
   organizational culture auditing, 4–5
   workplace diversity, 17
Tilford Group, 130

INDEX **237**

time
    challenges, 128
    commitment of Peer Research Advisors, 158–159
    saving through diversity, 37
Time magazine, 170
The Tipping Point: How Little Things Can Make a Big Difference (Gladwell), 38
Tolstoy, Leo, 55
Toronto Public Library, 54
training
    in CIRLA Fellows Program, 94–95
    at Frederick Douglass Library, 122–123
    of Peer Research Advisors, 158
    works on, 209
Trejo, Arnulfo, 83
tutorials, Frederick Douglass Library, 122–123

U

UC (University of California), 83
uncertainty, 19–20
University Diversity Advisory Committee (UDAC), 154
University of Alabama, 179
University of Arizona
    diversity in staffing at, 70
    GLISA program of, 83
    outreach initiatives of, 132–133
University of Arizona School of Library and Information Science, 84
University of California (UC), 83
University of Iowa Libraries, 78
University of Louisville Libraries
    diverse academic library environment of, 62
    as diversity case study, 66–67
    Diversity Plan, 217–218
    Intern Job Description, 223
University of Manitoba, 53
University of Manitoba Libraries, 53
University of Maryland Eastern Shore
    digital divide, 118
    distance education, 119–120
    impact of technology in library, 117–118
    integrated library system, 120–121
    laptops, wireless environment, 121–122
    online resources, 122–123
    technology history, 118–119
    training, instruction, 123–124

University of Maryland Libraries
    first diversity assessment, 6–11
    second diversity assessment, 11–13
University of Michigan, 3–4
University of Minnesota Libraries
    Training Institute for Early Career Librarians from Traditionally Underrepresented Groups, 197–198
University of Minnesota's Training Program, 102
University of Mississippi's Department of Archives and Special Collections
    background, 170–171
    donations to, 173–176
    exhibitions, 177–179
    integration anniversary and, 169–170
    Open Doors celebration, outcome of, 179–180
    Open Doors commemoration, 171–173
    Open Doors Oral History Collection, 176–177
University of Notre Dame Libraries' Summer Program, 106–112
University of Rhode Island Graduate School of Library and Information Studies, 77–78
"University of South Florida Libraries Strategic Plan, 2002-2007" (University of South Florida Libraries), 164
"University of South Florida Tampa Library Collection Development Policy: Special Collections Department—Tampa Campus Library" (University of South Florida Tampa Library Special Collections Department), 164
University of South Florida (USF)
    Tampa Library's Special Collections department, 163–168
University of Tennessee Libraries
    Climate Survey, 222
    Diversity Committee, 47–49
    Diversity Committee Mission Statement, 221
    Diversity Committee Web site, 219
    Diversity Definition Plan, 220
    Diversity Librarian's Network, 187–202
    diversity program of, 46–49
    Minority Librarian Residency Program, 48
    Minority Residency Program, 224

University of Washington, 78
university programs
    See library and information science (LIS) graduate programs
Urban Libraries Council, 14
U.S. Census Bureau
    diversity statistics, 16–17
    librarian demographics, 69
    U.S. demographics, 33
user services
    See library user services

V

Van Scoy, Amy, 152–161
Vanderbilt University Center for Services Marketing, 147
versatility, 41–42
Virginia, Johnson v., 17
vision, 153
vision statement
    HBCU Library Alliance and, 184
    in team-based strategic planning, 24
vos Savant, Marilyn, 96

W

"We Can Not Walk Alone" exhibition, 178
Weatherington, Elsie Stephens, 183, 185
Weaver-Meyers, Pat, 70
Web site
    Diversity Librarian's Network, 187, 188, 192–194
    Diversity Librarian's Network, design, 195
    Diversity Librarian's Network, feedback, 197
    Diversity Librarian's Network, implementation of, 190–192
    Diversity Librarian's Network, technical challenges, 198
    for diversity program, 39
    for library diversity program, 49
    for Peer Research Advisors program, 156
    of University of Tennessee Diversity Committee, 219

Webster's New Collegiate Dictionary, 17
Weil, Teri B., 117–124
White House Initiative on HBCUs, 182
Wilder, S. J., 93–94
William Winter Institute for Racial Reconciliation
    Department of Archives and Special Collections and, 180
    Open Doors commemoration and, 171
    Open Doors Oral History Collection and, 176
Williams, Jane
    "Assessing Your Library's Diversity and Organizational Climate", 3–14
    Open Doors Oral History Collection and, 177
Wilson, Charles, 176
Wilson, Richard, 175
Winnipeg, Manitoba, 52
Winnipeg Public Library, 54
Winston, Mark D.
    diverse library staff suggestions, 146–147
    on peer mentoring program, 152, 153–154, 156
    on role of Peer Research Advisors, 158
wireless environment, 121–122
work, 157–158
work curriculum, 94–95, 96, 97
workforce
    See library staff
workplace, diversity in, 17–18
"Workplace Climate Solutions" (CustomerSat), 147
"The World Is Changing: Why Aren't We?" (Grady and Hall), 102–103

Y

Yosso, Tara, 147–148

Z

Zangwill, Israel, 173

ABOUT THE EDITORS

Barbara I. Dewey has been Dean of Libraries, University of Tennessee, Knoxville, since August 2000. From 1987 to 2000 she held several administrative positions at the University of Iowa Libraries including Interim University Librarian. Prior to her work at Iowa she was Director of Admissions at Indiana University's School of Library and Information Science, Reference and Interlibrary Loan Librarian, Northwestern University Library, and Head, Reference and Adult Services, Minnesota Valley Regional Library in Mankato, Minnesota. She is the author or editor of five books. The most recent, *Leadership, Higher Education, and the Information Age*, was published in 2003. She has published articles and presented papers on research library topics including digital libraries, technology, user education, fundraising, and human resources. She holds the MA in library science, the BA in sociology/anthropology from the University of Minnesota, and the Graduate Public Management Certificate from Indiana University.

Dewey is past President of the Association of Southeastern Research Libraries (ASERL), a consortium of forty-three research university libraries in the southeast. She is chair of the Association of Research Libraries (ARL) Diversity Committee. She is on the Board of Directors for the New Media Consortium (NMC). She is active in the Association of College and Research Libraries, Educause, the Digital Library Federation, Council on Library Resources, African Studies Association, and the Tennessee Library Association.

Loretta Parham is Director and Chief Executive Officer of the Robert W. Woodruff Library at the Atlanta University Center. The Woodruff Library is a corporation organized to operate an academic library for the benefit of Morehouse College, Spelman College, the Interdenominational Theological Center, and Clark Atlanta University. The library has an impressive collection of resources to include Archives and Special Collections with extensive and rare collections on the African American experience. They include the John Henrik Clarke Africana and African American Collection and the Henry P. Slaughter and Countee Cullen Memorial Collection of graphic and performing arts (www.auctr.edu).

Most recently, Mrs. Parham served as the Director and University Librarian for the Harvey Library at Hampton University in Hampton, Virginia. Her experience includes serving as Deputy Director of the Carnegie Library in Pittsburgh, Pennsylvania; District Chief of the Chicago Public Library (CPL), where she managed the operations of twenty branch agencies; and other related positions at CPL and the City Colleges of Chicago.

Mrs. Parham has served as chairperson for several professional boards and committees, including the Board of Directors of the Southeastern Library Network (SOLINET); cofounder and chair of the Historically Black College and University (HBCU) Library Alliance; member of the Editorial Board for *College and Research Libraries*, a scholarly journal of the Association of Colleges and Research Libraries; on the Appalachian College

Association Central Library Council; and on the Members Council of the OCLC (Online Computer Library Center, Inc.). She earned her master's from the University of Michigan. Loretta was professionally distinguished in her industry when selected as a Library Journal Mover and Shaker for 2004. Loretta Parham is married and a proud mother of three.

ABOUT THE CONTRIBUTORS

Jennifer Aronson graduated with a master's in Library and Information Science from the University of Pittsburgh. She was the Curator of Visual Collections at the University of Mississippi from 2002 to 2004. Currently, she is a Project Archivist for the Guggenheim Museum in New York.

Rhea Ballard-Thrower was appointed in 2001 to the law faculty and named Director of the Howard University Law Library. Professor Ballard-Thrower earned a BA from the University of Cincinnati, a JD from the University of Kentucky, and an MLIS from the University of Michigan. Prior to her arrival at Howard, Professor Ballard-Thrower was the Associate Director at Georgia State University Law Library and a reference librarian at the University of Texas Tarlton Law Library. During her career as a law librarian, Professor Ballard-Thrower has been a legal bibliography instructor, conference presenter, author of several articles on law librarianship, and an active member of the American Association of Law Libraries.

Laura Blessing is the Director of Personnel Management at North Carolina State University Libraries. Laura received a BA from New Mexico State University in Las Cruces and an MLIS from the University of Texas at Austin. She served as the co-chair for the LAMA Diversity Officers Discussion Group from 1999 through 2005, and is actively involved in diversity initiatives on the North Carolina State University library and campus.

Kawanna Bright is currently Assistant Professor/Instructional Services Librarian at the University of Tennessee Libraries. She has been in this position since July 2005, after completing the libraries' two-year Minority Residency program. Kawanna is a graduate of the University of Washington Information School in Seattle. Her areas of interest include library instruction and reference services, with a special interest in the role of technology within these two areas; outreach; Web site design; and diversity in librarianship.

Sharon D. Brooks is employed at the University of Maryland Eastern Shore, Frederick Douglass Library, as a Librarian IV in Media Services. She received her undergraduate and graduate degrees from North Carolina Central University in Durham, North Carolina. Her interests are traveling, antique shopping, and reading.

John Burger has served as the Executive Director of the Association of Southeastern Research Libraries (ASERL), a nonprofit association of thirty-seven research libraries and five state libraries in the Southeast, for five years. ASERL is dedicated to communication and collaboration for the mutual benefit of member libraries. John's work includes coordinating the development of multiple consortial projects—including Kudzu, virtual reference, virtual storage, document delivery, and others—as well managing the day-to-day business affairs for the association.

Jametoria Burton is a 2002 graduate of the University of Rhode Island Graduate School of Library and Information Studies. She also participated in the original Project Prism, a program funded by the University of Rhode Island and Institute of Museum and Library Services (IMLS) which serves as a major recruitment effort in attracting talented candidates from underrepresented groups to the library profession. Mrs. Burton was a former Resident Librarian at the University of Iowa located in Iowa City, Iowa, during 2002–2004.

Jayati Chaudhuri completed the MLIS from the University of Rhode Island. She was a minority resident librarian at University of Tennessee Libraries from 2003 to 2005. Jayati has joined University of Northern Colorado Libraries as a science reference librarian during fall 2005.

Dr. Ganga B. Dakshinamurti is the Instructional Librarian at the Albert D. Cohen Management Library, the University of Manitoba, Winnipeg, Manitoba, Canada. She holds an MA from India, MLS from the City University of New York, and teaching certificates as well as a PhD from the University of Manitoba. Ganga is the current President of the Asian/Pacific American Librarians Association (APALA) and serves on the Steering Committee planning for the Joint Conference of Librarians of Color to be held in 2006. She has been a long-standing and actively participating member of the American Library Association, the Canadian Library Association, and the International Federation of Library Associations. Ganga is deeply committed to promoting diversity in workplaces and equality of opportunities, and as a member from Canada with its unique multicultural perspective, she is often invited to provide a different and meaningful viewpoint to the issues faced by Asian librarians in North America.

Jennifer Ford received her MA and MLS from the University of Southern Mississippi. She is the Head of Archives and Special Collections at the University of Mississippi.

Dr. Janice R. Franklin is Director, University Library and Learning Resources Center, Alabama State University, Montgomery. She previously served as a district chief for the Chicago Public Library (CPL) and as deputy director at the Carnegie Library of Pittsburgh. She co-chaired, along with Loretta Parham, the first meeting of the HBCU library directors in October 2002 and was instrumental in developing the HBCU Library Alliance. Dr. Franklin is past president of the Alabama Library Association, has published a book on copyright and library automation systems, and is active in many professional associations.

Tracie D. Hall is Director of the American Library Association Office for Diversity. She also worked at the Hartford, New Haven Free, and Seattle public libraries. She has served as visiting faculty member at the School of Library and Information Science at the Catholic University of America, and at Southern Connecticut State and Wesleyan Universities. Hall holds bachelor's degrees from the University of California at Santa Barbara, an MA from Yale University, and the MLIS from the University of Washington. She was designated a Library Journal Mover and Shaker in August 2004.

Dr. W. Michael Havener is Director and Professor at the University of Rhode Island Graduate School of Library and Information Studies. He has been Principle Investigator for multiple Library and Information Science grants, including a current $500,000 IMLS grant to recruit and educate librarians to serve diverse populations. He is the immediate Past President of Beta Phi Mu, the international honor society for library and information studies, and a member of the Spectrum Advisory Council.

Irene M. Hoffman is the Director of Library Personnel, Planning and Assessment at Georgetown University. She received an MS from the University of Illinois, and her career has included Business and Economics Bibliographer at the University of California—Davis, Library Instruction Coordinator at California State University—Los Angeles, and Manager of Sales and later Director of the OCLC, Inc. regional offices in California. Before coming to Georgetown she developed and directed a successful library fundraising and advancement program at Cal Poly San Luis Obispo.

Deloice G. Holliday has served as the Multicultural Outreach Librarian at the Herman B. Wells Library in the Information Common Undergraduate Services (ICUS) Department since August 2001. Her duties include developing outreach, educational, and collection-specific programs and activities to promote library services to students from different cultural and ethnic backgrounds at Indiana University Bloomington. Before joining the ICUS staff, she served as the Coordinator of the Science Information Center at the Helmke Library at Indiana University—Purdue University (IPFW).

Jessica Kayongo is the Catholic Studies Librarian at the University of Notre Dame. She has collection development and reference responsibilities. Her primary focus is on American Catholic history. Her educational background includes a BA, JD, and MA.

LeRoy LaFleur is the Public Policy and Management Studies Librarian at George Mason University's Arlington Campus Library. LeRoy has a bachelor's degree in Sociology from Michigan State University and a master's in Library and Information Studies from the University of Wisconsin—Madison. Previously, he worked as a Reference Librarian and Bibliographer for Social Sciences research at Cornell University.

Karen M. Brown Letarte is the Assistant Head of Cataloging and Head of Database Development at the North Carolina State University Libraries. Karen holds the AB from Dartmouth College and the MA in LIS from the University of Wisconsin—Madison. Karen is Aniiishinabe and an enrolled member of the Minnesota Chippewa Tribe. She is the 2005–2006 Vice-President/ President Elect of the American Indian Library Association.

Grace M. Mills was named Director of the Florida A&M University Law Library in 2002. She earned a BA from Wellesley College, a JD from Columbia University, and an MLS from Queens College. Prior to her arrival at Florida A&M, Ms. Mills was the Associate Law Librarian for Public Services at North Carolina Central University Law Library, a senior reference librarian at the University of California Boalt Hall Law Library, and a reference librarian and Assistant Library Professor at CUNY Law School. During her career as a law librarian, Ms. Mills has been a legal bibliography instructor, conference presenter, author of several articles on law librarianship, and an active member of the American Association of Law Libraries.

Maud Mundava is a former Fulbright scholar with an MLS from the State University of New York at Buffalo. She is currently working at the University of Tennessee as a Social Sciences Librarian. She completed UT's minority residency program in 2005. She holds the BA from the University of Cape Town and the MLIS from the SUNY at Buffalo.

Kate Nevins has been the Executive Director at SOLINET since 1994. Her previous experience includes positions at OCLC, the Library at Hobart and William Smith Colleges in Geneva, New York, and the Christiansted Public Library in the Virgin Islands. Kate has an MLS from the University of Wisconsin, a BA in Scandinavian Languages from the University of California—Berkeley, and an MBA from Ohio University. She served as President of the Association of Specialized and Cooperative Library Agencies, the ALA division devoted to cooperation and state library programs, and on many library and association committees.

Justina O. Osa, M.Ed, MSLS, EdD, is Education and Behavioral Sciences Librarian, Pennsylvania State University Libraries, University Park, Pennsylvania. Justina O. Osa is co-author of *The Social Sciences: A Cross-Disciplinary Guide to Selected Sources*, 3rd edition. She has published book chapters and articles including publications in *The Acquisitions Librarian*, *Education Libraries*, *The Reference Librarian*, *Science and Technology Libraries*, and *The Researcher*.

Emma Bradford Perry is Professor and Dean of Libraries, Southern University, Baton Rouge, Louisiana. She formerly worked at Texas A&M University, Harvard University Business School, Dillard University in New Orleans, the State Library of Louisiana, the Evanston Public Library, and other types of libraries. She has published several articles and served on many boards and has been a speaker on diversity in various venues.

Hannelore B. Rader has been Dean of the University Libraries at the University of Louisville in Kentucky since January 1997. She has more than thirty-five years of library, administrative, and teaching experience in higher education in Michigan, Wisconsin, Ohio, and Kentucky. Her background includes prominent leadership in international, national, and regional user instruction and information literacy activities. Ms. Rader has a teaching certificate, master's degrees in library science and German literature from the University of Michigan, and a specialist degree in educational leadership from Eastern Michigan University. She is currently an adjunct professor at the University of Kentucky School of Library and Information Science.

Lorel K. Reinstrom is an Assistant Librarian for Cataloging at the University of South Florida Tampa Library. Ms. Reinstrom began her career in the cataloging department at USF over five years ago, after completing her graduate work in Library Science from USF. Currently, she works with the Special Collections Department in processing various music collections.

Ira Revels is the project manager for collaboration between the Cornell University Library and the HBCU Library Alliance. Her duties include the administration and overall management of a multi-institutional digitization initiative aimed at preserving and providing access to HBCU institutional records. She received her MLIS from the University of Pittsburgh in 2001, where she focused on digital libraries, and her M.Ed in Instructional Design from Northwestern State University.

Marvella Rounds currently works at the University of Maryland Eastern Shore, Frederick Douglass Library, as a Cataloger. She has held this position for sixteen years. Her interests are reading, traveling, and meeting people.

Molly Royse has been an Associate Professor and Coordinator of Humanities at the University of Tennessee Libraries, Knoxville, since November 2000. Prior to her appointment at UT, she served as Coordinator of Multicultural Library Services at Kansas State University. At both Kansas State and at the University of Tennessee she has been active in campus and library diversity initiatives.

Dr. Theodosia F. Shields is Dean, Library Services, Frederick Douglass Library, University of Maryland Eastern Shore, Princess Anne, Maryland.

ABOUT THE CONTRIBUTORS

Tomaro I. Taylor is Assistant University Librarian for Special Collections and Latin American and Caribbean Studies at the University of South Florida Tampa Library. Ms. Taylor began her library career as USF's first recipient of the Dr. Henrietta M. Smith Residency Program, a two-year visiting appointment established to create opportunities in academic librarianship for members of underrepresented ethnic and racial groups. A certified archivist, her research interests include diversity in archival resources, museum-library collaborations, and the residency experience.

Amy VanScoy is Assistant Head of Research and Information Services at the North Carolina State University Libraries. In this capacity she manages reference services and reference collection development. Previously, VanScoy was Reference Librarian for Undergraduate Research at NCSU Libraries. She has the MLIS from the University of Alabama, the MA in French from Indiana University, and the BA in French from Pennsylvania State University.

Teri B. Weil received her in MA in Library and Information Studies from the University of Wisconsin—Madison in 1993. As a librarian, Teri has worked in several types of academic libraries, including two HBCUs. She has presented at several programs at local and national conferences.

Jane Williams directs planning and administrative services for the University of Maryland Libraries, College Park. She has also worked at the U.S. National Commission on Library and Information Science, the State Library of North Carolina, where she was state librarian from 1986 to 1989, and the Public Library of Charlotte and Mecklenburg County. Jane Williams received her library degree from UNC—Chapel Hill and her undergraduate degree from Pfeiffer University.